The
First
Year
Out

The
First
Year
Out

UNDERSTANDING
AMERICAN TEENS
AFTER
HIGH SCHOOL

TIM CLYDESDALE

The University of Chicago Press
Chicago and London

TIM CLYDESDALE is associate professor of sociology at the College of New Jersey. He received his Ph.D. from Princeton University and his B.A. from Wheaton College (IL).

The University of Chicago Press, Chicago 60637
The University of Chicago Press, Ltd., London
© 2007 by The University of Chicago
All rights reserved. Published 2007
Printed in the United States of America

16 15 14 13 12 11 10 09 08 07   1 2 3 4 5

ISBN-13: 978-0-226-11065-3 (cloth)
ISBN-13: 978-0-226-11066-0 (paper)
ISBN-10: 0-226-11065-6 (cloth)
ISBN-10: 0-226-11066-4 (paper)

Library of Congress Cataloging-in-Publication Data
Clydesdale, Timothy T. (Timothy Thomas), 1965–
   The first year out : understanding American teens after high school / Tim Clydesdale.
      p. cm.
   Includes bibliographical references and index.
      ISBN-13: 978-0-226-11065-3 (cloth : alk. paper)
      ISBN-13: 978-0-226-11066-0 (paper : alk. paper)
      ISBN-10: 0-226-11065-6 (cloth : alk. paper)
      ISBN-10: 0-226-11066-4 (paper : alk. paper)
   1. High school graduates—United States.
2. High school seniors—United States. 3. College freshmen—United States. 4. High School graduates—United States—Psychology. 5. High school graduates—Employment—United States.
I. Title.
   LB1695.6.C58   2007
   373.1'8—dc22
                                    2006029911

♾ The paper used in this publication meets the minimum requirements of the American National Standard for Information Sciences— Permanence of Paper for Printed Library Materials, ANSI Z39.48-1992.

To Dawn, Jonah, and Grace,
who graciously tolerated the
time I spent on this book and
generously demonstrated
their love and encouragement

Contents

Preface

Because most readers, myself included, like to have a sense of how the author has structured the text—let me start with a brief roadmap. I begin my first chapter inductively, telling the stories of four teens I met during my fieldwork at New Jersey High School (NJ High, a pseudonym). These teens are unique individuals, but their experiences and stories allow me to introduce many important aspects of teen moral culture and of the early transition to adulthood during the first year after high school. In the second chapter, I discuss starting points—of this project as a contribution to scholarly research and of teens as products of families, faiths, and communities. The remaining chapters lay out four life "arenas," which are of central to peripheral significance to teens during the first year out. Navigating relationships and managing gratifications are the primary foci of culturally mainstream American teens, while the realms of leisure, money, and work are of less recognized but striking import to teens' daily lives; these subjects comprise the third and fourth chapters. Of lesser significance to teens are their educational lives, and distantly trailing educational life are political, social, national, and global matters; these topics receive attention in the fifth and sixth chapters. Included in the final chapter is a discussion of the broader implications of this analysis, for various readers: scholars, educators, clergy, parents, and youth. An appendix supplies details about the research methods and process, and I also include a selected bibliography for those who wish to study these matters in greater depth—for little would be more satisfying than to find more joining the vital conversation about American youth and the transition to adulthood.

Conversations, of course, require partners—and I would be remiss if I did not gratefully acknowledge the many whose conversations with me made this book possible. My first thanks must go to the teens who agreed to sit for nearly two hours, *twice*, and share their thoughts, feelings, desires, goals, and experiences with me. My thanks also extend to New Jersey High's Class of 2001, who welcomed me into their lives and shared their senior year of high school with me. And my thanks also extend to the dozen teens who participated in a focus group on interpersonal relationships in April 2004 and to another two dozen teens who agreed to complete an open-ended survey about school rampages in October 2005. All of these teens must remain nameless here, but they know who they are, and I deeply appreciate their generosity of time and interest in this project. I am also grateful to the teachers, counselors, staff, and administrators at New Jersey High—who shared their stories and their perceptions with me, and who so kindly welcomed me into their workplace. They too must remain nameless here, but their contributions to this project have been invaluable.

This project could not have been done without the help and support of many good people. In particular, I wish to thank the many students who have assisted me in conducting, transcribing, cleaning, and coding this project's data. It was a massive undertaking, and I am deeply grateful to each one: Amy Ludeker, Holly Harrison, Greg Brown, Jessica Luciano, Michelle Booker, Marna Indico, Jen Dickson, Keith Brown, Vanessa Worm, Ann Rogers, Jennifer Schick, Kim Holzsager, Jen Pflugh, John Weiner, Andrew Blanco, Heather Ketchum, Kevin Cashman, Jessica Sautter, Dan Younkers, Christina Puglia, Maryann Mule, Joanna Pappa, Verena Schoch, and Christina Crispell. For the sake of narrative simplicity, I have written as if I were the only interviewer—but this is in no way an attempt to take credit for or minimize the contribution of my outstanding assistants. There have also been several other students who worked diligently on transcription: Scott Brown, Natalie Campagna, Ken Dahlenburg, Lisa Sepkowski, and Amanda Tobin. I have been fortunate to have outstanding supporters at several institutions: Susan Albertine, Carlos Alves, Steve Briggs, Barbara Cape, Dot Chappell, Chris Coble, Debra Compte, Lahna Diskin, Angela Domen, Craig Dykstra, Helen Rose Ebaugh, Sig Haenisch, Rick Kamber, Paul Kennedy, Jim Lewis, Elynn Mahady, Ray Maietta, Suzanne Pasch, Angela Sgroi,

Wolf Shipon, and Marcia Taylor. I am especially grateful for intelligent and generous colleagues: Rachel Adler, Nancy Ammerman, Robert Anderson, Dorothy Bass, Diane Bates, Elizabeth Borland, Alan Dawley, Chris Fisher, Mohamoud Ismail, Maria Kefalas, Regina Kenen, Rebecca Li, Lisa Ortiz-Villarelle, Beth Paul, Kim Pearson, Dave Prensky, Howard Robboy, Christian Smith, and Robert Wuthnow. I am grateful for the rich intellectual nurture I received as a student from Zondra Lindblade, Jim Mathisen, Alvaro Nieves, and especially from the late Ivan Fahs, who imparted to me his passion for empirical sociological research. I am thankful to the Society for the Scientific Study of Religion, the Faculty Development Program at Gordon College, the Support of Scholarly Activities Committee at The College of New Jersey, and to the Louisville Institute and the Lilly Endowment for generous financial support of this project during its many years. And I would be remiss if I did not acknowledge the warm encouragement and support of Alan Wolfe, Douglas Mitchell, Clair James, and Timothy McGovern during the writing and production process. Despite the able help and good intentions of all these folks, there are sure to be errors and omissions herein—and those are the sole fault of this author.

I want to thank the many friends, family, and neighbors who have graciously supported me during this project. I am blessed with wonderful friends like Arthur and Julie Eisdorfer, Jules and Virginia Grisham, Brian and Joanne Smith, and Steve and Tricia Wittekind, who often encouraged me and sometimes teased me, too, about whether I would "ever finish." I thank my parents, Thomas and Delores Clydesdale, for their constant love and prayers. I thank Lawrence and Betty Suydam for their love and kindness. Finally, I thank Dawn, Jonah, and Grace—and put this book aside to go out and play with them.

An Unexpected Journey

My first year out, that is, the first year that followed my own high school graduation, was a time of significant personal change. As a high school student, I had glimpsed a larger world through a voracious appetite for reading and through the liberal and cosmopolitan perspectives of my primarily Jewish, public school teachers. But growing up the youngest of five brothers in a blue-collar, urban, and Christian fundamentalist home kept that larger world at a distance. So I had, truly, an intellectually liberating and socially broadening experience during my freshman year at evangelical Wheaton College in Wheaton, Illinois. That was because evangelicals, especially of the sort found at Wheaton, took intellectual life seriously. They were not suspicious of new ideas or new theories, like the handful of Bob Jones University graduates who attended my otherwise blue-collar home church. Rather, they considered all ideas carefully and sought to learn all they could from them, no matter their source. "All truth is God's truth," they loved to say, "wherever it be found." At the same time, my first year out was socially broadening, because this blue-collar Philly boy met—for the first time—Midwestern teens who grew up in the suburbs, who attended schools without police assigned to them full time, and who had fathers who were physicians, lawyers, and business owners. Though building relationships with suburban, middle-class teens rarely counts as a "socially broadening" experience, it was for me. Given the subcultural shock of this transitional period in my own life, it is no surprise that I became a cultural sociologist who studies American religion and American education.

Thus, when I began working as a professor, I did not have to look far for a research project that interested me: I wanted to make sense of the first year out, for various sorts of teens, who head off into various settings, and who thus discover important things about themselves and the world. Generalizing from my own experience (always foolish, but I did it anyway), I believed that the majority of teens who headed off to college had broadening, if not liberating, experiences akin to my own during their first year out, while the majority of teens who stayed home did not.[1] That is, of course, what college admissions offices sell to prospective students. It is also what keeps an entire college admission industry in business—with guidebook authors promising readers "any one of the 40 colleges profiled here will . . . give you a rich, full life; . . . they will raise trajectories, strengthen skills, double talents, develop value systems, and impart confidence."[2] And it is also what professors like me tell each other after we toil all semester to convey something important to our students, to no observable effect. "Ah, but you are impacting your students even when they don't show it or realize it themselves," a senior and presumably wiser colleague told me. But as I would soon discover, neither he nor I was right.

Most of the mainstream American teens I spoke with neither liberated themselves intellectually nor broaden themselves socially during their first year out. Rather, most teens settled all the more comfortably into the patterns and priorities they formed earlier in their lives. What teens actually focus on during the first year out is this: *daily life management*. That is, they manage their personal relationships—with romantic partners, friends, and authority figures; they manage personal gratifications—including substance use and sexual activity; and they manage their economic lives—with its expanding necessities and rising lifestyle expectations. And to my surprise, they manage these things fairly well—or learn to do so rather quickly. Mainstream American teens navigate many changes in their personal relationships with friends and family; they generally moderate, though sometimes abuse, their use of adult substances and their expression of sexual freedoms; and they adapt to increased economic responsibilities and match consumption patterns with their peers (see chapters 3–4). This is quite a bit for teens to manage during their first year out, leaving most American teens with little time for, and little interest in, much else. The few teens who go beyond daily life management, the ones who demonstrate intellectual engagement and social broadening, are largely the ones pursuing careers that perpetuate these views of the first year out. They represent the next generation of professors and allied professionals—like therapists, deans, journalists, and guidance counselors—but they do not represent American teens in general.

Why is daily life management the paramount focus of teens? The reasons, I suggest, are both economic and cultural. The economic impetus lies in the new global realities of the American economy. Teens know all-too-well that good jobs are not certain and that even with the right credential there are no guarantees for the future. So unless teens receive a rich inheritance, they know they must complete their own educations and climb their own occupational ladder (affluent parents can make the process easier, but they cannot eliminate it). Post–high school education is therefore viewed instrumentally—as a pathway to a better job and economic security—with most teens accepting their educational hazing and orienting their attention to more immediate matters. Few teens, moreover, indicate any real interest in intellectual engagement or social broadening, which requires an exploration of cultural factors affecting teens' focus on daily life management during the first year out.

Culture, I tell my computer-savvy freshmen, is like our human "operating system." Just as a computer is no more than a mass of useless hardware without an operating system, so too are humans but a mass of organs and tissues without culture. Without culture we would have no language, no knowledge, no meaning, and no life. And just like a computer operating system, there are certain cultural "default" installation settings that, unless overridden, shape how individuals view the world and establish daily practices. I argue that the current default settings in the United States install a popular American moral culture that: celebrates personal effort and individual achievement; demonstrates patriotism; believes in God and a spiritual afterlife; values loyalty to family, friends, and coworkers; expects personal moral freedom; distrusts large organizations and bureaucracies; and conveys the message that happiness and fulfillment are found primarily in personal relationships and individual consumption. Put differently, the vast majority of Americans get a lump in their throat when they hear the wife of a slain police officer sing "God Bless America"; they hope that that slain police officer is now "in a better place"; they respect hard work and individuals who succeed through it; they strive for loyalty to families, friends, and coworkers; they are wary of politics, large corporations, and educational institutions; they accommodate moral liberties to drink, smoke, gamble, and be active (hetero-) sexually; and they generally pursue happiness through intimate relationships and personal consumption. Unless these default settings are altered, usually to install more specific religious or nonreligious subcultural settings, this constellation of beliefs and practices is characteristic of most Americans (see chapter 2).

The impact of popular American moral culture on the first year out is, consequently, substantial. Consider the place of education in this moral culture: as a large bureaucracy to be wary of and as the tacit means by which diligent individuals attain individual success. Education is the standard pathway to occupational achievement, but it is not a trusted institution beyond its supplying of necessary credentials. I argue that, rather than see schooling as an opportunity to examine oneself and one's place in the larger world, most American teens keep core identities in an "identity lockbox" during their first year out and actively resist efforts to examine their self-understandings through classes or to engage their humanity through institutional efforts such as public lectures, the arts, or social activism (see chapter 5). That lockbox preserves teens' mainstream American identity from intellectual or moral tampering that would put them out-of-step with the communities that shaped them or hinder their efforts to pursue the individual achievement they have always envisioned for themselves. As a teen planning to be a teacher told me plainly and unapologetically, "I know there's all this injustice and stuff in cities—but I could never teach in an urban school; I just want to teach in a nice school, live in a nice house with a big yard, and have kids." Though teens may have a variety of occupational interests, this teen's vision of success is widely shared. She therefore kept her lockbox tightly closed, lest she surrender her "safe and respectable" future for an unknown and dubious one.

Another way popular American moral culture fosters teen preoccupation with daily life involves the expectations it creates about the first year out. Most parents expect their teens to take on greater financial responsibilities following high school graduation, and both those who remain at home for their first year out and those who live at college experience a notable increase in financial obligations and expectations to earn money. This increased financial responsibility then combines with a rising American teen lifestyle to make both work and consumption major components of teen life during the first year out. Yet, as much as earning and spending occupy many teen hours during the first year out, teens are often oblivious to its effect on their schedule. Teens focus their attention instead on the semiadult relationships they now navigate and the adult gratifications (i.e., to consume substances and express sexuality) they now claim. It is in this arena that teens, with extensive support from American popular culture, expect to find fulfillment, satisfaction, and happiness. Whatever else it may be that teens are actually doing each day, one can be certain that in the back of virtually every teen mind are thoughts of past, present, or future friends, of partners, of family, and of good and bad times shared with others. Between meeting financial expectations, navigating adult relationships, and handling adult freedoms, it is no wonder that developing competence in daily life management preoccupies teens during the first year out.

As comforting as it may be to learn that teens manage their daily lives fairly well and can pitch their own "life tent" and live in it relatively independently, however, a dark cloud looms on the horizon. The dark cloud is this: most American teens do not question whether popular American moral culture provides a sufficient basis upon which to construct individual biographies or sustain shared lives. Can the private pursuit of happiness through personal intimacy and individual consumption, with a dash of patriotism and a sprinkling of theism, sustain these young Americans should daily life be significantly interrupted or permanently altered? I am dubious. Just as organizations must possess a combination of clear values, defined purpose, and good management to be successful, so must teens. But most teens possess only good management—and have inadvertently pitched their life tents in a flood basin. They remind me of G. K. Chesterton's "practical man," whom he contrasts with his thinking man: "A practical man means a man accustomed to merely daily practices, to the way things commonly work. When things will not work, you must have the thinker, the man who has some doctrine about why they work at all."[3] Contemporary teens are practical men and women. They pitch their tents and manage their daily lives fairly well. But they are not, by and large, *thinking* men and women. Few consider where they pitch their tents or question whether they should be so consumed with daily campground life. Should some calamity befall them individually, or befall us collectively, their tents will be damaged or destroyed and their occupants left without the resources or skills to relocate their campsite or reconfigure their lives. In fact, I suggest that an awful storm passed through the campground already, on September 11, 2001. But after a brief evacuation, American teens returned to their soggy tents and settled back into their daily, and now quite muddy, routines (see chapter 6).

It is ironic that in the same year that American teens gain competence in managing their day-to-day activities, they become equally accomplished in ignoring the longer-term direction of their lives and neglecting their interdependence with community, civic life, national politics, and global issues. Of course, American teens "know about" these matters, like they know about the Egyptian pyramids or the solar system. Teens know that these things matter to educated types like me. But it is abstract and trivial knowledge, to be regurgitated in an essay, and not useful or important knowledge, to be used to shape futures or determine pathways of action. Few and far between are teens whose lives are shaped by purpose, who demonstrate direction, who recognize their interdependence with communities small and large, or who think about what it means to live in the biggest house in the global village.

Perhaps this is because few and far between are American *adults* whose lives are shaped by purpose, who demonstrate direction, who recognize their interdependence with others, or who think about America's place in the global community—leaving teens with few such adults to model their own lives after. My study is about teens, of course, and not about adults. But my analysis offers readers a window through which they can observe the effect of American culture on youth and also infer something of the future direction of American culture as these teens take their places as the custodians of America for the next generation. No earthly creature knows the future nor what ordinary or cataclysmic events lie ahead, so inferences about the future come with the usual caveats. Still, I cannot help but find it sadly paradoxical that American culture, which is so associated worldwide with individuals who take initiative and pursue freedom, produces so few who actualize those core values.

The young Americans I interviewed and observed, who began their adult journeys between 1995 and 2003, learned to master digital technology as readily as they did walking and came of age knowing only an overscheduled and multitasking society. They are arguably a part of America's most time-efficient generation. The question is, do these new adults know where they are headed, and will they be satisfied when they get there?

Four Teens

I felt like a bright red pimple on a teenager's nose: blatantly obvious, socially awkward, and unable to disappear. Seventy seniors from the first lunch period had just left for their next class, no second lunch period seniors had yet arrived, and there I was with my notepad and twenty empty school cafeteria tables. The first lunch period, I will admit, could not have gone any better. Lowanda Smith,* one of the most outgoing seniors at NJ High School, walked me to the lunchroom from her social studies class and introduced me—*literally*—to every student in the senior cafeteria. But Lowanda and her friends were now gone, and there I sat, a 35-year-old pimple.

It was only then that I realized this senior cafeteria had no back door and no place to hide. Just the previous spring, I had watched, as millions did, the horrifying video images of teens fleeing Columbine High School, SWAT teams charging the building, and somber paramedics loading shrouded bodies into ambulances. My mouth began to feel dry, my hands began to shake, and I questioned whether I should proceed with this project—or run to my car and never return. The yelp of an arriving second lunch senior jerked me back to the present, and I took a drink from my half-pint carton of apple juice as I refocused.

---

* A pseudonym, as are all participant and place names.

Second lunch seniors would enter the cafeteria, scan the room, pretend to not see me, and find a seat beyond the 20-foot "no man's land" that apparently encircled me. This cafeteria, called the "senior café" by administrators but not seniors, was a 40-foot by 60-foot lunchroom adjacent to the main school cafeteria, wholly generic except that it was restricted to seniors and featured two wall-mounted televisions with cable hookup (tuned to music videos and *always* set at full volume). After five excruciatingly long minutes, a student I recognized from my presentation in Mr. Williams's class entered the cafeteria. Chuck Barker, a bright but mischievous student who asked a couple of half-serious questions during my presentation, acknowledged me with a nod before walking toward a cluster of boys in the back corner. That nod was all I needed. I followed Chuck back to the corner and asked if I could sit with him. "Sure," Chuck said, and then he turned toward a friend. "What?" he asked, but no one spoke.

The Back Corner Boys were silent. And Chuck gave no indication that he planned to introduce me. So I took the initiative myself. I extended my hand to each boy and said, "Hi, I'm Tim Clydesdale, and I'm writing a book about high school seniors—mind if I join you?" Poppy, Jim, Kato, Steve, and Scott all shook hands and told me their names. Chuck then asked, "What should we call you? Mr., uh . . . ?" "Just call me Tim." "OK, cool." Silence returned. So I asked a question about the food. Chuck said it is only good on "Domino's Day." Domino's day? "Yeah, every other Friday, they have Domino's [pizza] delivered and you can buy it—the rest of the time they serve fuckin' shit." Chuck was testing me. No NJ High administrator would tolerate swearing, and few teachers would either. I did not flinch, and I did not correct him. So Poppy decided to take a gamble: "Do you mind if we play cards?" "Go right ahead," I answered. "Do whatever you want." Immediately, the cards came out and the Back Corner Boys seemed to relax. Card-playing, you see, is against the rules at NJ High, as are gambling and swearing. The Back Corner Boys did all three, so they sat away from the door, where the thick-necked school security aide often stood, and directly below the security camera—in its blind spot.

Still, six boys huddled and laughing in the back corner attracts attention from even the slowest security aide, and he passed by just before the second lunch period bell rang. "Put the cards away, boys," he ordered and gave me a quizzical look. By this point, seniors throughout the cafeteria were packing up their things in anticipation of the bell, so the Back Corner Boys stood up and did the same. I said goodbye to each boy, using their names as I did so. Poppy Lopez was curious. "You gonna be here every day?" "Well," I answered,

"I'll be here for lunch every Friday, and I'll be around other times, too." "And you're writin' a book about high school," Poppy asked. "I'm writing about high school seniors," I answered, "about what happens to them and what they do after they graduate." I added, "I'll be keeping names and stuff like that confidential—I just want to learn about seniors." "Cool," Poppy replied, "I guess I'll see you next week then." And he did.

Poppy Lopez became the first male NJ High student I interviewed (and NJ High socialite Lowanda Smith became my first female NJ High interviewee). Poppy liked the $10 I paid him for doing the interview, but he agreed to do the 90-minute interview out of curiosity and because he had come to trust me during the five months that passed between our first meeting and our taped interview. Poppy and Lowanda were two of twenty-one NJ High seniors who agreed to in-depth, audio-taped interviews as part of the 2000–2001 school year I spent doing field research at NJ High. Both teens played critical roles in my transition from lunchroom alien to teen confidant, as their friends and classmates chose to talk to me, then befriend me, and ultimately trust me with the stories of their lives. I am still amazed by how willingly and openly teens would talk with me. Perhaps it was my promise of strict confidentiality; perhaps it was my efforts to convey genuine concern about teens and their lives. Perhaps the perplexity of contemporary teen life propelled teens to want to talk through issues otherwise left unexamined, or perhaps it was something else. But for whatever reasons teens felt comfortable talking to me, I am grateful that they did. Their openness gave me unparalleled perspectives on American teen life—gifts I can acknowledge but never repay.

This book is about high school seniors like Poppy and Lowanda. It is about the ways their lives unfold during their first year after high school graduation and about the cultural worlds they both live in and help create. This is not a book primarily about NJ High, however. Most of the 125 in-depth interviews that went into this book were conducted with high school seniors from Pennsylvania, Connecticut, Massachusetts, New Hampshire, New Jersey, Maine, and Oregon, and not with NJ High seniors. My goal in spending a year at NJ High was to better understand the culture of American high school seniors and to better diversify the project's interviewees (NJ High, a suburban public high school in a lower-middle-class township, is 50 percent white and 50 percent nonwhite). I simply start with four teens from NJ High because my fieldwork there provided more context with which to narrate their stories.

Just as I began my research by getting to know teens one at a time, I begin this book by introducing four teens, one at a time. I did not select these four teens because they are archetypal examples of teen experiences. I selected them because their stories, like those of all my interviewees, are interesting in their own right and because their stories allow me to introduce important themes and interpretations that I will discuss systematically in later chapters. Teens are the heart of this book—teens as they journey from high school student to young adult—so it is only right to begin with their stories.

POPPY LOPEZ

Poppy was downright bored with life in suburbia. Though born in Argentina, he moved with his family to Suburban Township, New Jersey, when he was one year old—and has never been back. Poppy yearned to travel, "I want to . . . just go *somewhere!*" But he admitted, rather embarrassedly, "Well, the farthest I have ever been is Florida on vacation." Short of traveling, Poppy would settle for more opportunities to "have fun."

Twenty-two times during my first interview with him (as a high school senior), Poppy used the word *fun.* Explaining why he stopped playing soccer after his first year of high school, Poppy said, "They were, like, so serious. Like, I just didn't have fun when I played." When asked about his plans following high school graduation, Poppy said, "Hopefully have a fun summer, then go to college." When I asked what he hoped his college experience would be like, he gave the following list: "Fun, do good, get a diploma." When we talked about work experiences, Poppy said that although his job at a mall watch repair booth was easy, it was "not much fun." When I asked what kinds of work Poppy might like to do, he answered, "I don't know, have fun." So I pressed him to give me examples of what he considered fun:

> POPPY: Be with friends, hang out. I don't know, just do things.
> INTERVIEWER: Yeah?
> POPPY: [Go to] Great Adventure [a Six Flags amusement park] or something.
> INTERVIEWER: Can you give me other examples of something you did that was fun?
> POPPY: Went to a party this week—that was fun.
> INTERVIEWER: OK.
> POPPY: I got a new car—that was fun.

For Poppy, fun was an emotional state triggered by external activities, some of which he could pre-identify (like parties or amusement parks), and some of which were purchased goods (like a new car), but most of which oc-curred, seemingly, by accident. Since Poppy did not have any hobbies, play any sports, or participate in other activities, he had a lot of hours to fill, and his challenge was finding enough fun.

Part of Poppy's thirst for fun may have come from observing his family. His father worked as a maintenance man for the county government, his mother as a hospital lab technician, and his much older sister as a mailroom clerk—after dropping out of community college. All had worked for many years in their jobs. When I asked Poppy what he saw as the greatest injus-tices today (a question I thought would elicit concerns about poverty, the environment, etc.), his answer was revealing:

> That most people aren't really getting a choice of what to do. That people are kind of raised the same, kind of, now. Like kids are supposed to go to school, do well in school, and then they're supposed to go to college, and they're supposed to get a job. But that doesn't seem fair. Not anymore. I hope that I'm not like that, but, like, once people get with their job, they stay with their job. They get a house, and they just stay there. Not that much fun in their life. They look forward to their once-a-year vacation. I just don't want to get tied down in a job and place.

Poppy resented the monotonous life his parents and sister led and resented his parents for forcing him to attend college.

Poppy also resented his parents for forcing him to attend church. "They tried to introduce religion to me, but it just didn't take." Poppy's parents, like many American parents, seemed to believe that sending children to religious education is analogous to encouraging children to eat their veg-etables—even though many parents possess little zeal for vegetables (or religion) themselves. Poppy thus developed an aversion to religion—one of Poppy's responses to my question about three things he would like to change about the world was "no more religion." Poppy knew what he did *not* want: he did not want to follow the standard middle-class pathway of college to job to a settled life of house, family, and church.

Perhaps Poppy's resentment of suburban monotony and his desire for excitement facilitated his experimentation with and use of illegal sub-stances. Though Poppy did not volunteer information about this, he will-ingly answered my questions about substance use directly and without hesitation. He said he drank alcohol, usually beer, perhaps twenty times over the last year. Poppy would consume three to four beers at a time—"not that much," because he knew he had "a really low tolerance." Poppy told me he "tried marijuana," then explained that he used to smoke marijuana regularly—during his junior year—but stopped doing so because "I just realized I wasn't having as much fun as I used to." As for other illegal substances, Poppy reported trying "acid" once:

> POPPY: Only half. You're supposed to take a whole one from this paper thing, but I only took half, and my friend took the other half. It keeps you up. . . . We didn't go to sleep until 7:30 in the morning. I didn't feel out of control or anything, I just felt really awake. It was kind of weird.
> INTERVIEWER: Did you ever try it again?
> POPPY: Um, no.
> INTERVIEWER: Why?
> POPPY: I don't know, I just don't like it. It's supposed to be bad. That stuff messes with your backbone, so I don't want to mess with that.

Given Poppy's willingness to experiment with alcohol and drugs, his reluctance to attend college, and his average academic performance, I expected Poppy to immerse himself in the college partying scene and end his freshman year on academic probation—if he made it even that far. I was wrong.

When I reinterviewed Poppy, I learned that he "really liked" college, that he was "happy," and that although he wished he could have done better academically, he stilled earned C's and B's. Part of Poppy's satisfaction came from entering college with no expectations and having a frank, straightforward goal for college:

> POPPY: Just don't fuck it up (laughing)!
> INTERVIEWER: Yeah?
> POPPY: That was one of my goals. Have fun, but you gotta do your work, you gotta go to class, and I gotta do good enough in school, or else it's not even worth being there.
> INTERVIEWER: And do you think you achieved that goal?
> POPPY: Yeah. Like what I said. I wasn't gonna like go wild over every assignment, just cause I'm out of high school, like, "Oh yeah, appreciate this, work so much and so much and so much," because I just couldn't do that much work. But I set the goal for myself that I would go to every class as much as I could. I only missed like two or three classes the whole year. And, I did most of my work, some better than others, but the important ones I did good enough.

Hearing this, one might think (as I did initially) that Poppy steered clear of the party scene, that perhaps he immersed himself in intercollegiate athletics, a long-term romantic relationship, or a job he really enjoyed. But none of these was true.

Poppy *did* immerse himself in the college party scene—even hosting parties with his college buddies—and still performed acceptably in his classes. By the end of his freshman year, Poppy said, his partying "was actually getting worse—almost every day." He drank enough to "feel good"—usually five or six beers and sometimes shots of whiskey or other hard liquor. And he smoked marijuana "one to two" times a day, though he emphasized, "There's some days where I'm just not gonna smoke. It's not a big deal." While two of Poppy's partying buddies "failed out," Poppy attended class and completed his class work "good enough" for himself and his parents. Although one might think Poppy was exceptionally lucky and that his substance use would result, sooner or later, in Poppy's academic, if not personal, demise, I found Poppy's story to be quite common and that of his failing friends to be quite uncommon.

Poppy demonstrated an amazing yet widespread skill I call "managed gratification." He neither delayed his desire for gratification nor indulged it uncontrollably. Rather, Poppy spent an evening at college drinking heavily and getting high—then woke up the next morning, wrote an acceptable philosophy paper, and turned it in at his 2 p.m. class. If the next day's schedule was particularly intense, Poppy would limit his alcohol consumption and forgo getting high, so that he could perform adequately on his exams—then celebrate twice as much the following evening. Poppy actively managed his gratifications alongside his other responsibilities. Many of the teens I observed and interviewed possessed a remarkable ability to involve themselves in the teen partying scene and still complete school, work, family, and community obligations acceptably. (I will develop this argument, and present the evidence to support it, in chapter 3.)

As for the other realms of his life, Poppy described little change since high school. Though Poppy is Latino, his friends were uniformly white, and he demonstrated little racial consciousness, beyond affirming the presence of a certain number of prejudiced people in the United States. He was "antigovernment" in his political views, indicating an interest in the Libertarian Party as a high school senior and offering similar sentiments as a freshman:

POPPY: I'd never vote in this country.
INTERVIEWER: You wouldn't vote in this country?

POPPY: No choice. It's like bad or worse. What am I going to do, throw my vote away?

INTERVIEWER: What type of party, or what type of person, would it be that you'd want to vote for?

POPPY: Independent Party. Just a party that's, you know, not about the same crap that they're always about. You know, all excited, "Oh, I'm for this." And then they get in and they don't do anything. They just chill.

Though Poppy began his freshman year just days before September 11, 2001, I was struck by how little he was affected by the horrific events of that day. Yes, he was initially shocked, saddened, and angry. "It was just, like, anger, you know. Like, what are we going to do?" But when I asked whether that day had any long-term impact on him, Poppy answered no, and he was being honest. Poppy's answer to my question about what he wished he could change about the world confirmed his September 11 answer. Unlike a number of post–September 11 interviewees who wished to "end violence," Poppy described immediate, personally significant changes—"decriminalize marijuana" (saying it would "make my life a lot easier") and "legalize abortion" (not *keep* abortion legal—actually *make* abortion legal). Poppy's focus during his first year out was not politics, it was not the world-at-large, and it was not his college studies.

Poppy's primary focus was managing his own life: what made him happy, who his friends were, and how to live with little supervision from adults. And in this regard, Poppy was wholly typical. High school graduates do not set out to "experience the world" or find their unique role in it—despite the earnest entreaties of high school valedictorians. Their focus is intensely and almost exclusively personal. Poppy's story, and the stories of virtually all teens interviewed for this project, serves as an important corrective to a number of common assumptions—including some of my own—about the first year out. First, for teens who attend college, as 76 percent of high school graduates from households earning $25,000 or more do,[1] the first year out is *not* about abandoning religious faith or moral upbringing to experiment with new philosophies or alternative lifestyles, as numerous scholars and producers of popular media presuppose.[2] Teens who appear to do this are only making public how they had previously determined to live as early adolescents. Second, the first year out is *not* about becoming a well-rounded world citizen, nor is it about discovering the values of a liberal arts education. The "liberal arts" rhetoric of so many college administrators is just that—rhetoric—and illustrates just how out of touch college administrators and many faculty are with the lived realities of their freshmen's lives. Third, the first year out is *not* that different between teens who remain at home to attend community college or vocational programs and teens who leave home to attend college. Wide parental latitude combined with increased time and financial responsibilities make the lives of commuting freshmen more similar than different from residential college freshmen.

The first year out, rather than being a time when behavior patterns and life priorities are reexamined and altered, is actually a time when prior patterns and priorities become more deeply habituated. What the vast majority of teens focus on during their first year out is *daily life management*: they manage the semiadult relationships that now characterize their social interactions; they manage their adult freedoms to use substances and be sexually active; and they manage expanded responsibilities for their daily life, including money, food, and clothes. *This* is the common experience that culturally mainstream American teens share during the first year out, and this is what occupies the attentions of most teens during the entire year. In other words, the upper-middle-class young woman who attends a private, four-year liberal arts college and the working-class young man who attends a local community college are both focused on day-to-day life management. What differentiates them is not the colleges they attend, but rather their family, faith, and community starting points. I will develop this argument later (in chapter 2, and discuss its implications in chapter 6), but the evidence to support this interpretation resides in virtually every teen story contained within this volume—as it does in Lowanda Smith's story, next.

LOWANDA SMITH

"Are you *really* gonna eat this food?" Lowanda asked me again as I stood in the cafeteria line behind her at NJ High. "You brave!" Before I could answer, Lowanda screamed—"Woo-hoo! Hell-o, Doenisha! You lookin' good today, girl!" Lowanda screamed a lot, not in anger or fear, but in sheer delight at seeing her friends. And Lowanda had no shortage of friends—I would wager $100 that she could name every senior at NJ High. She walked me from Mr. Williams's social studies class to her locker, then to the cafeteria (where we stood in line to eat lunch at 10:20 a.m.), and then into the senior cafeteria—talking nonstop the entire time. Occasionally, I would answer "yes" or "right," but mostly I just nodded and watched this NJ High socialite perform at peak speed. After introducing me to every senior in the cafeteria (some 70 students), Lowanda insisted that I sit with her girlfriends: Cookie, Tadia, Shatoya, Jo, Dorothea, and Mary.

From that point forward, I ate lunch with the "Girlfriends Seven" every Friday at 10:20 a.m. These energetic black NJ High seniors made sure they thoroughly enjoyed their 30-minute lunch period, telling stories and laughing often, using street vernacular so heavily I had difficulty following their conversation—which was a source of much good-hearted amusement for the Girlfriends Seven. (Lowanda later explained she was biracial: Puerto Rican/African American; but she identified herself as "black" primarily. All seven seniors insisted that I say "black" and not "African American"—a request I honor here as well.) Eating with the Girlfriends Seven became a favorite activity; these young women not only welcomed me into their world, but they took the time to explain it to me, too. Cookie, Tadia, and Shatoya all agreed to taped interviews, and their words appear in subsequent chapters. But I want to introduce Lowanda's story here, as it reveals another side to the fascinating story of American teens and the first year out.

At that first lunch together, and at every subsequent lunch, Lowanda made a point of fervently praying over her food tray. Lowanda would place her elbows on the table, clasp her hands together, close her eyes, bow her head, and pray silently for 10–20 seconds. She would then genuflect as she finished her prayer, and eagerly dig into her food. The rest of the Girlfriends Seven respected this daily ritual, keeping quiet and not teasing Lowanda for this very public demonstration of religious faith. I thought religion might be a common bond among the Girlfriends Seven—and at a foundational level it was, as there was a culture of respect for Christian faith among black students at NJ High. But Tadia was the only other regular churchgoer among the seven. Cookie, Shatoya, and Dorothea attended church infrequently at best, while Jo and Mary never attended church and had no interest in religion. Except for Lowanda's exaggerated prayer ritual, religion was absent from the conversations of the Girlfriends Seven and even from Lowanda's own conversations with me outside of our audio-taped interview. The primary bond among the Girlfriends Seven was not religion, it was shared history: they had been friends since grade school, often assigned to the same classes for eight years or more. And though the friendship among the Girlfriends Seven appeared quite close, they were "just school friends"; Lowanda's only friendship that extended beyond the school day was with Tadia.

Lowanda and Tadia shared a common faith and occasionally attended each other's churches (both are black Protestant congregations). Because my interest lies in how teens make moral sense of their lives, I was interested in how religious teens like Lowanda, or nonreligious teens like Poppy, used available cultural resources to interpret their lives. During our interview, and *only* during our interview, Lowanda drew upon her faith extensively. Lowanda reported she had "absolutely" no doubt about her belief in God and told me her relationship with God is the most important part of her faith. "You gotta have your own special relationship [with God]—if somebody else believes in something it doesn't mean you should. You gotta have your own special relationship with God, because God has his own special relationship with you." Lowanda was not always so committed to her faith, however. She did not like the church she attended with her mother: "I went to a [primarily white] Methodist church before, and everybody was, like, quiet, and I didn't like that. I wanted everybody to get up and start clapping and praising God like that—like that's the kinda church I wanted to go to. So . . . before, I wasn't into church. I just went 'cause my mom . . . made me go to church, then *she* stopped going to church." Most teens who attend religious services regularly do so with their parents—but Lowanda was by that time the only member of her family who attended religious services. Lowanda attended Pentecostal House of Faith and Prayer with her best friend, Terri. "I used to go every Thursday and Sunday, but now I go every Sunday 'cause my mom says I go out too much. So I usually go every Sunday now for both services, night and morning." When I asked Lowanda who was most influential in the development of her faith, Lowanda said it was "Terri, because she's really into it."

Yet, as involved as Lowanda was in her church, she had not accepted its very traditional view of women. Lowanda struggled to explain this.

> All right. I'm a Christian. But my friend Terri, she's a Christian and she only wears skirts, because she believes that women should dress as women. Now, I'm a Christian, but I wear pants, too. . . . I think I gotta work on that because somehow I'm trying to fit into what one church might think [is] the right thing to do, when another church . . . I don't know. I believe that women should dress modestly. Meaning they shouldn't wear like tight pants with holes all in them and butt cheeks all hanging out. I don't want to say [wearing skirts is] what God meant—because I don't know what God really meant, but I believe in the Bible and I believe that whatever is in there is real. But some things I don't abide by and I sin everyday—but you just have to repent.

Lowanda recognized the limits of her ability to follow church teachings, but she also recognized that her church was not the only version of Christian faith available to her. She knew that neither Terri nor her church would go to college with her, and while she wanted her future commitment to faith to increase, she hoped at least that it would "stay the same—I don't want it to decrease; I really don't." Lowanda ended up getting her wish, though I doubt the circumstances that facilitated her increase in faith were ever part of that wish.

I am getting ahead of the story, however, for besides Lowanda's words during our first interview and her lunchtime prayer ritual, there was little else publicly religious about Lowanda. True, she did not dress as revealingly as she could have, but she still dressed like most senior girls, which meant a tight-fitting top paired with snug jeans. Lowanda also knew the words to every hip-hop BET or MTV video, singing along to lyrics that would surely shock fellow church members. Socialite that she was, Lowanda relished NJ High gossip, salting her stories with occasional obscenity—though always apologizing to me afterward (despite my efforts to convince her it was unnecessary). Besides classes and church, Lowanda danced with NJ High's "step team," spent time with her boyfriend, and worked long hours at a local sandwich shop so she could buy and maintain a car. I recall vividly the week Lowanda was "on punishment" for staying out late with her boyfriend and talking back to her mother: she had not combed her hair, she wore dirty sweats and no makeup, and she barely spoke to anyone. Lowanda was in many ways a typical suburban teen girl—just more outgoing and more religiously involved.

In Lowanda's mind, however, she believed her relationship with God had made a profound and observable difference in her life. "People can tell if you are a spiritual person by just looking at you," Lowanda explained. To make her point, she twice contrasted her life as a senior with her life as a freshman. Lowanda first described how she now apologizes to and forgives her friends, rather than gossiping or holding grudges. Lowanda then described her present state of sexual inactivity with her prior state of intense activity: "In ninth grade, you know, sex was something, like, everybody was doing. It was, like, ninth grade! But now that I'm, like, in eleventh and twelfth; when I was, like, in eleventh and twelfth I was, like, 'Whoa, people are crazy!' I'm not, I'm not going to [have sex] because it's not worth it. It's not worth having partners that you're not going to be with. You understand what I sayin'? I can't say that I might be with [my boyfriend] for ten years down the line. I don't know that." In Lowanda's own self-understanding, faith had brought about major change—from grudge-holding to forgiving, from sexually active to sexually abstinent—making her a visibly "spiritual" person. Though

I could not discern a visible difference, the shared history of the Girlfriends Seven must aid their perception, and their respect for Lowanda's daily prayer ritual attests to the change she proclaims.

Like other American teens, Lowanda spoke earnestly of pursuing one field of study in college, only to return home just as earnest about a different course of study. Lowanda planned to become a counseling psychologist, because "you can change somebody's life just by listening to 'em and then giving them feedback." But she returned from her first year at Historically Black College with a major in public relations. Her new goal was to earn $70,000–$90,000 as a public relations "specialist" for Coca-Cola, because she wanted "to be a 'big dog'—I want to have the money." Part of her drive for financial and occupational success surely stemmed from growing up in a single-parent, working-class family. Her hard-working mother worked in a government office and moonlighted as an insurance agent, but never finished her associate's degree. Her mother's efforts bought her a house in the suburbs, but that surrounded Lowanda and her younger siblings with more affluent peers, creating a standard-of-living gap that only widened for Lowanda at Historically Black College.

Lowanda's first year of college, then, was neither "good [n]or bad, I would just say that it's been a learning year." For the first couple of months, Lowanda just wanted to come home. Everything had gotten off on the wrong foot—quite literally. During freshman orientation week, her college held a large student activities fair, with fraternities, sororities, and other groups staffing tables in a large hall with a high ceiling, a balcony, and a wide staircase. The freshmen entered the hall en masse, descending the staircase. As Lowanda descended, she lost her balance and fell down several steps. Physically unhurt, Lowanda's fall silenced the room, and she became known for the rest of the week as "the girl who fell down the stairs." "I was like, 'I just don't belong here.' I called my mom, like, [all the] time. I was like, 'Mom, come get me, because I don't think I belong here.'" Though Lowanda laughed as she recounted the story, she did not find it amusing then. It only added to her rough start, because she also had to deal with a "mess" in the financial aid office (her loan checks had not arrived), and then broke up with her boyfriend of two years during her second week of college. Yet Lowanda spoke with pride about resolving the financial aid problems herself, and she formed a close friendship with another freshman "who also is Pentecostal. I met her in the first week. And I just knew that was just God, you know, trying to say that, trying to keep me on the right ground, trying to keep me in check. So I found a church [near the college]." Lowanda attributed making it through her first year out to the work of God in her life. Finding and getting involved in a church while at college was one example of God's involvement in her life. But returning home created another way she would rely upon her faith.

Although Lowanda broke up with her boyfriend at the start of her freshman year, she stayed in regular contact with him, and both agreed to reunite when she returned for the summer. When Lowanda returned in May, however, it was only to have her ex-boyfriend break her heart:

> We talked off and on during college—and he did have another girlfriend, but I never thought it was that serious. We always talked about getting back together. But when I came back from school, my mother called me. She was like, "Did you hear from [your boyfriend]?" And I'm like, "No, I haven't heard from him." Or whatever. And she's like, "Well, your boss is telling me that he's gonna be a father." . . . So I kind of pulled my hair back and grabbed my car keys and went down to [her boyfriend's workplace]. And I just went in the back, gathered my thoughts, [and] I came up to the [bakery] he was working at and I said, "Is it true?" And he said, "Is what true?" And I said, "Are you gonna be a father?" And he said, "Yes." And I just started cryin' right there, I mean, it's so hard for me. And then later on I called him that same day, he said they're getting married. And now [six weeks later] they're married and they're having a child. And this is the person I was going with for *two years*—and they've been going together for six months and all this has taken place! So it was so hard for me to grasp and I just kept praying to God, like, "God, heal my heart. Please, someday, make me whole again." My heart was just so torn apart, I just stayed in the car for half an hour just cryin'. . . . We always talked about getting back together, we always talked about God and stuff, and then when I came back to hear this, I was just blown away. So I just kept asking God to keep me moving, don't let me just give up now. Just, "God," you know, "help me. Make me whole. Just fill this void in my heart." And he has. And day by day—I mean, I'm not gonna sit here and say that it doesn't bother me anymore—but day by day he is healing my heart and I just can see it.

Lowanda's eyes filled with tears as she spoke, and she vividly demonstrated how relationships—romantic relationships in particular—are crucial to teens during the first year out. Few things are more significant during the first year out than romantic love: seeking it, finding it, keeping it, losing it, believing in it, or rejecting it. As another teen told me succinctly, romantic relationships are "just always in the back of your mind." (I examine the crucial realm of relationships—romantic and otherwise—in chapter 3.)

Lowanda found solace for her broken heart in God. She got her senior year wish of a stronger faith in God—and reinforced that faith by increasing her attendance at religious services to four times weekly: Tuesday, Thursday, and twice on Sunday. For all the "learning" that Lowanda claimed during this first year out, however, she remained much the same person at the end of the first year out that she was as a high school senior. Lowanda still loved to socialize, still looked up to her mother as an outstanding example of what a woman should be, still worked long hours but could not track how she spent her earnings ("I'm a shopaholic with no money."), still demonstrated the keen awareness of artificial race boundaries that many biracial Americans possess ("I attend Historically Black College . . . but I miss the diversity of NJ High; I miss my white friends . . . and my other-race friends"), and still had no views on politics ("I don't really have any—I should have some, but I don't").

Lowanda's political apathy was particularly striking, as she, like the other three teens in this chapter, had just begun her fall semester on September 11, 2001. Unlike Poppy, Lowanda reported that that day had a long-term impact on her—a religious impact. She was mad that Americans pray only during a time of crisis and that the interest in both the tragedy and prayer had already faded away. She wished Americans would remember the tragedy and make prayer a priority in their lives—as she endeavored to do. Religion, then, provided the primary lens that Lowanda employed to view her own life and the larger world. Lowanda did use other lenses—such as those imparted to her by being both biracial and from a single-parent, working-class family—but the religious lens was foremost. Or, to return to my earlier analogy of religion as vegetables, Lowanda had a passion for vegetables and liked to consume several helpings, though she stopped short of the exclusivity that characterizes "religious vegetarians." (Chapter 2 examines teens and the cultural lenses they use to understand the world—giving particular attention to the role of family, faith, and community starting points. Subsequent chapters explore how these starting points affect the first year out.)

ROB ROBERTSON

Though each of the four students I present in this chapter is a unique individual, their stories often share commonalities with other American teens. This young man, however, shares fewer commonalities than the other three.

There are surely other American teens whose lives resemble Rob Robertson's, but I came across precious few during the years I collected data for this project. I include Rob here because he is the progressive educator's "dream teen"—community-engaged, intellectually curious, athletically gifted, self-confident, and politically conscious. Rob is the exception that proves the rule: the vast majority of contemporary American teens have little interest in world or national affairs and view a "broad education" as an annoying hurdle that separates them from their primary goal of obtaining the necessary educational credential for the type of occupation they desire. I argue (in chapter 5) that a handful of "Robs" make it to most colleges—sufficient to perpetuate the myth of liberalizing education and supply the next cohort of college professors—while the vast remainder of college students quietly endure their liberal arts hazing. As unrepresentative as Rob is, he warrants a close examination, for I find atypical teens like Rob reveal important dimensions to teen culture that are less apparent among more typical teens.

Rob reversed the usual pattern. Though I introduced myself to Rob, it was Rob who directed our first conversation by asking questions of me. As the student government vice president, Rob made it his business to know what was happening at NJ High—and that meant finding out who I was and what my purpose was. He already had his answers before we began talking:

> ROB: So you're a professor at TCNJ [The College of New Jersey]?
> INTERVIEWER: Yes.
> ROB: And you're writing a book about high school seniors?
> INTERVIEWER: Yes, I hope to, with cooperation from seniors like you.
> ROB: And when is the book coming out?
> INTERVIEWER: Well, that'll take a few years, because I'm interested in studying what happens during the first year after graduation, and you all haven't graduated yet.
> ROB: Yeah, I guess that would take a while. Well, I'm the vice president of the student government at NJ High, and I'm happy to welcome you to the school.

Rob was quite comfortable speaking as a leader and took his role as an elected representative seriously.

Rob's work in various student organizations meant he often arrived late for lunch or skipped it entirely. I often saw Rob huddled with the principal, vice principal, or athletics director in the hallway, and every teacher I saw passing Rob made a point of greeting him. Because Fridays were my regular day at NJ High, I often saw Rob wearing the shirt of his sports uniform, as he played on several teams and Friday was a frequent game day. As capable a leader as Rob was, though, he was not the center of attention at the honor student/athlete table (i.e., Popular Kids table). About a dozen seniors, all of them honor students and all of them athletes, student leaders, or cheerleaders, sat together every lunch period. All but two students at this table were white. Other students would call this group "the stuck-up, popular clique," and, unlike the Back Corner Boys or the Girlfriends Seven, the Popular Kids were aloof. For example, one time when Rob arrived early to lunch, I joined him and a fellow wrestler, Chris, at the Popular Kids' regular table. But rather than join us, the rest of the Popular Kids opted for a different table across the room, and soon even Chris abandoned Rob and me to sit there, too. Though I asked four of the Popular Kids to sit for an interview, three turned me down directly, and only Rob agreed to talk to me. So I respected the implicit wishes of the Popular Kids that I leave them alone and did so.

Rob, like the student government officers I recall from my own high school, hoped to be elected president of the United States. If not that, he wished he could be Michael Jordon. Why Michael Jordon?

> Well, first of all, just because I like basketball a lot. But I really admire his, like, excellence. That's one thing I really admire in life is excellence. And I think for him to be as good as he is, with the kind of integrity he has, and his reputation on the line as much as it is, I think to be as upstanding as he is—is *something*. And I think the way he excels at his task . . . he's so fine-tuned, and so focused. And, like, I personally think he's a genius.

Politically, Rob admired former New Jersey Senator Bill Bradley. "He was the athlete and then the politician." Rob admired Bradley's integrity and "his political viewpoints," because they meshed with Rob's own "liberal" views. Unlike most teens who lacked political interest (like Poppy and Lowanda), or even the few teens with political leanings (like Kristi, whose story is next), Rob could describe both his general political views and his specific policy positions in detail—and they tracked quite closely to the moderate Democratic positions of Bill Clinton and Al Gore. Yet Rob would vote for "John McCain over a Bill Clinton—because I think that *who* the man is, or the woman is, is more important than [their policies] sometimes. Especially now when we've just had Bill Clinton with all his moral failings." Rob knew his political awareness and interest made him unique. Only his best friend, John, and the student government president, Randi, were "probably as interested in politics as I am." Rob attributed his interest in politics to his parents.

Rob's father earned a master's degree in public administration from an Ivy League university and managed a state government office; Rob's mother was a social worker with the county government. Both, then, were public employees with graduate degrees, and both were surely proud of their son, who said with utmost sincerity: "I feel like I need to do something that kind of helps the world." To Rob, that meant becoming president of the United States. But Rob was not waiting for adulthood to "help the world." As a high school senior, he already had years of experience with volunteer groups and had been involved in school activities since elementary school. Reflecting on his work as NJ High student government vice president, Rob reported,

> That has really been a positive experience—I think we did a lot, we accom-
> plished a lot—and especially compared to what we've done in years past. . . .
> Actually one of the more rewarding things . . . from high school has been
> that it's become more of a community since I got here. . . . When I first got
> here, it didn't really feel like I was belonging to anything special, but . . .
> now, it seems like . . . I was kind of part of something special when I was at
> [NJ High].

As evidence, Rob pointed to the increased attendance at sport games, the successful class competition week he helped create, and the general in-crease in NJ High "school spirit." I was particularly struck by Rob's use of the word *community*—so I asked him about it. He defined it well, saying community is a place where "I like to interact with a lot of people . . . and feel like I'm part of a group."

That type of community was one of the things Rob appreciated most about NJ High—and one of the things he would miss in college. Rob de-scribed Elite College, where he would attend college in the fall, as "almost a utopia, you know. It's kind of nice; everybody gets along, everybody's edu-cated, everybody respects everybody else, everybody listens to everybody else." Rob preferred NJ High, because it was "the real world." Rob knew that he would miss "the adversity—where people, you know, clash—[while, at Elite College], there isn't as much poverty and stuff like that. . . . [At NJ High], you kind of have problems to deal with, you know. People have their prejudices, in just about every aspect—like, prejudiced about school, prej-udiced about race and gender, things like that. . . . I don't know, I kinda like dealing with that for some reason; I'm not sure why, but I do." I expected

Rob to become the freshman class president at Elite College; he possessed strong leadership skills, was recruited to play varsity sports, and had a strong desire to serve. But Rob's experience at Elite College was anything but utopian.

Rob had a miserable first year at Elite College. He knew he did not fit in by his second day, when his teammates—a bunch of "snobby rich kids"— whined throughout the first practice about the heat, the coach's drills, the temperature of the drinking water, and the like.

> ROB: Like, whoa—I don't like these people. I was pretty uncomfortable from the second day.
> INTERVIEWER: So how did you deal with that?
> ROB: I don't know. I mean, I just kinda kept going.

It did not get any better. At the "meet your new hall mates" group gathering the next week, each student was to share something about themselves that others might initially misunderstand. Hall mates shared information like "I'm grumpy in the morning" or "I don't like people borrowing my stuff." Rob shared that he liked occasional off-color jokes. "It was like, you know, 'I might make a joke, but it's not meant to offend anybody,' and everything like that. And then, everybody goes around and goes, 'Yeah, I, I'm really offended by certain types of jokes,' and stuff like that." Though many freshmen transfer to other schools for lesser cause than this, Rob was not accustomed to giving up. So he hunkered down and pushed through both fall and spring semesters. But it took a toll on him. The stalwart NJ High leader and future U.S. president found himself spending an hour each week in the college counseling center as he struggled to cope. "I don't know if I would admit to myself that I was depressed. [Pauses.] I mean, I might just say, you know, 'I'll work through it,' or something like that." Rob vacillated between three interpretations of his first year difficulties: that he chose the wrong school (i.e., that he should have chosen a large public university), that he was clinically depressed, or that he needed to be "born again." The first interpretation was his primary one when I reinterviewed him—though his concern about being a "quitter" kept him from making a final decision about transferring. The second interpretation was his counselor's diagnosis—but Rob was unwilling to accept it. And the third interpretation was from one of his closest friends at Elite College—yet, as much as he respected this friend, he was "not in any kind of position to decide anything new about religion."

In fact, Rob—a self-described but congregationally unaffiliated Unitarian—knew more about Christianity than many of the Christian teens I interviewed. Some of that came from attending church youth groups with his friends—one at a conservative Baptist church, another at a mainline Presbyterian church, and a third at a Roman Catholic church. The rest came from Rob's intellectual curiosity and love of learning. Rob was one of few teens I interviewed who enjoyed reading, and one of very few who preferred nonfiction books. At the time of our reinterview, Rob was reading political scientist Samuel P. Huntington's *Clash of Civilizations and the Remaking of the World Order.* He was reading this because "as I told you last year—if I wanna be president, you know, I gotta know some stuff." But the breadth of his intellect was apparent as he talked to me, for he mentioned this book while answering a question about long-term, personal effects of September 11, and in his answer he covered global political change, altered bases of identity, and his own view of God. Rob explained that Huntington wrote the book in 1995:

> ROB: But it really explains what's going on right now [in 2002]. And how things are shifting from kind of a bipolar politics of the cold war—where ... the question during the cold war was, 'What side are you on?' Now the question is, 'Who are you?' And I think there's a real return to people's traditional beliefs and practices right now. . . . I'd say even in America, I think, people are looking back at their religious roots. . . . People are starting to define themselves and find themselves differently than they would have, before that.
>
> INTERVIEWER: Have you?
>
> ROB: Sort of. I mean, I think about things a little bit differently, like what's important to me. I mean, I was brought up with no religion. But I mean, I think I told you last time I believe in God. . . . I wouldn't even call myself agnostic. I'd say I believe in a literal God. But, you know, I don't have ... a church to identify with. But, in terms of ... life values ... I think I've become a little bit more solid ... somewhat because of the [Elite College] environment I was in.

Few college students would ever read such a book voluntarily, much less use it to interpret global change after September 11 or reflect upon their own identities in light of that global change. Most teens view politics, national issues, and global issues as important in theory but irrelevant to their present daily lives. (I examine teens' narrowed perspectives on the larger world in chapter 6.) But on this matter, Rob was again an exception, as he refused to secure critical identities, like his political and religious identity, in an identity lockbox like most teens do.

Most youth secure critical identities and beliefs in a lockbox during their first year out, and I believe they remain there for quite some time thereafter. I suggest two reasons for this phenomenon. First, Americans in general are suspicious of large institutions, and higher education in particular. Education is respected for its credentialing role but not for much else. Second, because young Americans must earn their own degrees and climb their own occupational ladders (though affluent parents can make the process easier), culturally mainstream American teens are deeply affected by the reality of downward social mobility and the desire to avoid it. Anthropologist Katherine Newman calls this "falling from grace," and essayist Barbara Ehrenreich calls it the "fear of falling," and both make compelling cases for its commonality among mainstream Americans.[3] Consequently, few teens care to explore diverse interests or question critical identities, because doing so could put them out of step with the mainstream of American culture they yearn to stay within. Besides, the pressure to successfully manage an increasingly complex daily life leaves little time for anything else.[4] (I develop these points in chapters 2 and 5.)

That one of Rob closest college friends would be an evangelical Christian might seem unusual—until one hears Rob describe the peer environment at Elite College. First, Rob complained about the politically liberal, "antiestablishment" ethos of the campus in general: "I think most of them come from a pretty upper-class environment. And I think a lot of them are kind of disgusted with it. And you know the upper-class benefits from 'the establishment,' so they're antiestablishment." Rob, politically liberal himself, was not bothered so much by the liberalism. But his tolerance for privileged teens spouting antiestablishment views was not high—and plummeted as he watched his classmates' response to September 11, 2001. "September 11 . . . OK, you know how the rest of the country was 90 percent approval of Bush, 10 percent disapproval? I think it was probably the flip of that there. . . . I mean, after that happened, it was like . . . there's only one thing I can support right now [i.e., the president]." Second, Rob had no respect for the sexual mores of his peers. Rob's parents "instilled" their sex views early. His mother taught Rob—well before any of his peers even knew about sex—about the dangers of sexually transmitted diseases, the risks of pregnancy, and the value of abstinence. "I don't think my Mom meant to, but I think she might have scared me and my little brother out of dating a little bit." Thus Rob, a handsome and popular high school athlete, surprised me when he confided during his first interview that he had "never kissed a girl"—even though he was 18 and just weeks away from high school graduation. Rob arrived at Elite College, then, from a very different place than most of his classmates did.

When I asked Rob whether his views on sex had changed since our first interview, I hit a hot button issue for Rob:

> I think it's stupid to say that—this is me talking to [Elite College] right now, because they're all like, they're still in the '60s. It's the sexual revolution, and anybody who tells them that they're not ready to have sex is "an asshole." And I think that's crap. They say, "It's none of my parents' business whether I have sex or not." It's *totally* my parents' business whether I do that, because if I have a kid, it's totally gonna affect their life. If I get AIDS, it's totally gonna affect their life. Their responsibility is to bring me up to be an adult, so that I can live on my own, make my own money, [and not] depend on them. . . . I'm not gonna be healthy if I get any diseases, and I'm not gonna be financially well off if I have a kid. Neither are they. They're gonna have to raise my kid. My kid is gonna grow up in kind of a weird environment, because if I have sex as a teenager, if I get married to the girl, it's probably not gonna last—if you look at statistics. And it's just stupid. . . . Having sex as a teenager is stupid. And I think having sex as an adult is OK when you do it responsibly. . . . Kids have sex like kids. . . . They don't take precautions about it. . . . Have sex like an adult, you know? Or just practice abstinence. What's wrong with that? . . . You know, that's another thing—it's like, "Oh, you're copping out to the establishment if you practice abstinence." What the hell are you talking about? . . . I don't care if I'm not having sex right now!

By proclaiming abstinence and supporting President Bush in the days after September 11, Rob found himself seriously out of step with his peers—and in a position to share a lot of common ground with an evangelical classmate.

The biggest change during Rob's first year out—besides going from NJ High leader to Elite College outsider—was a new ambivalence about his long-term career goals. Rob was no longer certain he wanted to be U.S. president, and not even sure he was interested in his fallback career as a high school teacher and coach. Instead, Rob was seriously entertaining the idea of getting a Ph.D. in history or American studies and becoming a college professor, after he completed two years in the Peace Corps. But this redirection of Rob's occupational plans confirms my argument about liberal arts education: only a handful of students on each campus find a liberal arts education to be deeply meaningful and important, and most of those end up becoming college professors themselves (while the rest choose other fields where progressive ideals are valued—such as educational administration or counseling psychology). And so the liberal arts paradigm perpetuates itself, while remaining out of sync with the vast majority of college students.

Though Rob's first year out was not the triumphant one that NJ High faculty would have predicted, Rob demonstrated remarkable continuity in behavior patterns and life priorities. And in this respect, Rob is wholly typical. Rob, Lowanda, and Poppy each ended their first year out with the same behavior patterns and life priorities they began with—in fact, they seem more established in those patterns and priorities at the end of the year than at the beginning. Poppy found the fun and excitement he was seeking in high school, Lowanda experienced the deepening of faith she wished for, and Rob identified the Peace Corps and higher education as the specific ways he wanted to help the world. Even Kristi, who was engaged in active identity work when I first interviewed her, returned to her roots just months into her first year out.

KRISTI KRAMER

Chuck and Jack liked to flirt with Kristi in the crude, unpolished way 17-year-old high school boys do: "Come with me, Kristi, and I'll satisfy *all* your feminine desires." "Yeah, right," Kristi retorted. "I'd sooner be dead." But Kristi smiled as she said this, and while it was clear she was not interested in having sex with either Chuck or Jack, Kristi regarded the conversation as more amusing than offensive. After introductions, Chuck and Jack headed off and Kristi apologized for the boys' comments. "Those guys can be really gross sometimes; just ignore them, that's what I do." In any event, the guys knew Kristi was involved in a serious relationship with a 22-year-old Marine, and they flirted with her more because Kristi was good-humored about it than out of any expectation of success.

Kristi was an enigma. Attractive and outgoing, Kristi sat with just one or two other NJ High seniors—and not the same seniors every lunch. Sometimes Kristi sat with Dale, a shy and somewhat obese, white senior male. Sometimes she sat with a couple of black senior females. And sometimes she sat with Chuck or another of the Back Corner Boys. Kristi was the first NJ High senior to complain to me about the cliques at NJ High, where "all they care about is what you're wearing." Because most of the white females at NJ

High dressed similarly, the fashion differences that distinguished cliques were too subtle for this 35-year-old, fashion-oblivious male to identify. Perhaps Kristi did not fit in with the Popular Kids because she was not in honors classes or because she had blue-collar parents. Perhaps she did not fit in because her best friend, Raquel Johnson, was black, while most NJ High students have only "school friends" across racial lines. Or perhaps she did not fit in because she decided "she didn't care anymore" what other students at NJ High thought of her—and "got into" the coffee shop "scene" of folk music and poetry readings.

Kristi worked nearly thirty hours each week. She waitressed at a small restaurant and was a cashier at a local music shop, too. At the music shop, "The people I work with are poets and I love to write [poetry]. So they took me out to the [Funky Downtown Café], which is in [Small City], and I just loved it. I loved the whole writing thing and the speaking in front of people and letting my emotions out to different people." This "poetry scene" could not have been more different from Kristi's military family background, and Kristi had just begun to explore this scene in the weeks preceding our first interview. Yet Kristi had already integrated language from this subculture into her own speech—describing how she liked to "slam" poetry; how her new friends were "different," while her old friends were "all alike"; and how everything she used to do for entertainment was "so clichéd," while now she wanted and needed "diversity" to enjoy herself. Kristi, it seemed to me, was engaged in active presentation work at the time of our first interview—working more consciously than other teens on what sociologist Erving Goffman calls "the presentation of self."[5] Thus, Kristi emphasized how she was "open-minded" and wanted to "experience as much as she possibly can," and she talked about her sexually intimate relationship with her boyfriend freely. Kristi only balked at answering one question—telling me her SAT scores. That refusal came during a conversation in which Kristi told me she planned to "be in school for the rest of her life," obtaining a master's degree and then a Ph.D.—but admitted she had "no interest" in teaching at the collegiate or any other level and no desire to do research. Though interviewees often seek to impress their interviewers, Kristi made a concerted effort to do so.

Kristi was far from one-dimensional, however. Safe inside the interviewing room, Kristi described a strong commitment to her family and a notable involvement in her local Roman Catholic parish. Kristi's mother and father were both 22 years old when she was born, and Kristi was soon joined by two younger brothers. They lived in various apartments during

Kristi's preschool years, eventually settling into one apartment located two blocks from Kristi's maternal grandmother. Almost every day, Kristi would "have tea" with her grandmother, and they would talk about books, about school, and about religion:

> I saw her every day or I would talk to her every day. There wasn't a day I can remember that went by that I never saw or talked to my grandmother. . . . Every day we'd have tea. That was our thing—tea time was our thing. And we'd talk about life and religion, 'cause she was very religious. We'd talk about books. We'd talk about anything I wanted to talk about. We'd talk about anything she wanted to talk about. . . . And that kind of shaped me, talking to her. I miss that.

Just eight months before our first interview, Kristi's beloved grandmother died and her family had moved into her grandmother's house. "I hate living in that house," Kristi told me. "Because when my grandmother was sick, we used to go there every day. And she had her bed in the corner of the living room, and I was there when she died. So to me, I hate the living room and I hate the kitchen and I hate the bedroom. So I try to avoid those rooms as much as possible. . . . I can't be in that house half the time. I hate it." Watching the long and painful death of her grandmother—who was devoutly Catholic—left Kristi "angry with God" for several months.

Then Kristi underwent a profound "turnaround." She began to eagerly attend Mass weekly, read her Bible, give money weekly to her church, and go to confession. "I was mad at him [God] for three months, because he took the one person that meant so much to me away from me. And she was in pain until her last breath, and I did not understand that. I did not understand that. . . . And then, all of a sudden, I did a complete turnaround. I don't know what happened. I guess it was her—I swear it was her [my grandmother], saying, '[Kristi], knock it off!'" Kristi had always attended Mass weekly, because her parents required all of their children to attend with them. The difference was that Kristi began to really enjoy attending. Sunday Mass provided Kristi with a regular and meaningful religious experience, though she struggled to articulate that meaning:[6] "When you're sitting in church and you can go in and feel so completely able to get your thoughts out of your head . . . like you're sitting there and just getting your thoughts out and feel so completely satisfied after you leave—there's *something* there." As committed as Kristi was—even teaching confirmation classes at her local parish—Kristi admitted she was far from perfect. "If I want to do something, I'm gonna do it and not have to worry about breaking a commandment." Kristi, like many teen Catholics I interviewed, did not follow church prohibitions on birth control or premarital sex. "The sex before marriage, well yeah, I just broke that commandment. I mean, I believe in it, I fully do believe in it." Yet Kristi followed Catholic doctrine on abortion, saying she would "keep the baby" if she ever got pregnant and using birth control to reduce her likelihood of becoming pregnant.

Kristi did not "get in" to her first-choice college, a small Catholic college located near Big East City, nor did she get into her second- or third-choice colleges, so Kristi planned to attend the local community college and transfer to a four-year college after her first semester. Kristi complained that she "did not get any guidance" from NJ High, but admitted part of the problem was that she "had no idea what I wanted to do or where I wanted to go." Once she got into the "poetry scene," Kristi thought she would like to study writing or "something in the arts," but even that desire was tentative. Because her mother never attended college (because Kristi's grandfather had "skipped out with all her college money") and Kristi's father had earned a vocational certificate only, Kristi received no parental advice during her college decision process. Hence, Kristi applied to three colleges, all very respectable—and all well beyond Kristi's average academic record.

Kristi had "misaligned ambitions," to use sociologists Barbara Schneider and David Stevenson's term for teens with high ambitions but little knowledge of occupational pathways.[7] Schneider and Stevenson attribute the rising number of teens with misaligned ambitions to parents and teachers not doing enough to guide teens toward clear occupational choices. Schneider and Stevenson's work, however, overlooks two critical cultural factors that were readily apparent during my fieldwork. The first of these cultural factors is college application and admission as a status competition: Kristi, like many other NJ High seniors, would often name drop the colleges she applied to during conversations at lunch (conversations probably made more frequent by the presence of this college professor at the table). Other seniors would do the same. "I hope to go to Georgetown," said one NJ High senior, who a week earlier admitted to failing her remedial science class. I suspected many seniors were overreaching and seeking to impress listeners with the names of schools to which they had applied. My suspicions were largely confirmed: exit surveys revealed that a few seniors would be attending private colleges (some prestigious, others not), many would be attending state colleges (some well-regarded, most not), and many would be attending the local community college.

The second cultural factor contributing to misaligned ambitions is, ironically, teen nonchalance about actual fields of study, occupational interests, or future matters in general. The majority of NJ High seniors had "no idea" or "no clue" what occupational field they wanted to study, and many seemed to relish their cavalier approach to these matters. In fact, NJ High seniors often stereotyped peers who resisted this culture of nonchalance—disdainfully describing "straight-A types" who wanted to be doctors or politicians, or "vo-tech kids" who planned to work in building trades or beauty salons. Only in response to a direct question about intended college majors or career plans could I get seniors to talk about the future, and they generally offered vague statements like, "Maybe I'll do something in business," or negations like, "Definitely not anything in science." It is as if a new, race-neutral "oppositional culture"[8] was emerging at NJ High that labeled career or life planning as something that only "straight-A types" or "vo-tech kids" did. If true and if widespread, no increase in career guidance by parents or teachers will reduce the prevalence of misaligned ambitions among contemporary teens. (In chapter 5, I develop these points at greater length.)

Returning to Kristi's story, I learned during our second interview that Kristi had not transferred to a four-year college, but instead attended both semesters at her community college. In fact, Kristi now planned to finish her associate's degree in psychology before transferring to a four-year college. Kristi "loved" her professors at the community college and made a number of new friends in her classes. She decided she "wants to work with inner-city kids" and planned to get a master's degree in counseling or social work. Kristi made no mention of writing or the arts, and only after I asked did Kristi say she did not have "much time" to write poetry anymore. Kristi and her new friends sometimes went to coffee houses to listen to the blues, but not often, and she refused to "do the party scene" (in fact, she drank only once during her entire first year out—at a family dinner celebrating her high school graduation). Kristi's social life was limited, in part, because she developed a medical issue soon after high school graduation that took several months to stabilize. It was also limited because she worked three different jobs for a total of forty-five hours per week, in addition to taking a full load of classes at the community college. And it was limited because Kristi's spent a lot of time with her family, in part because Kristi's other grandmother died in late August, exactly one year to the day after her first grandmother died.

Kristi described how she went from "itching to leave" home for college as a high school senior to not "being in a hurry about it" anymore:

KRISTI: In the past year, we've gotten [my parents and I] a lot closer. I don't know why, but we have.

INTERVIEWER: Do you think it has been a change at their end, your end, or both?

KRISTI: My end. Actually, both. We communicate a lot more than we did last year because of everything that was going on, and then after the second death in our family in a year, everything changed. We started appreciating each other more. 'Cause I think you get to the point where you live together, you see each other every day, so you take it for granted that they're in your house and whatever. But . . . we talk now and we have dinners together at least twice a week so we can talk and stuff.

INTERVIEWER: Is there a moment in time or a particular period that you can point to when this change happened?

KRISTI: I'd have to say the middle of my first semester in school . . . the middle of October [2001] it changed.

Though Kristi pointed only to the loss of her second grandmother in August 2001 as the cause of his new family togetherness, I was struck that the change also occurred just weeks after September 11. So I pushed Kristi a little further about the timing of this change, and she narrated her family's October events.

KRISTI: My parents went away for a weekend. . . . I took care of my little brother . . . 'cause it was their anniversary, so I told them to get out. I was just like, "Just go away." So they went and I took care of my brother. And [then] they came back, and it just . . . everything changed. I don't know why. I still to this day have no clue why.

INTERVIEWER: But you started eating more meals together?

KRISTI: No, we just started enjoying each other. My mom and I became real close, and now my dad and I—'cause I really didn't talk to my dad, . . . but then we became closer. We started talking more. 'Cause my dad's not one to talk. So all of a sudden he started talking to me more.

A bit later, I asked Kristi about September 11 and whether it had a long-term effect on her. Her response was immediate and personal. "I'm not taking anything for granted. Like my relationships with people and the way I think now. 'Life's too short to be miserable' is my new thing. 'Cause I've noticed everybody walks around miserable, but the people who died that day didn't have the chance to finish out their lives. Some of them were in their 20s, and that was ridiculous, I thought. They had their lives taken away from them for no reason." Kristi saw her own life affected by that horrific day but did not connect her changed family dynamics to the possibility of a similar effect on her parents. Of course, Kristi's own maturation is a possible factor, too. As literary legend Mark Twain famously said, "When I was 16, my father was a fool. When I turned 25, I was surprised at how much he had learned in nine years." Though Kristi was only turning 20, she had apparently gained an appreciation for her father (and mother) that Mark Twain gained at 25.

Part of understanding youth during the first year out is distinguishing maturational effects from institutional effects. Maturational effects become clearer when institutional differences are compared. Thus, I drew teen participants from two broad institutional contexts: those who attended four-year colleges and those who worked nearly full-time and attended community colleges or vocational programs—usually full time. (Though this pool is less diverse than I initially desired,[9] my analyses of U.S. Census Bureau statistics indicate that about 80 percent of teens from households earning $25,000 or more annually end up in one of these two categories. So while the teens whose stories are told here do not represent all high school graduates, they are selected from the statistical and cultural majority.[10])

That Kristi had definite plans to transfer to a four-year college and to complete both bachelor's and master's degrees distinguishes her from many community college students. That Kristi juggled a full-time course load while working forty-five hours weekly, however, is wholly typical of community college students. Almost all community college students are employed, and many are employed full time.[11] Kristi further represents new community college freshmen in that she lived at home and stayed with her same employers during her first year of community college (briefly adding a third part-time job as a nanny). Kristi's experience prompts two observations. First, by continuing with her employers, Kristi made her first year out somewhat easier, but she did so at the expense of gaining more career-related work experiences. Many American teens view their current work as little more than a source of money and do not explore options that would expose them to new opportunities or move them closer to their long-term career goals. Second, wide parental latitude and increased personal and financial obligations made Kristi's first year out more similar to than different from the first year out of residential college freshmen. If anything, the greater personal and financial obligations of most teens who live at home during their first year out brings about *more* maturity than for those teens who live at college and have schoolwork as their primary obligation—as the latter activity rarely consumes more than thirty-five hours per week. (I develop these observations in chapters 4 and 5.)

Kristi worked because she had to pay her own tuition, books, and college fees, pay her own car expenses, plus cover her basic living expenses—clothes, meals, phone, and entertainment. As a blue-collar teen, Kristi's parents could not fund the "American teen lifestyle" that Kristi and virtually every other teen I interviewed sought to live. This lifestyle (described in chapter 4) requires cars, clothes, food, entertainment, and technology and costs $500 to $1,500 monthly. Because few parents can or will impart such sums directly to teens, Kristi's parents allowed her to start working during her sophomore year of high school. Blue-collar teens like Kristi often reported working sooner than their more affluent peers and went to great lengths to live as similarly to their more affluent peers as they possibly could. Thus, Kristi worked more hours, drove an older car, wore the same clothes more frequently, and had more credit card debt than her middle- and upper-middle-class peers. But she generally succeeded in blending in with these same peers, which was an important, if unexamined, goal of hers. (I take up the economic life of Kristi and the rest of my interviewees in chapter 4.)

All of this kept Kristi very busy during her first year out and may have affected Kristi's decline in church attendance. Kristi said that she had "shunned away from the church for a while. I don't know why, but in the past year I have. And I think it drives my parents nuts, but I haven't had any interest in it in a while. I don't know why." I asked Kristi why she was "shunning" church, when it had been an important part of her life at the end of her senior year. Kristi agreed that church had been important to her, saying, "I went and I got a lot out of it." But "then, right after my other grandmother died, I said, 'Forget it—I'm done.' I don't know why. I guess I was angry. I don't know. I guess I still am." Yet Kristi had not abandoned her identity as a Roman Catholic nor notably altered her basic religious beliefs. She described herself as "spiritual, I guess," and offered as evidence that "[I] pray every night" and "believe in my religion." In fact, Kristi prayed the Rosary every night and then prayed more after that, spending approximately twenty minutes in prayer nightly. Kristi further believed that the Roman Catholic Church is the "one true church," accepted the church's authority, wanted to be "married in a Roman Catholic church," and planned to "raise [her] kids Catholic." Kristi also taught confirmation classes at her parish, which she admitted "is hypocritical in a way, 'cause I don't go to church, and I'm preaching to these kids, 'You have to go to church.'" Further driving a wedge between her and the Catholic Church is Kristi's continued relationship with her Marine boyfriend, with whom she remained sexually intimate. Still, Kristi did not "think I'll be shunning away from the church my whole life" and planned to attend Mass weekly "at some point." Kristi viewed her avoidance of Mass, then, as a short-term reaction to the "unjustified" deaths of her two grandmothers, rather than a permanent alteration of her religious practice. I got the sense that Kristi, by "shunning" weekly Mass, thought she was punishing God for allowing her grandmothers to die—and that she knew she would eventually make amends with God.

I did notice that Kristi was far more articulate about political and social issues during her second interview than during her first. When we first spoke, Kristi was quick to say that she despised racial prejudice and offered "The rich get richer and the poor get poorer" as her explanation for economic inequality—but she did not want to describe her political views ("I'm not into the political thing anymore"). When pressed to choose a political affiliation, she answered hesitantly, "Probably on the Republican side, I think." A year later, Kristi's hesitance was gone. She still despised prejudice and still offered "The rich get richer . . ." as her explanation for global disparities in wealth. But Kristi had become keenly interested in politics, articulated strong pro-life and proeducation positions, reported she "always voted Republican," and readily answered my "three things you wish you could change" question as follows: (1) end all war, (2) end global poverty, and (3) make economic opportunity available to all. Perhaps Kristi's new articulateness was aided by her college writing, history, and sociology courses (which also gave her a better sense of what college professors like me want to hear); perhaps it came from spending more time with her father, grandfather, and boyfriend—all past or present members of the Armed Forces and all staunchly Republican; or perhaps it was a return to an earlier interest in politics that was temporarily jettisoned ("not into the political thing *anymore*") during Kristi's exploration of the "poetry scene" in her senior year. Kristi did not know herself, and I hesitate to assign cause. I suspect, however, that all three factors were important and all three influenced Kristi's interest and perspectives.

Kristi's first year out did not work out the way she hoped. She was living at home and not at a four-year college near Big East City. She would stay two years at community college, and not transfer to four-year college after her first semester. And she no longer had time to write poetry or be engaged in the arts. But Kristi was not complaining. She liked her community college professors, she identified a career path that excited her, and she came to truly enjoy the time she spent with her parents and her brothers during her first year out. By earning good grades in her classes, she was putting herself in a good position to transfer to a four-year college and eventually complete a bachelor's degree. If she does that, Kristi would be among the minority (35 percent) of community college students who pursue four-year degrees. Because the state of New Jersey requires its public colleges to maintain transfer agreements with its community colleges, Kristi's odds of completion should increase if she chooses an in-state public college.

Though some might conclude Kristi abandoned her dreams of writing, getting involved in the arts, and living in the city, I would not agree. Her interests in these things were more of a flirtation, and her average academic skills combined with her blue-collar background suggest she would have had a low probability of breaking into, much less succeeding in, that highly competitive field. Planning to work with needy children in nearby Small City, with a nonprofit agency like the Catholic Youth Organization, was a realistic future goal that would likely provide meaningful work for Kristi and even provide opportunities for her to connect her lingering interests in writing and the arts with youth development. It was also a goal that would fit nicely with her newfound appreciation for her family and her desire to marry and have children. Kristi's exit from NJ High's culture of nonchalance, her enjoyment of several college courses, and her new family connectedness following September 11 may have encouraged Kristi to open her identity lockbox somewhat and, by reflecting more deeply upon herself and her relationships, to gain a greater sense of purpose or direction for her life.

SEATED AT A WOBBLY TABLE

Poppy's, Lowanda's, Rob's, and Kristi's stories illustrate many important aspects of American teens' first year out, and I have used their stories to introduce several observations and general interpretations. In this closing section, I will describe a "table" schema I use to organize these interpretations into a more meaningful whole. I envision a table around which the vast majority of American high school graduates gather; that table is the first year out. Tables serve a number of purposes in America—meals, conversations, negotiations, displays, work, and play—and we have all had to tolerate a wobbly one at some point. Though any metaphor is admittedly imperfect, the one I believe best summarizes the first year out for Poppy, Lowanda, Rob, and Kristi is one that positions them (and their peers) around a wobbly table.

Two pedestals support this first-year-out table. One pedestal represents the new economic realities of global America. That is, it represents an American economy that is inextricably tied to the worldwide economy, that has outsourced manufacturing and now is outsourcing technical and support functions, that prefers short-term contracts with an on-call workforce to the long-term consistency of career employees, and that demands long hours from ever more credentialed specialists. The other pedestal represents the popular moral culture of mainstream America. That is, it represents the default American socialization process that generates citizens who celebrate personal effort and individual achievement; express patriotism; believe in God and affirm a spiritual afterlife; value loyalty to family, friends, and coworkers; expect personal moral freedom; distrust large organizations and bureaucracies; and pursue happiness primarily through personal intimacy and individual consumption. (These two pedestals, connected yet distinct, are discussed further in chapter 2.) But note that the first-year-out table, though generally sound, does have a noticeable wobble. This is partly because the moral culture pedestal is starting to crack and partly because the new economic realities pedestal has an internal hydraulic lift that raises or lowers its end of the table on a schedule of its own choosing.

The teens who gather around this wobbly table find two items on it. The first item on the table is an *identity lockbox*, into which teens can place their critical religious, political, racial, gender, and class identities for safekeeping during the first year out (and beyond). Because the table does wobble, most teens make quick use of the lockbox. Besides, everyone else at the table seems to be doing it, and teens like to fit in. The second item on the table is a complex but engaging board game known as *daily life management*. This game has a myriad of pieces and complicated rules: there are pieces representing relationships with peers, family, and various authority figures (e.g., instructors, bosses, coaches)—and a host of possible combinations thereof; there are monies to be earned, managed, and spent; there are social activities to choose and navigate; and there are refueling requirements (e.g., food, clothing, and health) for each player (see chapter 3 for a fuller description). Given the intensity of the game, its interactive nature, and the range of strategies one can apply as it is played, most teens never give a second thought to their use of the lockbox and forget its presence on the table. Some teens, for various reasons, will occasionally peek inside the box, while a select few will keep their critical identities out of the lockbox and try to inject them into the daily life management game.

The encouraging news is that the majority of teens learn to play the daily life management game fairly well. They gain valuable skills in intimate and peer relationships, adjust to changes in their relationships with their families, learn how to satisfy the authority figures in their lives, manage their gratifications, and forge strategies to meet their food, clothing, and money needs. The discouraging news is that widespread use of the identity lockbox diminishes teens' willingness to connect their daily lives to deeper values or larger purposes, or to consider those values and purposes thoughtfully. This not only impedes teens' immediate sense of purpose and direction, it also reduces teens' likelihood of recognizing and valuing their connectedness to larger communities—from voluntary organizations to localities to state, nation, and world.

Please do not view this, however, as just another professor's rant about a new generation of college students—as I have become convinced that my own generation of college students was little different. (In fact, political scientist Philip Jacob demonstrated that college students in the 1940s and 1950s were also similar, which suggests that the 1960s and 1970s—when many campuses witnessed political turmoil and when progressive educational ideals became institutionalized—were the aberration and not the norm.[12]) Rather, my concern is fourfold. First, it is for the teens themselves, who simply seek to pursue happiness as they have been taught, but who find themselves ensnarled by a culture that prioritizes short-term efficiency to the detriment of long-term effectiveness and celebrates superficiality while ignoring those whose lives have been shaped by purpose and connected to community. Second, it is for the parents, educators, and clergy who wish to enrich the lives of youth but who have unknowingly underestimated what adolescents can learn and overestimated what they can meaningfully integrate on their own. Third, it is for scholars who may overgeneralize their own *atypical* youth experiences to youth in general and then become frustrated by the disengaged pragmatism of these newly emerging adults. And fourth, it is for Americans in general, who too readily tolerate lives dominated by everyday urgencies and too quickly distract themselves from the thought that life is not what it should be. (I expand several of these points in chapter 2 and return to all four in chapter 6.)

Though some readers may wish these identity lockboxes would be unlocked and their contents thoughtfully considered and meaningfully evaluated during the first year out, I believe that hope is unreasonable. The global economic forces and slowly deteriorating popular American moral culture that give the first-year-out table its wobble are not about to alter anytime soon. But more can be done to encourage those teens who do want to examine the purpose or direction of their lives—by engaging them at deeper levels *before* and *after* the first year out and by supporting them as they learn the daily life management game *during* the first year out. There is a window of opportunity, for example, to engage some teens more fully with their communities prior to the first year out, when teens have less daily life to manage and more time to integrate community with core identities (particularly if one recognizes the dubious value of most teen employment and the value of community engagement—see chapters 4 and 6). There are also windows of opportunity during the first year out: to earn select teens' trust (which they are surprisingly willing to give to those who demonstrate genuine concern); to ask simple questions like, "Where are you headed?" or "How do you want your life to influence others?" and to listen carefully and thoughtfully to their answers. Some teens do stumble while playing the daily life management game, and this too offers a window of opportunity for adults to suggest that what lies within teens' identity lockboxes might help them sort out some problem. And of course one can relocate programmatic efforts to evaluate identities and form connections to the larger world to points after the first year out, when teens have gained confidence in their ability to manage daily life, and when they may be more willing to peek inside their identity lockboxes. I will expand these suggestions in chapter 6, but must caution here that these nonetheless are heroic efforts that must compete against enormous economic and cultural forces.

The first year out is not the time of dramatic personal change that so many assume it is or it should be. Yet it is a critical time of life management and interpersonal adjustment. Because past patterns matter far more to teens than new options during this year, I found it essential to understand the family, faith, and community starting points of contemporary teens. By understanding these starting points, I was well-positioned to understand—if not predict—the journeys most teens took during the first year out. I examine those starting points in chapter 2.

TWO

Starting Points

Poppy Lopez was unimpressed with his parents, reported that their half-hearted attempts to instill religion "didn't stick," and was disengaged from his school, local community, and ethnic heritage. Lowanda Smith respected but struggled with her mother, had a deep religious faith, and was quite involved with her local and ethnic communities. Rob Robertson described parents whom he very much wished to please, firmly believed in God but did not follow any specific religion, and possessed a deep passion for building community. Kristi Kramer loved her "awesome" parents "to pieces," had an on-again, off-again Roman Catholic faith, and could barely find time for herself, much less for community involvement. In chapter 1, I introduced these four teens with four distinct family, faith, and community starting points. To understand their starting points, I contend, is to understand much of what differentiates the patterns teens forge during the first year out. In this chapter, I examine the starting points of family, faith, and community in turn.

But first, I must address a more pressing matter. It involves a question I often heard from teens: "Why are you writing a book about teens?" And a similar one I heard from adults: "Why are you writing about the first year out?" To teens, who wanted a simple but honest answer, I would say that I wanted to understand teens because they represent the future and that I was not sure if what researchers knew about teens from a couple of decades ago was still true. That answer would satisfy teens, and some would concur that their lives were "nothing like" their parents' lives as teens. But adults, especially well-read ones, deserve a more detailed answer, so I begin this chapter on teen starting points by first describing this project's starting points.

WHY STUDY THE FIRST YEAR OUT?

It was a poignant question from a smart colleague: "Aren't there enough books on this already?" Truth be told, there are too many books about American teens that oversensationalize their subjects' lives or falsely reassure their readers.[1] This may be due to authors' fascination, as high school graduates occupy an ambiguous and even exotic cultural position, enjoying many adult freedoms while having fewer adult responsibilities. This may be due to authors' desire to confirm cherished assumptions, as teens are sufficiently diverse that authors can readily find a few teens whose stories support a pet theory. And this may even be due to authors' convenience, as many authors work with teens full-time and thus have a steady supply of adolescents about whom they can write. I will admit that a combination of exotic fascination, cherished assumptions, and even convenience initially launched this project. I quickly learned, however, that teen lives are not nearly as exotic as fictional, nostalgic, and popular accounts suggest, that many of my cherished assumptions about teen lives were flat wrong, and that teens can be quite inconvenient to study. In the process, I discovered that teens who graduated from high school between 1995 and 2003 are much like American adults, that the daily concerns and personal goals of these teens are remarkably conventional, and that although most teens learned to handle personal daily matters fairly well, teens are also products of and participants in a popular American moral culture that prioritizes attention to everyday matters and gives short-shrift to deeper, wider, or longer-term matters. There are no books, I contend, that tell *this* story or explain *its* implications for scholars, educators, clergy, parents, and teens themselves. Thus, I endeavor to do so here and describe important issues that this book will address with regard to education, American culture, adolescence, family, religion, and community.

Many readers will be acquainted with the weighty tomes on the impact of college by Astin, Pascarella and Terenzini, Feldman and Newcomb, and Bowen.[2] These works, summarizing legions of cross-sectional and quantitative studies, generally report that (residential) college students grow smarter and somewhat more liberal during their college educations. Other well-known works, by Nathan, Moffat, Holland and Eisenhart, Levine and Cureton, and Horowitz, combine qualitative and historical methods to extend our knowledge of college student culture, relationships, use of time, expectations, and behaviors.[3] All of these works have commendable qualities, and I interact with these texts at numerous points later on. But this book is *not* primarily about gaining a college education, *nor* is it primarily about the student cultures that teens create on college campuses. While I do include a chapter about the educational lives of American teens, I use that chapter to evaluate teen experiences within secondary and postsecondary educational settings and do not limit myself to residential college student experiences. In this book, *I seek to describe the moral culture that mainstream American teens inhabit and express, to understand how teens transition from relatively structured high school experiences to fairly autonomous post-high school activities, and to investigate the ways family, faith, and community do and do not influence teens during the first year out.* I argue that it is *these* factors that are critical to understanding how teens experience their first year out, that the organizational and ideological effects of obtaining a postsecondary education are modest at best, and that there are far more similarities than diversities across various college student cultures.

Observers of American education should find much that is relevant to their interests herein. But my direct contribution to the "impact of college" and "college student culture" literature is my focus on the significant influence of family, faith, and community during the first year out. Many hold to the view that these traditional influences should be reevaluated as youth explore new possibilities during their first year out. One finds this most famously expressed in psychoanalytical theory about youth, by Sigmund Freud's daughter, Anna Freud, and her colleague Erik Erikson.[4] But this view is also evident in a lot of writing about college education, both scholarly, such as Richard Light's *Making the Most of College*, and popular, such as Loren Pope's *Colleges That Change Lives*. And, I submit, it pervades the speeches heard at virtually any college's or university's opening convocation for incoming freshmen.[5] I find, however, that the vast majority of contemporary American teens are quite uninterested in seeking new self-understandings and instead carry forward patterns of living previously established within their family, faith, and community origins. This is because, as readers will see, most teens become absorbed by daily life management during the first year out and relegate critical (if underdeveloped) identities to a lockbox. In this chapter, I build my case by examining teens' starting points and by describing teens' continuity with respect to family, faith, and community origins during the first year out. In subsequent chapters, I evaluate how these starting points do and do not influence teen patterns during the first year out.

Because I do not place this book into the "impact of college" genre, nor do I place it alongside popularized tales about teens, readers deserve to know where and how I do place this book. With some trepidation, I place it in the qualitative sociological tradition of classic works such as *Street Corner Society*, *Middletown*, *The Lonely Crowd*, and *Habits of the Heart*.[6] By carefully observing, listening to, and participating in the lives of American teens, I hope to tell a story about the cultural world that teens inhabit and, in the process, offer perspectives on the larger culture that Americans share. My target audience is students, scholars and observers of American culture, and particularly those interested in connections between American culture and education, youth, family, religion, and community life. Of course, classic works like *The Lonely Crowd* are brilliant and original analyses of American culture, and I by no means purport such brilliance or originality in this book. I seek simply to identify the proper genre for this book and understand full well that my book will be an ugly stepsister to Cinderella books like *The Lonely Crowd*. Hopefully, readers will find that even an ugly stepsister has a few useful insights of her own.

One potential insight involves understandings of culture's impact on social behavior. Anne Swidler, sociologist and coauthor of *Habits of the Heart*, theorizes that youth are "trying out (and trying on) the possible selves they might become" and therefore possess "unsettled lives." In unsettled lives, culture has a "greater, or at least more obvious, influence over action" than it does in "settled lives," where "well-established life patterns" make the influence of culture "nearly invisible."[7] I do not agree, however, that most youth try out possible selves or that most youth possess unsettled lives—at least not during the first year out. Most of the youth I studied, in fact, demonstrated remarkably settled lives and continued well-established life patterns during their first year out. There were critical exceptions, of course, among youth with extreme positions on religion (e.g., religious zealots and atheists), and these exceptions reveal a powerful influence of (sub-) culture on social behavior.

Sociologist Christian Smith argues that religious subcultures thrive in American pluralism precisely because they are embattled.[8] I concur with Smith, extend his argument to include *antireligious*[9] subcultures and propose that religious and antireligious subcultures *manufacture* what Swidler calls unsettled lives, while those who swim with the American cultural mainstream establish settled lives. Unsettled and settled lives are, therefore, as much a (sub-) cultural construction as they are the result of social structural change (e.g., divorce, economic change, disaster). In fact, given the widespread lack of response among this project's teens to the powerful structural change of September 11, 2001, settled lives may be even more a cultural product than a structural one (see chapter 6).

Placing my book within this classic tradition of cultural analysis does not, of course, eliminate its connections to other streams of important research. I have already described two such literatures—the voluminous research on the impact of college and studies of college student culture. There are several others, including research on adolescents and the transition to adulthood, adolescents and the family, adolescents and American religion, and adolescents and community. The first field is striking, as sociologists have long been outnumbered by psychologists in the study of adolescent life transitions. Particularly rare have been macrosociological and cultural analyses of American adolescents. Although sociologists produced important works on 1950s teens,[10] macrosociological interest in American adolescents has been largely episodic until recently, with the publication of Schneider and Stevenson's *The Ambitious Generation*, Mortimer's *Working and Growing Up in America*, Settersten, Furstenberg, and Rumbaut's *On the Frontiers of Adulthood*, and Milner's *Freaks, Geeks, and Cool Kids: American Teenagers, Schools, and the Culture of Consumption*.[11] Schneider and Stevenson focus on the gap between teens' ambitions and their actual plans, Mortimer focuses on teen employment and its outcomes, Settersten et al focus on the stage between adolescence and adulthood occupied by Americans between 18 and 34 years of age (with primary emphasis on 20-somethings), and Milner focuses on developing a theory of social status using high school students and U.S. consumerism. Each of these studies has much merit, and I make connections to them throughout the book. But none examine much about the larger moral culture of American teens, and thus readers do not see the ways this larger moral culture affects teen plans for the future, patterns of employment, consumption preferences, or understandings of adulthood. Teens, like all humans, are profoundly cultural beings, and thus this book will contribute a cultural analysis of this emerging generation of Americans to the sociology of adolescence.

Closely linked to research on adolescents is research on the family. Several fine studies have examined the ways class, race, and urban locations affect how children are reared and how they fare as teenagers and young adults. These include Furstenberg, Cook, Eccles, Elder, and Sameroff's *Managing to Make It: Urban Families and Adolescent Success*, Lareau's *Unequal Childhoods: Class, Race, and Family Life*, and Kaplan's *Not Our Kind of Girl: Unraveling the Myths of Black Teenage Motherhood*. I focus, however, on teens from culturally mainstream American families and seek to tell a story about teens whose challenges in life are more ordinary. These teens inhabit a mainstream American teen culture that takes for granted its opportunity to follow mainstream American life scripts. I do endeavor to follow in the even-handed tradition of the scholarship above and to resist the "teen crisis" interpretation that is prevalent in many trade publications. Some examples of the latter include Currie's *The Road to Whatever: Middle-Class Culture and the Crisis of Adolescence*, which examines middle-class family life and teen crime; Thompson's *Going All the Way: Teenage Girls' Tales of Sex, Romance, and Pregnancy*, which examines teen families, sexual behaviors, and teen pregnancy; and David Elkind's *All Grown Up and No Place to Go: Teenagers in Crisis*, which examines families that rush childhood and the effect of this on teen lives. Though I argue that there are troubling gaps in how American families and American culture at large prepares teens for a rapidly changing and globally interdependent future, there is also much to acknowledge about the warmth that most American teens feel toward their families and their success in managing their increasingly complex daily lives. Hopefully, then, this book will serve as a continuation of the careful research recently begun on adolescents and their families and as a corrective to overly quick conclusions about a "teen crisis."

Observers of American religion should also find much of interest in this book, as it continues an important tradition of research on religion and American youth, extends important new research, and challenges a widely cited but surprisingly flawed report on college student spirituality by UCLA's Higher Education Research Institute (hereafter, HERI). Early research on teens and American religion, appearing in academic journals primarily,[12] documented the decline in religious involvement by later adolescents and largely attributed it to the 1960's cultural shift and the liberalizing impact of higher education. The impact of the 1960's cultural shift on religion has been well documented, and it is sometimes labeled the "third disestablishment" of religion in the United States.[13] But conclusions by early researchers about higher education's liberalizing effects on religion have not garnered equal support, as subsequent research demonstrates strong life-cycle and aging patterns with respect to religious participation in the United States.[14] The seeming liberalization of college students in the late 1960s and early 1970s may have been a unique period effect or a shorter-term cohort effect.[15]

More recent research, such as Flory and Miller's *Gen X Religion*, Cherry, DeBerg, and Porterfield's *Religion on Campus: What Religion Really Means to Today's Undergraduates*, Clark's *From Angels to Aliens: Teenagers, the Media, and the Supernatural*, Lytch's *Choosing Church: What Makes a Difference for Teens*, and Smith's *Soul Searching: The Religious and Spiritual Lives of American Teenagers*, reveals a widespread religiosity among American teens. Though religious involvement is often superficial and occasionally transient, there are sizable proportions of American teens for whom religious life is important and influential and relatively few American teens for whom religion is anathema. None of these works, however, examine teen religion longitudinally, and several study religious teens only. Smith's research provides the most comprehensive review of the religious life of American teens at large, and many of my findings overlap with his (see discussion below). However, our projects are distinct in important ways: I examine religion among 18–19 year olds, while Smith does so among 13–17 year olds; I contrast religion's influence with that of family and community, while Smith focuses on religion exclusively; and I evaluate religion over the course of teens' first year out, while Smith's research is cross-sectional.[16] My project can be viewed, then, as a partial extension of Smith's research, but it is more an analysis of teen religion *in context*—in the context of teens' everyday lives and in the context of the larger moral culture that American teens inhabit and perpetuate.

Because I examine lived religion among American teens, I draw very different conclusions about religious and spiritual life among college-age teens than survey analysts at HERI did.[17] Asking incoming American college freshmen whether they "have an interest in spirituality" is like asking a soldier in a trench whether he has an interest in world peace or an arguing spouse whether she has an interest in honest and loving communication. To learn that most would agree should not surprise us in the slightest. The critical questions are whether indicating interest in religious and spiritual life, world peace, or loving communication makes a difference in present activities and long-range goals, and to what extent. The first of these is the question of lived religion, and it is the question that I investigate. To answer it requires spending many hours where teens live and many hours in confidential and wide-ranging conversations with them. As a survey researcher myself,[18] I endorse survey methods when appropriate to the question. But analysis of a static questionnaire gives little basis to conclude, as HERI does, that teens "are actively engaged in a spiritual quest and are exploring the meaning and purpose of life." I do concur that most teens are on a quest during their first year out, but that quest is to successfully navigate interpersonal relationships and manage everyday life (like eating, working, attending class, doing laundry, and having a little fun). Religious and spiritual identities are peripheral to that quest and stowed in an identity lockbox for a later point in the life cycle. The exceptions are found among the approximately 30 percent of American teens for whom religion is of great importance, who seek to maintain or increase their religious faith during their first year out (see discussion of national estimates below).

Finally, this book examines the impact of various communities on American teens and addresses several issues of relevance to observers of communities in America. To those concerned that Americans may be "bowling alone" and that their social capital is in critical condition—as political scientist Putnam alleges[19]—I describe those teens who have been affected by their local community involvement, examine how teens forge interpersonal connections and navigate relationships, and report how teens comfortably disengage from larger social and political matters. To those interested in the role "communities" of gender, race, and class[20] play in teen lives and in teen moral culture, I note how and to what extent teens differ, given their gender, race, and class origins. And to those curious about the role of generational "communities" (like the World War II or the Baby Boom generations), I describe ways that Americans who graduated from high school between 1995 and 2003 have been influenced by the specific cultural and historical events of their adolescence and suggest ways this generation in turn might influence America's future.

Community is a broad concept, but one that nevertheless deserves careful attention. There is little that is more important on this globe, I suggest, than building and sustaining healthy communities. This whole chapter is, in many ways, about community. It is about how various communities of learners might benefit from this book. And it is about how teens are shaped by the first communities of their families, the elective communities of their faith, and the larger communities of neighborhoods and municipalities, of gender, race, and class, and of shared birth cohort. To that profoundly important first community of family, I now direct your attention.

STARTING POINTS: FAMILY

It does not take a Ph.D. to understand that families powerfully influence their children. But what I learned by talking to teens is just how dynamic and busy American families have become, how warmly most teens describe their parents, and how deeply the family's infrastructure and its relationship to faith and community establishes teen patterns and trajectories. Take, for example, Megan Morici's family. Both of my interviews with Megan, a white, middle-class teen, occurred in the evening at her family's suburban townhouse. While there, I observed a busy yet affectionate single-parent family with two teenage children that was planning meals, coordinating transportation, sharing chores, arranging shopping trips, and spending time together. The logistical details alone made my head spin, and Megan's mom teased me, saying, "Just wait till your kids get older!" But I soon realized that most American families with teenagers are as busy as Megan's—and particularly those housed in suburbia, where automobiles reign and teenagers do not yet drive.

Megan's family was only atypical in that it had experienced more extreme family dynamics: Megan's father left her mother for another man, her mother moved Megan and her brother out of the city and into a suburban townhouse, and Megan herself became addicted to cocaine. The latter, brought to light after an awful, early morning automobile accident, caused by Megan, that seriously injured Megan and two friends, ultimately restored communication with Megan's father and connected Megan with some valuable psychological counseling. Because I learned all of this as "past history" from Megan during my first interview with her, I thought that Megan's extremely high opinion of her mother might have been overly influenced by her mother's support following Megan's accident. Megan described her mother, for example, as "my best friend these days," because "I know that no matter what I do—no matter how much I screw up—she's gonna love me." And when I asked Megan whether there was anyone she thought exemplified what being a woman is, Megan again praised her mother. "She's great! She raised my brother and I by herself. She's got a good job, and she cares about the house. She moved us out of the city so we could get a good education up here, and she just did everything she possibly could for us. I hope to be like her when I'm a mother." Megan's high opinion of her mother was not, however, a short-term reaction to her mother's care following Megan's accident. Megan reiterated her high opinion of her mother more than a year later, and the majority of other teens I interviewed expressed similar warmth toward their own mothers and fathers. Megan simply had more immediate and dramatic evidence to support her high opinion of her mother than most teens did.

Megan's family, then, was a busy, dynamic, loving, and supportive family. But it was also Megan's "life infrastructure." As such, it facilitated certain possibilities, limited others, and supplied Megan with a recurring system of relationships that in turn cultivated certain patterns and weeded out others. Hence, Megan's family shaped her economic, social, and cultural opportunities. For example, Megan's mother and father maintained separate households and possessed middle-tier, middle-class occupations, so Megan was restricted to public education and did not have the opportunity to consider private or more exotic opportunities. Yet Megan's college-educated parents deeply valued education, which led her mother to relocate to a "good suburban school district" and her parents to advise Megan to apply to residential, four-year colleges only.

Similarly, Megan's family provided a recurring system of relationships to kin, faith, and community, which established a number of important patterns for Megan. It facilitated, for example, an important relationship between Megan and her paternal grandmother, which helped Megan "learn to accept" her father's homosexuality. It connected Megan to Christian faith, of a couple of varieties, which played a part in Megan's early recovery from drug addiction. And it established a pattern of disengagement with the wider community, beyond obligations to work and school, which provided Megan with ample time to spend privately with her boyfriend and her "drug friends." These patterns, combined with the limits and possibilities of a middle-class economic and cultural infrastructure, established Megan's trajectory for her first year out. Understanding these patterns and identifying this infrastructure makes it easy, in fact, to predict Megan's post–high school trajectory.

Megan had a good first year out, learning "a lot" and growing up "a lot." Megan learned how to study and earn good grades, by adjusting her schedule and prioritizing her time to prepare for an examination or assignment: "I learned how to discipline myself. Like if I had a test, I shouldn't go out even though I wanted to—because there was this huge party or something. I didn't have my Mom to say, 'No, you're staying in tonight.' I had to shift things around so I could work it out myself and just, like, fix it by myself. Like, I taught myself study habits and stuff like that." Megan also explained how she "grew up a lot . . . because it was my first year on my own." Yet Megan still had "the same perspective and stuff," by which she meant the same core identity and outlook on life. This included her gregariousness, her propensity to act first and think second, and her willingness to take risks. The first netted her a host of friends at college, the second put her on disciplinary probation for punching a "Barbie doll" hall mate, and the third reconnected her with regular use of marijuana and alcohol. But Megan's own history and the death of a high school girlfriend from a drug overdose helped Megan restrict herself to smoking pot and drinking beer only. "Hard drugs, like, I've tried them. You know, I've basically tried almost everything. And I think that it's not fun. Like when you do coke or something, you're all strung out, and you're weirded out, and . . . your heart is beating—and what's the fun in that? Like when you smoke pot, like you laugh and you have a good time. It's just like everybody is chillin' and, like, it's fun. But I think the other drugs—I don't see the point in them." Megan's first year out did not, then, involve experimentation with new adult gratifications, but rather involved Megan's selection and careful management of gratifications with which she had had a long experience. (I discuss gratification at length in chapter 3.) Nor did Megan's first year out involve alterations to her core identity or general outlook on life. For example, she still wanted to get married and have children ("I want, like, eight kids—just kids all over the place!"); she still maintained her connection to Christian faith (self-identifying as a Christian, attending Mass numerous times with her college roommate, and visiting a couple of Protestant churches too); and she still had no interest in voluntary activities, school clubs, or social and political issues of any sort. Megan, like most teens, entered a new educational institution and made new friends, but largely carried over the patterns and outlooks she had previously established within the context of her family. Though impetuous and willing to experiment, Megan kept within the trajectory that her family had facilitated and that she and her family had established.

It may seem ironic that the family, whose direct influence wanes early in the senior year of high school, remains the most influential factor in how teens proceed through the first year out. The popular self-help literature refers to the senior year of high school and the first year after as the "launching period."[21] That is, in some respects, an apt term for this transitional period for parents (who are the readership for these self-help books). But parents and everyone else must understand that trajectories are not set during the launching period.[22] Trajectories are established long before the senior year of high school, and the launching period is but the ritualized enactment of that trajectory. It is akin to a traditional, mainstream American wedding: the "trajectory" of the wedding is planned long before the wedding day, leaving the wedding party and family members to do little more than don their wedding clothes and smile for the photographer on the wedding day itself. There are, to be sure, brides and grooms who fail to show up and marriages that soon fizzle, just as there are teens who founder during their first year out and others who radically alter course soon thereafter.

But the latter, I suggest, are the likely product of launching periods that tried to alter established trajectories—of artistic teens forced to choose a college major in accounting, for example, or of passionless teens sent to "thirteenth grade" at community college. For most of the teens I observed and interviewed, launching periods matched established trajectories, relegating families' chief influence during the launching period to their teen's choice of a post–high school educational program.

How, then, do families establish trajectories with and for their children? It is a lengthy, dynamic, and complex process that includes both intentional planning and unconscious patterns. It involves where parents choose to live and their expectations about the kind of neighborhood and community in which they wish to rear their children. It involves the schools and activities that parents enroll their children in and the friendships that they facilitate or hinder for their children. And it involves the wider connections that parents establish with kin, neighbors, friends, and larger communities—including more defined civic and religious communities and less defined communities of race, gender, class, and nation. Consider Kasim Douglass, a black, working-class senior at NJ High. Because his parents were concerned about the urban environment of Small City, they moved Kasim and his siblings to Suburban Township for better schools and less crime. They also supported Kasim's involvement in school athletics and his participation in the youth group at the mostly white Pentecostal church they attended. Kasim reported a warm relationship with his mother, but a more tumultuous one with his father: "Sometimes me and my dad are, like, near fist fights—literally. Like one time he, like, grabbed me and stuff, and like, he had his fist cocked. . . . My dad says I have a lack of respect for authority, and he may be right." Still, a couple of weeks after graduating from NJ High, Kasim—like his father—enlisted in the armed forces. And Kasim—like his father and mother—carried forward his parents' Pentecostalism as his own. Not all teens follow as closely in their parents' footsteps as Kasim, but few wander far from the trajectories their families establish.

Perhaps teens stay within their established trajectories because baby-boomer parents have largely succeeded in forming closer relationships with their offspring than baby boomers themselves experienced with their more role-constrained parents,[23] thus establishing their offspring's trajectories more collaboratively. Most teens describe relatively close relationships with at least one parent and plan to marry and have children themselves (see chapter 3). Or perhaps teens stay within their trajectories because culturally mainstream American families have conveyed that happiness resides

in two places, in personally fulfilling relationships and in individual consumption, and teens recognize that the trajectories that their families have
established give them the best odds of attaining such happiness. For example, Tammy Biggs, a white, working-class senior at NJ High, hopes to meet
and marry her "soul mate and best friend," have three children, and be oc-
cupationally and financially "successful." Similarly, Sam Postman, a white,
upper-middle-class senior, hopes to marry his current girlfriend, have kids,
and live in a nice house in the suburbs. Thus, Sam plans to choose his occupation based "definitely on [its] salary," as he knows his salary is what will
make him "happy there in the long run." I contend that teens like Tammy
and Sam stay within their established trajectories because these culturally
mainstream teens are products of, participants in, and even proponents of
a popular American moral culture that envelops their families and the other
mainstream American institutions in which they are reared.

Popular American moral culture is, therefore, conveyed to children by
most American families unless that family chooses to alter it through involvement with a particular (usually religious or ethnic) subculture. While
popular American moral culture is dynamic, adapting itself over the years
in response to historical and social changes, it is deeply rooted in American art, folklore, entertainment, social history, and discourse. As such, it
celebrates personal initiative and achievement; demonstrates patriotism;
believes in God and a spiritual afterlife; lauds loyalty to family, friends, and
coworkers; expects personal moral freedom; distrusts large organizations
and political processes; and, increasingly, defines happiness and fulfillment
as accomplishments found primarily in personal relationships and individual consumption. Evidence for widespread endorsement of this constellation of beliefs and values can be found in many national surveys, including
the General Social Survey.[24] Families are not the only teachers of popular
American moral culture, but they are its first teachers and its primary facilitators. They either reinforce its inculcation through mainstream socializing
agents, such as schools, churches, community organizations, and media, or
alter its content through immersion in the parallel organizations of particular subcultures. Thus, understanding teens' families is essential to understanding teen trajectories during the first year out, but understanding the
role of faith and community in teens' lives is also critical.

Before I turn to that task, I must note that, while a clear majority of teens
describe a warm relationship with at least one parent and follow the trajectories that they have established within their families, there are some
teens who lack warm relationships and some whose parents did little to

inculcate trajectories or aim them particularly high. Shatoya Barkley, one of the Girlfriends Seven from NJ High, was one of four children born in rapid succession to adolescent parents. When they abandoned Shatoya at two years old, she was taken in and reared by her godmother. This godmother had very simple goals for Shatoya: that she "stay out of trouble" and finish high school (unlike her parents). Shatoya sought more. She wanted a "nice house" with a "three-car garage and a pool," and she knew that required a bachelor's and possibly a master's degree. But "that's a lot of school and I don't like school," Shatoya admitted during our first interview. To her credit, Shatoya did graduate from high school, "stayed out of trouble," and even completed two semesters at the local community college. However, Shatoya did not like college much, gave vague answers about finishing her college degree, and mostly talked about moving out of state. Lacking both the family infrastructure and emotional support that many teens possess, and without connections to religious or other community supports, Shatoya was beginning to realize that her dreams of a higher personal trajectory demanded more than she had (or wanted) to give. At a minimum, the odds were stacked against Shatoya, as they were against other teens whose families set low or undefined trajectories.

STARTING POINTS: FAITH

Dwight Stevens, a white, suburban high school senior, was proud of his parents. Despite the collapse of his father's insurance business—for reasons "beyond his father's control"—and the effect of that collapse in limiting Dwight to in-state public colleges only, Dwight was proud of his father's "amazing talent" as a self-employed handyman and his mother's underappreciated skills as a teacher's aide. (Dwight emphasized that his mother earned a college degree in teaching, but received it before coming to the United States, so "it doesn't count here.") Dwight was also proud of his parents' efforts to give him a religious upbringing; he attended the local Lutheran church with them each week and believed it had positively influenced him. He explained: "I don't go around, like, preaching to people, but I think [attending church] affects me morally, and like, I just think I'm a better person because I have a conscience, more of a conscience, and stuff like that." To Dwight, religion was about "morals," and he admitted that "a lot of the time" he attended church just to make his mother happy. Still, he "definitely" wanted "to instill religious beliefs in" his own children, especially "at a young age, because as they get older it's kinda harder to, you know, get it into their heads." As for his own future, Dwight said he hoped his own religious commitment "will stay the same, [and] hopefully it won't decrease." Then he reversed his answer:

> DWIGHT: Hopefully, it will increase. Only because right now I say, "Alright, I'll believe that later." I mean, "I'll practice that later." Hopefully I will, but . . .
> INTERVIEWER: Can you give an example?
> DWIGHT: Like, you know, even the small example of my mom reading the Bible all the time. Like, right now as a teenager, that's so hard to do. But hopefully I will do that in the future.

Dwight, like most of the high school seniors interviewed for this project, viewed religion positively and believed it plays an important role in the lives of children, parents, and older adults (such as his grandmother). Thus, Dwight identified himself as a Christian and, more precisely, as a Lutheran, but he largely assigned religion to his postteen to-do list.

Dwight, then, was much like other high school students, as Christian Smith's national study of teen religion confirms. Most American teens, Smith reports, consider religion to be "a very nice thing" and, despite their particular religious affiliation, adhere to what he calls "therapeutic moralistic deism." Smith defines this as a faith in "divinely underwritten personal happiness and interpersonal niceness."[25] While I concur, I suggest the following analogy conveys a fuller picture of American teens and religion. American teens, or at least the culturally mainstream teens I observed, seem to approach life like a grand buffet, and religion as its vegetable table. Vegetables are "good for you," of course, "everyone" knows you should eat them, and most buffet diners will include items from the vegetable table. In fact, it would not be a proper buffet without a vegetable table. Most diners, therefore, take a serving or two of vegetables and pick at them, others take several servings and consume them eagerly, while some ignore the vegetable table completely, and a few mutter something about vegetables being "sissy foods." Strongly religious teens, that is, buffet diners who eagerly consume several servings of vegetables, comprise 25 to 35 percent of American teens nationally, with percentages varying based on the indicators used.[26] Nonreligious teens, that is, buffet diners who skip the vegetable table and may even despise vegetables, comprise 12 to 18 percent of American teens nationally. This leaves the majority of American teens in the semireligious middle ground. Like Dwight, these teens believe in God, identify themselves with a religious tradition, indicate some interest in religious life, but generally assign religion to a future period in their lives. For efficiency's sake, I will set the proportion of semireligious American teens at 55 percent, of strongly religious teens at 30 percent, and of nonreligious teens at 15 percent—with a margin of error of plus or minus 5 percent.

I have two questions about semireligious teens like Dwight and about his strongly religious and nonreligious peers. First, what role does religious faith (or its absence) play in the moral culture of American teens? Second, how, and to what extent, does religion's role alter during the first year out? I will begin with the first question. For Dwight and other semireligious teens, faith primarily serves to underscore the popular American moral culture that most American families inculcate. The practical creed of these semireligious teens goes something like this: *God exists, he wants me to be a nice person, and he'll help me out if I am.* Though semireligious teens identify with specific religions that possess quite different creeds, in the end they affirm this far simpler creed, which hews rather closely to Benjamin Franklin's "God helps those who help themselves." Thus, this practical teen creed possesses a distinguished American history—and its prevalence may be why Will Herberg's observation in 1955, that "America seems to be at once the most religious and the most secular of nations," remains apropos.[27]

For strongly religious teens, such as Lowanda Smith (introduced in chapter 1), faith takes on a more complex role. It can be used to critique personal behavior, as when Lowanda used it to alter her sexual behavior, and to critique collective behavior, as when Lowanda used it to critique the revealing attire of classmates and music video dancers. It can provide a source of comfort, as when Lowanda explained her utter confidence in the existence of God and in God's desire to have "his own special relationship" with her. And it can also serve to reinforce popular American moral culture, as when Lowanda explained that her efforts to be nice to others were the products of her faith in God. Among strongly religious teens, I suggest, faith enlarges the niceness creed of semireligious teens to include more specific behavioral norms and more specific assurances. It can even supplant niceness with pointed criticism of others—though I found few strongly religious teens who transgressed the niceness norm outside of their own religious circles or past the door of an interview room. In other words, strongly religious teens may denounce the morality of certain peers, but only among similarly religious individuals and never to the face of the ones whom they criticize. The norm of niceness, at least on a superficial public level, is virtually unquestioned among the culturally mainstream teens I studied.

Even among nonreligious teens, niceness is the norm. I found, like Christian Smith, that most teens who are nonreligious are so for no particular reason and generally describe religion as a preference they simply do not happen to share (similar to how one might say, "I don't like peas").[28] Most nonreligious teens have, in fact, been exposed to religion, usually because a semireligious parent or a strongly religious family member (such as an aunt or grandparent) insisted on it. Most nonreligious teens report simply that religion "didn't interest me" and say nothing more, perhaps out of habituated concern for the feelings of family members or friends who might be religious. Only a few nonreligious teens qualify as antireligious. By antireligious, I mean teens who largely view religion as erroneous and as harmful to its adherents as well as to the world at-large. One such teen was Nick Lawrence, a white, middle-class senior at NJ High. Though Nick attended both his mother's church and a friend's church youth group, he nonetheless concluded—with polite caveats—that religion is "very plastic," consumes itself with "power" and "hierarchy," and is "not about what it's supposed to be about." Though high school seniors with skeptical to atheist opinions on religion were rare, the ones I met, like Nick, were an intelligent bunch and often articulated humanistic ideals. By contrast, most other nonreligious high school seniors concerned themselves with maximizing their moral freedom and qualified as semihedonists. I say "semi" because, although they are primarily oriented toward obtaining access to adult gratifications, they still fulfill basic school, work, and family obligations as necessary (see further discussion in chapter 3).

In sum, religious faith functions differently for different types of high school seniors. For the semi- and strongly religious majority, it reinforces popular American moral culture and offers assurances that being nice and doing the things that culturally mainstream Americans do will pay off. For strongly religious teens, it also adds specific moral and behavioral norms and supplements popular ways of interpreting one's personal life and the larger world. For nonreligious teens, religion's absence does not diminish adherence to popular American moral culture except for its theistic elements, though its absence does seem to facilitate more extensive pursuit of personal gratifications.

Which brings me to my second question: How and to what extent does religion's role alter during the first year out? The answer may surprise some readers: other than a drop in rates of active religious involvement,[29] faith's role hardly alters at all. Teens described virtually the same religious faith at the end of the first year out as they did at its beginning, except that their frequency of attendance at religious services declined. It was as if my teen respondents had secured their religious identity (or nonreligious identity) in a lockbox soon after graduating from high school. Though they may not have checked on that identity during the year, when I asked teens whether it was still there, they opened the box and confirmed, "Yes, it's still there." This pattern, moreover, is not unique to my sample; it has been documented by analysts of two different national, longitudinal surveys.[30] Except among three specific sorts of teens, namely, strongly religious teens who enrolled at religious colleges, antireligious teens who enrolled at public colleges, and future intelligentsia teens enrolled at any college, most American teens preserve core identity constructions (including religious, political, civic, racial, and gender identities) by keeping them in separate compartments within a secure lockbox, so that they can focus on the more pressing management of daily life during the first year out.

Identities, whatever else they may be, are products of social interaction. Thus, identities both form and change through social interaction.[31] Teens can preserve certain identities, however, by removing them from interaction and resisting efforts to alter them. Doing so, I argue, ensures teens that they will keep within the cultural mainstream of America—that they will fit into the popular American moral culture that shaped them and that they will remain within the individual achievement and personal happiness trajectories that they have been socialized to seek. If religious identities, for example, were to shift to a religious or antireligious extreme, they could ruin teens' mainstream standing and long-term future. Therefore, most teens stow their religious identities away, because most religious identities in America provide crucial reinforcement for popular American moral culture. (Other identities, such as political, civic, racial, and gender identities, are likewise secured in lockboxes because "wrong" choices here would also put teens critically out of step with mainstream culture and jeopardize their plans for a mainstream future—see discussion below). The new American economic realities,[32] moreover, underscore the importance of not tampering with either culturally mainstream identities or their corresponding trajectories, so that teens maintain the best odds of attaining the private happiness they have been socialized to seek. The "fear of falling" and of "downward mobility" are deeply rooted in culturally mainstream American identities.[33]

This may well explain why American teens are, as Smith puts it, religiously "inarticulate."[34] From the perspective of historic religious traditions, they are quite inarticulate—but they articulate the "therapeutic, moralistic Deism"[35] of popular American moral culture rather well. This may also explain why religious faith is more widespread in the United States compared to Europe and Canada. The fabric of mainstream American culture is woven through with the religious thread of "divinely underwritten personal happiness and interpersonal niceness." Thus, being semi- or even strongly religious is simply part of what it means to be an American.[36] That teens place religious and other identities into lockboxes reveals how, in spite of their seeming inattention to such identities, keeping these identities within the American cultural mainstream is essential. Lockboxes are, after all, for the preservation and protection of treasures.

Observers should not be fooled, then, by the decline in religious participation of American teens during the first year out. Lowanda, for example, sometimes missed church on Sundays while at college, but mostly she attended each week. That represents a decline, of course, from the twice weekly attendance of her senior year of high school. And if Lowanda had received a survey asking whether her rate of attendance at religious services declined since starting college, Lowanda's answer would have been yes. Nick would have also answered yes to this question, as he moved out of his semireligious mother's home after graduating from high school and into his nonreligious father's home fifty miles away. Thus, Nick ceased attending church with his mother. But neither Nick's nor Lowanda's survey answers would reveal much about their religious faith itself—as Lowanda's stayed strong and even grew during her first year out, while Nick's nonattendance was now consistent with his nonexistent faith. As for Dwight, he did not attend religious services while at college but continued attending with his parents. In fact, Dwight's parents switched to a nondenominational church and "became born-again Christians," making his "household a lot more peaceful and pleasant now." Dwight attended the new church with his parents whenever he was home and, being impressed with its pastor, described "learning a lot" about Christian faith when I interviewed him the second time. But Dwight's "real life"—that is, his on-campus fraternity life—"is totally different," and Dwight was unwilling to sacrifice his current life for the evangelical one his parents now embraced.

Most semireligious teens do not, of course, come home to discover born-again parents, most strongly religious teens do not attend religious services multiple times each week, and most nonreligious teens do not articulate a passionate and thoughtful concern "for humanity." Neither Dwight, Lowanda, nor Nick should be viewed as an archetypal example of a semireligious, strongly religious, or nonreligious American teen. Rather, Dwight illustrates how semireligious teens may not see their specific religious affiliation as terribly relevant to their first year out, but that does not imply that their religious identification is insignificant or fading. Lowanda illustrates how strongly religious teens wish to maintain faith during their first year out and do so in a variety of ways. And Nick illustrates how nonreligious teens often choose to express, verbally or behaviorally, their nonreligiosity during their first year out. Taken together, Dwight, Lowanda, and Nick illustrate that teens chiefly stay within the religious trajectories they establish before their first year out begins.

This brings us back to the role of families and parents in establishing teen trajectories, including religious ones. Parents may not get what they hope for with respect to their children's religiosity, but as Smith reveals and I confirm, most will "get what they are."[37] Parents will generally observe the same religiosity in their offspring's lives as they do in their own—after that religiosity is stripped of its hypocrisies. Hypocrisy is much of what sociologists of religion study, and as one, I have no doubt that a fair measure of hypocrisy exists within all religious groups (just as it does within all scholarly disciplines, including the sociology of religion). And because children observe their parents closely, it should not surprise parents that their children know their hypocrisies—religious and otherwise. A baby-boomer father, for example, who only attends religious services on holidays to please his in-laws, should not be surprised when his children profess nonreligiosity as young adults. Though that father might still claim a religious identification himself, he is effectively nonreligious and will likely observe the same in his adult children's lives. As James Baldwin famously observed in *Nobody Knows My Name*, "Children have never been very good at listening to their elders, but they have never failed to imitate them."[38] This is not, of course, a nomothetic relationship—Lowanda, for example, was *more* actively religious than her mother. Nick, on the other hand, saw his mother's religiosity as superficial and adopted the nonreligiosity of his father. And Dwight saw the moral and interpersonal value of his parent's faith and planned to uphold it. Though teens may attend fewer religious services during the first year out, at the year's end, they continue to affirm the religious identities that they formed within their family context. And they continue to affirm the political, civic, racial, and gender identities that they formed within their family, faith, and community contexts, as I discuss next.

STARTING POINTS: COMMUNITY

Just listening to Moesha Anderson list her *thirteen* different school and community activities made me tired. Moesha, a black, middle-class senior at NJ High, participated in two academic clubs, two music groups, student government, yearbook committee, varsity soccer, a community service club, and two recreational sport teams, in addition to taking dance lessons and attending two church youth groups. Some of this was possible because Moesha neither worked for nor needed much money (a point I return to in chapter 4). And some of this was possible because Moesha was smart and focused, so she did her homework both quickly and well. But most of this was possible, I suggest, because Moesha valued community and sought to contribute to others. Moesha told me, for example, that Americans with money "need to get over themselves and give back to community; I know I plan to." Instead of just planning to, however, Moesha was already giving of her time and abilities to affect NJ High and the wider Suburban Township community.

Moesha grew up in a dynamic, multigenerational household. She lived with her sister, her mother, and her grandmother in a home that was frequently visited by one or more of her mother's six older siblings and various cousins. Moesha's home was also a diverse one. Though Moesha primarily identified herself as a black American, her grandparents crossed racial and cultural boundaries to marry, producing seven biracial children, several of whom also crossed boundaries to marry and have children. While every family represents a child's first community, Moesha's family was an especially large, diverse, and seemingly healthy one, and thus Moesha's appreciation for community and diversity has its likely origins here. But Moesha was no head-in-the-clouds idealist; she was growing "tired" of her classmates and was quick to express annoyance with NJ High's rules. At the same time, Moesha reported that her favorite part of school was "the people." Like many who interact extensively with people, Moesha found that relationships with people provided both feelings of deep satisfaction and feelings of deep frustration.

Moesha was unlike most teens, however—and not just because of her commitment to community or her unique family history. Unlike most of her peers, Moesha understood that her interactions with others were significantly shaped by her gender and her race. (Let me pause to acknowledge that there are no monolithic communities of gender or race; for example, there is no single black community in the United States. But because ascribed characteristics often form a basis for sustained social interaction, I place my discussion of these under the rubric of "community.") Most teens recognize that gender and race affect behavior, but they do so in stereotypes. For example, NJ High boys may boast that they are "always ready" to have sex and complain about having to "wait" for the girls to be "ready," while NJ High girls may bemoan the immaturity and crudeness of high school boys. Similarly, white NJ High students would sometimes complain about the loudness of their black classmates, while black NJ High students would sometimes complain about "stuck up" white classmates. Such stereotypes do, in fact, match my own observations of and conversations with *some* NJ High teens. But Moesha's gender and race observations were at a deeper and more subtle level.

With respect to gender, Moesha described how women approach issues more relationally and holistically, unlike the men she knew: "We have a totally different understanding of a lot of things. . . . We see things a lot of times based on our emotions, and just more deeply. Like we see how it's gonna affect the person more. So we really think a lot . . . into things." Moesha drew similar conclusions, in fact, about gender's impact on reasoning and decision making as Harvard psychologist Carol Gilligan.[39] Yet, while Moesha acknowledged these gender differences, she affirmed the importance of gender equality. She emphasized, for example, how her (future) children would play sports *and* take dance lessons, girls and boys alike. She also cited the need to improve the status of African and Middle Eastern women.

With respect to race, Moesha described how frustrated she got when her black peers followed black stereotypes, such as "dressing like thugs" and "the whole chicken thing [i.e., liking fried chicken]." She explained how her black classmates "need to be shown how we're appearing to other races, like the stereotypes and everything. . . . They [should] be shown that that's *not* what they need to do. Their priorities are all wrong. They need to come up, and they can if they just believe they can." When black teens follow black stereotypes, Moesha explained, they are "just letting the oppression affect them totally." The "oppression" that Moesha spoke of is, of course, racial oppression. (Moesha was, by the way, the only teen who used the term *oppression* with me.) Moesha saw racial oppression when NJ High's faculty selected a white student over several black students for a special travel award, she saw it in the New Jersey State Police's profiling of racial minorities (a national news story at the time), and she saw it in whites' opposition to affirmative action. But she also saw it when black peers questioned whether Moesha deserved to "be with us," since she has light brown skin. While other minority teens sometimes spoke of racism, they generally placed it in remote places and distant times (see chapter 6). Moesha spoke of it as local, real, and multidirectional.

So how did Moesha fare during her first year out? Moesha had a "great" year, loved her Well-Known Black University, and did well academically in her accelerated BA/JD program. Moesha scaled back her participation in extracurricular activities so she could focus on study. Yet Moesha continued to attend church weekly, maintained daily contact with her mother and frequent contact with her grandmother and extended kin, and developed a core group of close friends. Moesha also met and began to spend a lot of time with her "hardworking . . . and cute" boyfriend, who lived in the public housing project adjacent to her residence hall. She met her boyfriend while volunteering in a tutoring program that her university ran at the project. Seeing poverty up close for the first time, Moesha said, "You really see how it's, like, the rich people stay rich, and the poor stay poor—or get worse." Seeing this also reinforced Moesha's longstanding commitment to public interest law, so she could go after the city that provides "awful, horrible schools" and does "nothing" to maintain the housing projects. Thus, Moesha expanded her prior perceptiveness about gender and race to include social class as well, and all three convinced Moesha about the importance of following local politics and voting in local elections. Or, to frame it another way, Moesha refused to use an identity lockbox, and, perhaps because she felt safe within a historically black and Protestant university, Moesha found her self-understanding as well as her perception of the world both expanded and better integrated.

I tell Moesha's story because it illustrates how profoundly community engagement and awareness *can* affect the lives and future of American teens. I attribute Moesha's concern for community primarily to her family (particularly to her grandmother, who possessed a deep interest in and active concern for the lives of all who surrounded her), secondly to her faith (which her family nurtured and which facilitated several of her involvements), and thirdly to the emotional rewards she accrued from her activities themselves (as helping others almost always produces positive feelings within the helper). Engagement with others did not reduce Moesha's drive to succeed; rather, it helped her identify a goal to pursue. And pursuing her personal goal did not mean Moesha had to lock away core identities out of concern that she might not fit within the American cultural mainstream (though her enrollment in a historically black, Protestant university likely made this easier). Rather, Moesha's engagement with others became the site wherein she nurtured her various identities and forged her larger purpose.

It does not require involvement in thirteen activities, however, for teens to nurture identities or determine larger purposes. Other teens did so through more moderate involvement with school, religion, civic organizations, or informal social networks. Dave Olsen, a white, middle-class, high school senior, played varsity lacrosse and "started and ran a Bible club for two-and-a-half years at my high school." This experience helped Dave select the ministry as his career and focused his college applications on religiously affiliated universities only. Similarly, Rob Robertson (from chapter 1) sought a career in politics based partly on his high school experience as a student government leader. At the end of the first year out, both Dave and Rob began to consider other, related career options—with Dave considering research with youth and Rob considering political science—because both teens refused to use identity lockboxes during their first year out and thus continued their efforts to understand and integrate their various identities.

Still other teens, though few in number, use awareness of gender or race to nurture identities and determine direction. Andre Kendall, a black, working-class senior at NJ High, was one of these. Seeing what the civil rights movement accomplished despite "the odds against them" made Andre "feel responsibility . . . for the black man." So Andre planned to own and operate a business in Suburban Township to give "something back to the community." (I return to Andre's story in chapter 4.) Few teens, including minority teens, demonstrate such an awareness of race or gender, and none that I spoke with had more than a passing awareness of social class. For those few teens who do possess a measure of race or gender consciousness, however, the impact of this awareness on their first year out is substantial and sustained.

The majority of teens, though, show little interest in their identities as members of various communities—be those local or civic communities or the more amorphous communities of race, gender, or class (and none show awareness of an emerging generational "community" that results from the intersection of history and culture on their particular birth cohort). Most teens describe no voluntary involvements or, at best, limited involvements chosen to burnish college applications and résumés. In fact, a survey of St. Paul, Minnesota, teens found that, although high school volunteers largely continue to volunteer as young adults, just 18.4 percent of 18 year olds reported any volunteer work in the previous twelve months.[40] They assert that race, gender, and class have little contemporary significance for social life, and they have little sense of what their distinct, generational perspective might be on the wider world (neither did I for the longest time—see chapter 6). Instead, what most teens do is immerse themselves into a micro-world of school, work, and leisure consumption and focus on the friendship networks they maintain within each sector (see chapters 3–5). Thus preoccupied, and moreover concerned to stay within the American mainstream due to the larger economic and cultural changes that make the first year out "table" wobble, they assign core identities to lockboxes and give passing attention (if any) to what lies beyond their micro-worlds. Although teens manage these micro-worlds rather successfully, and deserve our respect for doing so during an era when these micro-worlds have become quite complex, they seem blind to the tenuousness of these micro-worlds. Such a widespread pattern is, of course, a product of American culture. Popular American moral culture produces efficient teen managers of micro-worlds, whose daily living patterns keep numerous institutions and much of the global economy humming. But it also creates young adults whose narrowed perspectives on wider, deeper, and longer-term matters have unwittingly placed them within a low-lying cultural campground, located adjacent to the flood-prone river of history (see chapter 6).

The next three chapters evaluate the primary life arenas of culturally mainstream American teens who graduated from high school between 1995 and 2003: relationships and gratifications; work, money, and leisure; and education. The last chapter examines how teens understand and engage themselves with what lies beyond their micro-worlds and presents the book's key implications. These four chapters, combined with the starting points evaluated above, convey the lived experiences and shared moral culture of mainstream American teens. Though most of what affects teen trajectories and patterns during the first year after high school has been described in this chapter, it is striking to see how teens carry forward the patterns they forged within their family, faith, and community contexts and stay within their trajectories during the first year of their emerging, adult lives. America has just cause to be proud of its youth, but it also has reason to give pause. The next four chapters will illustrate why.

THREE

Navigating Relationships, Managing Gratifications

Barb Miscoski was a bright, clean-cut marathon runner with well-defined plans to become a teacher of deaf students. The youngest of four children born to white, middle-class parents, Barb parlayed her high SAT scores and excellent running record into a sizable scholarship at Ordinary Private College. I sat down with Barb a few days before her high school graduation, so the end of her high school years became a natural topic of conversation. Barb had mixed feelings. On the one hand, she was "sick of school" and more than "ready to move on . . . [because] some people just haven't grown at all in the four years." On the other hand, "it's going to be sad, like, saying goodbye to everyone; and some people I know won't stay in touch—so that's kind of like a reality." Barb knew her friendship circle was about to alter permanently. Leaving behind classmates who had not grown up would be a welcome change, but the loss of friends would not: "I don't think it will be a problem on my end—like keeping in touch with everyone. . . . I'm just hoping that they'll try to keep in touch too."

Still, Barb looked forward to life after high school graduation and especially to going away for college. Not that Barb was unhappy with her home life or struggled with her parents. In fact, Barb selected her college partly for its proximity to her parents: "I want to be close enough where they'll come get me if I need them." Rather, Barb was eager to attend college because she felt ready to "test herself" and to live "without parents always around." When I talked with Barb the following summer, she reported passing her own test: "I liked being on my own; I liked making my own decisions.... I don't think I made a wrong one anywhere." Barb loved her parents, but, living back at home after her first year at school, she once again had "someone to answer to" and she preferred just having "to answer to myself." Barb was independent in every way except financially, and her relationship with her parents had reached an awkward moment: "I like being home," she told me, "but I'd rather not be here—you know what I mean?" Apparently, the awkwardness went two ways. Barb said of her parents, "They missed me. Now they have me again; they don't know what to do with me." An important part of Barb's first year out was navigating this changing relationship with her parents—as it was for virtually every other teen I interviewed.

Barb's changing relationship with her parents was not the only relationship she had to navigate, however. Barb fell in love with another freshman at college, she had to live with her first-year roommate, she saw relationships with several "very close friends" from high school grow distant, and she discovered that even her closest friends from college made little effort to stay in contact during the summer. Barb's relationship with her boyfriend was "pretty serious, I guess," but she struggled with how much of herself to reveal to him: "I'm, like, should I bother him with this?" Barb's relationship with her roommate was tolerable, but they had to work at it and they did not become close like other roommates she knew. Barb's relationships with her high school friends changed as she had expected, but more mutually than she anticipated: "Maybe they've changed, or maybe I've changed. [My friendships] are just different, like not as close." Perhaps the most surprising change for Barb, however, was seeing how quickly her college friendships cooled off: "It was weird 'cause, like, all during school, I maintained friendships [with college classmates], and then it's just like coming home that it was, like, 'Oh, this feels kinda different.' Oh my god, we talked *all year*.... [Sighs.] I guess I'm close with them because I live with them. It's kind of a forced closeness." Barb recognized that shared context, like a college dormitory, fosters friendships, and that without that context, friendships grow distant and wither. Navigating these shifting relationships kept Barb quite occupied during her first year out.

At the same time, the independence Barb sought and so enjoyed during her first year out imposed additional obligations on her: managing the myriad of adult gratifications now freely available to her. Adult gratifications were not new to Barb; high school students can obtain access to sex, drugs, and alcohol. But the removal of parental and school oversight, together with the legal definitions of 18 year olds as adults gives teens wide freedom to gratify themselves as they choose. Thus Barb reported, "I'm partying a lot more" than she did as a high school student, by which she means consuming alcohol more frequently with other teens at parties of various sorts. But Barb "learned her limit" with respect to alcohol:

> BARB: Well, I'm small, so I can't drink a lot at all. Like, I'd be just a mess.
> INTERVIEWER: How much do you typically drink?
> BARB: Like three or four beers probably. . . . Like that'd be it for a whole evening. . . . I just don't like not knowing where I am and things. I think it's just from observation of seeing other people like that, and I just do *not* want to be like that. So I try to keep myself under control at school. Throwing up—I just do not enjoy that. I've learned my limit. I've learned my limit.

Barb learned her limit by exceeding it a couple of times and feeling the consequences. She also chose to restrict herself to alcohol only. "No, no illegal substances for me," she declared. While some of her friends "smoke pot," and Barb considered that "their choice," Barb said she "frowns upon" those who use "cocaine, heroin, and . . . hard-core stuff." Barb described herself as a "social drinker," occasionally consuming one or two beers with her family, drinking three or four beers when with her friends, and "like maybe . . . once a month"—and only at college—drinking five or six beers.

Of course, teens do more than drink at their parties. They talk, flirt, dance, and pursue romantic and/or sexual relationships. Barb was quite familiar with the pairing off that often follows these parties, and she did not approve of it. She had firm views about sex: "I think it's something some people, like, take for granted, or rush into. . . . I think if you, like, truly believe you're in love with someone then it, it's fine. But in the world today, I definitely frown upon just, like, random sex . . . like pure lust as the reason. . . . I don't think people take the time to consider, like, how big it is." Barb acknowledged that she was sexually active with her boyfriend and that she was no advocate of abstinence: "Not to say I'm, like, 'Miss Moral Upstanding.'" But she also said she "really frowns upon people that just don't care" about their sexual partnerships. Barb asked rhetorically, "What's the point of that?" For Barb, serial monogamy was the only justifiable way to manage sexual gratification, and that was how she managed her own sexual behavior.

Barb is like a lot of teens in two important ways. First, navigating relationships and managing gratifications were critical aspects of Barb's first year out and consumed a large share of Barb's energy. Second, Barb's choices of moderate alcohol use (with occasional heavy use), no illegal substance use, and serial monogamy are the most frequent choices of teens during the first year out. The first confirms the primacy of daily life management during the first year out, while the second runs counter to many popular images of teens, including ones they hold themselves. This chapter will tell a story of teens consumed with daily life management and, in particular, with navigating relationships and managing gratifications. For the most part, these teens prefer relatively conventional relationships and moderate their use of new adult freedoms. There are exceptions, to be sure, but they do more to introduce interesting side observations than they do to challenge the primary story.

The primary story of the first year out, then, is not the story that repeatedly emerges from reports by investigative journalists, public health experts, and profamily pundits. Abuse of drugs and alcohol, disregard for sexually transmitted disease, and incapacity for emotional intimacy are all, to be sure, valid cause for concern,[1] but these do not represent the lived realities of the vast majority of mainstream American teens during the first year out. Conveying an accurate and representative story, and explaining this story via identity lockboxes, popular American moral culture, and increased economic uncertainty, is, therefore, the major contribution that I seek to make to the scholarly literature on American youth. An accurate and broad understanding of American teens' primary foci during the first year out, moreover, holds important implications for several American social institutions and a variety of different readers (see chapter 6 for a specific discussion of implications).

PLAYING THE DAILY LIFE MANAGEMENT GAME

In the first chapter, I suggested the first year out was analogous to teens gathered around a wobbly table. On the table is an identity lockbox for the storage of critical identities and next to it is the game of daily life management, which seems to engross all those gathered around the table. At the risk of pushing this analogy too far, I will describe this game board and its pieces, the rules of play, and the goals of the game. Doing so conveys not only "what" the key components of the first year out are, but also "why" managing these components so engrosses teens during the first year out.

THE GAME BOARD AND PIECES

Visualize a Monopoly-like game board, with four corner spaces and ten spaces running along each side. The ten spaces along the sides are variously labeled with one of the following: "Class," "Work," "Buy," "Added Obligation," "Eat, Sleep, and Wash," and "Party." The four corner spaces are labeled "Go (or Exit)," "Extra Work," "Extra Study," or "Sick." In the center of the board is an illustration of a beach, with young people surfing, wading in shallow waters, sunbathing, or playing beach volleyball. Instead of Monopoly money, there are time chips, class credits, and debt points. Instead of "Chance" and "Community Chest" cards, there are "Buy," "Added Obligation," and "Surfing" cards. And instead of houses and hotels, there are five types of relationship tokens. Finally, there is a six-sided die to roll and playing pieces of different colors for each player to move around the board.

BASIC PLAY

Each player receives fifty time chips and must "spend" them as specified on each board space. Each player also receives ten relationship tokens: one romantic partner token (platinum), one best friend token (gold), two good friend tokens (silver), three acquaintance tokens (bronze), and three "blow-off" tokens (plastic). To start, players select a playing piece, place it on the "GO" corner, roll the die, and advance to the corresponding space.

* If players land on "Eat, Sleep, or Wash" or "Work" spaces, they surrender one time chip and wait for their next turn.
* If players land on a "Class" space, they surrender the number of time chips specified and receive one "class credit."
* If players land on "Buy" or "Other Obligation" spaces, they must take a card from the respective stack and follow its instructions.
  · "Buy" cards are of two basic types. One type lists items a typical teen can afford, like a music recording. The other type lists items that assign debt points, like a car.
  · "Added Obligation" cards describe obligations to family, sport, exercise, voluntary organizations, religious organizations, extra work,

extra study, or recuperation from illness or injury, and each card requires time tokens and occasionally assigns debt points, too.

* If players land on a "Party" space, they surrender one time chip, choose between beach volleyball, sunbathing (with an occasional dip to cool off), wading in shallow waters, or surfing.

  · If they choose surfing, they must take a "Surfing" card. "Surfing" cards are of three different types: most prevalent are injury-free or minor injury cards, sporadically appearing are major injury cards, and there are a couple of cards that list a shark attack. Injury-free cards cost players nothing. Minor injury cards cost players one time chip for recovery. Major injury cards put players in the "Sick" corner space and cost three time chips and one class credit. Shark attack cards end the player's game immediately.

* At any point during a player's turn, that player can approach another player sharing the same space and propose a relationship token exchange. If both players agree, they secretly select one token and exchange it with the other player. The ideal exchange nets players matching tokens (for example, romantic partner token for romantic partner token). But any exchange is possible, and mismatches are common.

The goal of the game, which runs continuously as new players enter and seasoned players exit, is for each player to accumulate eight class credits and at least three valid relationship tokens without running out of time chips, exceeding eight debt points, or getting attacked by the shark.

GAME OBSERVATIONS

The beach party is an enticing place (especially when compared to work, class, or other obligations), and teens enjoy socializing with each other there. Most teens try out surfing, and some become regular surfers. But the possibility or experience of injury keeps most teens closer to the shore and keeps some out of the water entirely. The ocean waters represent the gratifications of sex, drugs, and alcohol. Surfers represent those who choose to immerse themselves in one or more of those freedoms. And the shark represents the remote—yet real—possibility of addiction.

Surfers, nonetheless, command the attention of just about everyone at the beach—even though they do not represent the majority of those attending the beach party. Those who wade in ankle- to knee-deep waters face the ocean and watch the surfers, often unaware of the sunbathers or volleyball players behind them. Those who sunbathe or play volleyball likewise look out at the ocean, but the glare from the sun can make it hard for them to distinguish between waders and surfers. The surfers themselves focus on the waves, hoping to enjoy a good ride on the next big wave, hooting and hollering when they do get a good ride, inviting waders to join them, and laughing at beginners who get "thrashed" by the waves.

All board spaces offer a view of the beach party. By that I mean that teens at work reminisce about past visits to the beach, talk about the beach with their coworkers, and plan their next trip to the beach. The same happens to teens at class, those engaged in shopping for products or services, those fulfilling added obligations, and those attending to daily needs such as eating or washing. In fact, the beach party—and the relationship token exchanges that occur there frequently—so dominate most players' attentions that they fail to realize how much time they spend on the "work" or "buy" spaces. Teens so focus on having newer cars to drive to the beach, new clothes to wear at the beach, and new surfboards, volleyballs, or beach towels to use at the beach that they are oblivious to the hours they devote to both working and shopping that they could forgo to spend more time with their friends at the beach (though admittedly with older possessions that some friends might not find acceptable). At the same time, teens are all too aware of the time they spend on the "class" space, and most attempt to reduce the hours spent there to some personally acceptable minimum. (I take up work and money issues in chapter 4 and education issues in chapter 5.)

If all of this sounds like a rather complicated game, it is. And this game analogy unquestionably oversimplifies the first year out, as relationships have far more levels and combinations than the game allows, and as countless other factors can affect a teen's actual first year out. Still, this game description conveys why playing the daily life management game so consumes teens' time and attention, why it is that teens opt to use the identity lockbox, and why virtually everything that lies beyond this game (such as social or political issues, personal or community development, or thinking about the future) is simply off the radar screens of mainstream American teens. (On the latter point, see chapter 6.) Because this is the first time American teens have been cleared to play the daily life management game as adults, it takes time for teens to settle into a game plan that works. Still, most teens adopt a successful game plan during the first year out. The rest of this chapter describes how they do it.

EARLY PATTERNS

High school seniors do, of course, navigate relationships and manage gratifications. But their experiences are qualitatively different during high school, as their social contexts are both more stable and more limited than those they enter during the first year out. As liberal as some baby-boomer parents may be, there are precious few who invite their 17-year-old daughter and her boyfriend to spend the night together in her room, or who encourage their 17-year-old son to become so intoxicated that he staggers home, vomits on the lawn, and falls asleep in the flower garden. The oversight of parents and the constraints of school combine to present teens with relatively stable social networks in which to navigate relationships and with reduced access to the adult gratifications most teens desire.

In this section, I examine teen relationship and gratification patterns at their point of departure: the senior year of high school. Having already presented the general warmth that most teens express toward at least one parent in the previous chapter, I offer a couple of additional observations about how teens navigate relationships with their parents before moving on to peer relationships and long-term relationship expectations. After that, I examine gratification cycles during high school, that is, how teens surreptitiously test the waters at several points and begin to form patterns of management that they carry over during their first year out.

RELATIONSHIPS WITH PARENTS

Most teens express warmth toward at least one of their parents, and most teens describe that relationship as a close one (see chapter 2). That does not mean, however, that teens who report having close relationships truly have close relationships—that is, relationships defined by honesty, vulnerability, respect, and deep concern for the other. Rather, they are making a judgment based on comparisons with their peers. Because most teens' relationships with their parents are not as tumultuous as some that they know of, teens infer that their relationships are "close."[2] Raquel Johnson, a black, middle-class senior at NJ High, confirmed this relativity of judgment: "My relationship with my parents is good compared to stories I hear from other people. . . . I was talking to [Kristi] on the phone [about an argument with her parents]. She's like, 'You think that's an argument?' And I was like, 'Yeah, it's a big deal. They're all in my business.' She's like, 'Get a life!'" Bill Keiser, a white, middle-class senior, was unusual because he realized that frequent conversations with his parents did not mean his relationship was truly close. Describing his relationship, Bill explained, "It was kind of close *and* distant. Because, I mean, we talked—but we didn't talk about things that were real deep. You know, it was just on the surface. It was in that way that we were close. We talked a lot, but it wasn't about anything, really." I suspect many teen reports of close relationships are like Bill Keiser's description. Truly close relationships with parents were as rare as truly poor relationships, at least among the mainstream teens I interviewed. Most teens have relationships with their parents that are *relatively* close, while some have relationships that are *relatively* distant.

Perhaps that is how teens can report close relationships with their parents one moment and the next moment describe intentionally deceiving them. For example, John Snow, a white, upper-middle-class, high school senior, reported a "fairly close" relationship with his parents. By that, he meant that he talked to his parents often and could tell his parents a "fair amount" of things about his life. But John did not tell his parents everything, keeping his "partying" secret. Similarly, Joann McBride, a white, upper-middle-class senior, found no irony in this description of her "very close relationship" with her parents: "My parents—they just basically adore me because I'm their only child. I am Daddy's little girl, I am Mommy's little girl, all wrapped up in one! I can talk to them about things, but they also give me my space and we have a good relationship. I don't do anything *too bad* that will upset them. I know their rules and I try to make them proud. And at the same time I try to make myself happy, so it works out good." Deception of this sort is widely described by teens, and widely accepted—so long as it is parents, and not peers, who get deceived. I am certain that Joann and John would be angry if they discovered a friend or romantic partner had deceived them about an agreed upon matter. But *deceiving parents is an accepted and unquestioned aspect of American teen moral culture*, and one that characterizes teen relationships with authority figures in general, be they coaches, bosses, or teachers (a point I take up in the next two chapters).[3]

RELATIONSHIPS WITH PEERS

Many teens find high school graduation to be a bittersweet moment. Teens describe exuberance, to be sure, upon leaving an institution that controls and bores most teens and upon moving symbolically closer to full adulthood. But teens describe sadness, too, about saying "goodbye to all my friends there." Perhaps this is what propelled teens at NJ High to hug and high-five each other on that humid graduation night in June 2001 and prompted some two dozen seniors who passed by me to do the same. But the emotion of graduation night was not about me, nor the half-dozen teachers who received similar farewells. It was about moving on and about saying goodbye—without trying to say goodbye—to one's classmates.

Part of what makes sorting out the meaning of graduating from high school so difficult is teens' loose use of the term *friend*. Midway through my field experience at NJ High, I realized an important distinction that teens made among their peers: "school friends" and "other friends." For example, Sam Postman, a white, middle-class senior, described different sets of friends, one set that he saw during the summer and another set that he saw at high school. Sam enjoyed going to school, because "I think it's a good opportunity to see more people. . . . In the summer, you usually only see one set of friends. But during the school year you see everyone. You get to talk with everyone." But beyond these two sets, teens describe different levels of friendships, variously referred to as "close" friends, "good" friends, or occasionally "best" friend. Rachel O'Leary, a white, upper-middle-class senior, described having two "really good" friends at school—friends she rarely talked to on the phone and had never gotten together with outside of school: "In school, like, they are *good* friends. . . . We are all in the same classes all the time. . . . I've talked to them on the phone like a few times, [but] I don't hang out with them or anything." There is no culturally standardized definition of a "really good" friend, of course, but I was struck by how many teens quickly labeled classmates as friends, friends as "close" friends, and so on. I suspect many teens inflated not only the numbers of friends they had, but also the closeness of those friendships, as a way of demonstrating their social acceptance. As much as teens eschew the notion of popularity, their drive to be accepted by others remains powerful indeed. So much so, that some teens would describe impossibly large numbers of "close friends." When asked to list three of his closest friends, Okapi Ahmed, a black, working-class senior, identified the "whole school"—over 1,500 teens—in that category: "I have, like, a lot of friends. Everyone—the whole school is my friend! I'm a friendly person." Some of this friendship inflation comes from inexperience and immaturity; as friendships fade or endure over the years, adults grow more selective about whom they count as a close friend. But more of it comes from another source.

That other source of friendship inflation is American culture itself, namely, the compartmentalization of most Americans' social relationships, its consequent weakening of the notion of friendship, and the American equation of quantity with success. By that I mean: (1) Americans have sets of relationships at work, school, home, and a few other realms, such as congregations, neighborhoods, voluntary organizations, or shared leisure activities; (2) Americans generally keep these sets of relationships distinct; and (3) Americans often equate popularity with individual worth. The result is that American friendships are often context- or institution-bound, not particularly deep, and valued more for personal utility than for their own sake.[4] This is a part of what sociologists describe as the social consequences of modernization,[5] and teens are as affected by these consequences as adults are. Schneider and Stevenson conclude that "the fluidity of friendships is perhaps a dominant characteristic of the social life of today's adolescents,"[6] and I agree—except for the "perhaps" part.

If teens do not, then, spend much time with their "school friends" outside of school, with whom do they spend their time? The answer is that they spend their limited "free time" with their "other" or "hangout" friends. (Teens have no common term for such friends.) Hangout friends are teens of two types: those who share a current context with a teen (such as work, church youth group, leisure activity, or occasionally school) and those who once shared a context with a teen and have maintained a friendship. Joann McBride reported maintaining friendships from previous contexts: "It seems that I have one really close friend from every stage in my life." But Joann described over a dozen "close friends," including several she sees quite infrequently. Rob Robertson, by contrast, spent most of his time with two buddies, one from his neighborhood and one from his high school sports team. Yet even Rob described only one as a close friend. The other buddy is just convenient—he lives across the street, he and Rob both like to shoot hoops in the driveway and play video games, and he has his own car. Hangout friends are not necessarily, then, any closer than teens' school friends.

Occasionally, teens will describe a "best friend" with whom they spend a lot of time and connect with on a deeper level. For Tremaine Owens, a black, middle-class senior, it was his friend Jamel: "We do the same activities—just for college [applications]. Same neighborhood—we live like two minutes from each other, we go to the same school. We were born like four days apart. He could be, like, my brother. We're like the same person. We think the same." For Lowanda Smith, it was Terri, a friend from a previous school whom Lowanda goes to church with at least twice weekly. For Kristi Kramer and Raquel Johnson it was each other, as both spoke their minds freely and found a significant connection with each other during their senior year. These teens were atypical, however, as most teens did not report a best friend or classified their romantic partner as their best friend. Perhaps because teen contexts change so rapidly (school terms end, jobs change, families move, peer groups realign, etc.) or perhaps because teens choose to keep their "free time" so limited (see chapter 4), relatively few teens have formed lasting and truly close friendships.[7] Perhaps this is also why teens emphasize the quantity of their friends.

RELATIONSHIPS WITH ROMANTIC PARTNERS

Even though most high school seniors are not in a romantic relationship at any given moment, most wish to be in one. Infatuation and sexual desire are as common in high school as tiles on classroom floors. But to understand how teens approach the whole realm of romantic partners—be they actual or potential partners—it is essential to distinguish public teen discourse from private teen discourse. Public teen discourse about romantic partnering is variously loud, shallow, humorous, demeaning, and crude. Private teen discourse is variously confused, tender, insecure, desperate, and sweet. That teens must commute between these two discourses makes this crucial dimension of their lives all the more difficult to navigate.

Publicly and collectively, teens appear obsessed with romantic and sexual relationships. At NJ High, teens gossiped about who liked whom, who was having sex, who was not having sex, who might have gotten pregnant, which couple was going out, which couple broke up, which girls were "sluts," and which boys were "players." And the public teen discourse split along gender lines, with senior girls predominantly talking about relationships and senior boys predominantly talking about sex. It was very immature, often painful, frequently malicious, and the most difficult part of the whole project for me to observe dispassionately. It also made for a NJ High social environment that was sexually hostile and intimidating. Lisa Smith, a working-class senior at NJ High, described conversations she participated in:

> LISA: Like, the next day you find out this person slept with you-know-who. That should be kept between two people and [not shared] with like twenty other people. . . .
> INTERVIEWER: Did you hear that a lot?
> LISA: Yeah, you hear things. I don't know if everything's true or not, but you know, you hear things. And I've been known to just go, "Oh yeah, that must be true; look at her."

But Lisa, without a moment's hesitation, added, "I wouldn't want that to happen to me." To those to whom it did happen, it was painful indeed.

Sadly, NJ High's administration was not only oblivious to this environment, they inadvertently made it worse. The principal told me proudly how he arranged to have two large televisions with cable service installed in the senior lunchroom, as a "reward" for the seniors. These televisions were controlled by successive cohorts of male athletes at each lunch period—mostly but not exclusively black—who ensured that they were tuned to cable's Black Entertainment Television's (BET's) raunchy music videos (or MTV, if it happened to have raunchier offerings) and set at full volume. They would then eat their lunch and amuse themselves with crude remarks about the women in the videos. Sitting adjacent to these male athletes was a handful of senior females, dressed as provocatively as the school dress code would allow, who bantered with the athletes about the videos and about sexual matters in general. Though the total size of this group numbered no more than a dozen, its control of the televisions affected the lunchroom atmosphere significantly. Many senior girls expressed their displeasure with the videos to me and to each other, and a number of the boys were embarrassed by their response to the videos' titillation. None of these teens attempted to challenge the athletes' control of the television channels directly (by changing the channels) or indirectly (by appealing to the administration). Mostly, these teens resigned themselves to the videos and the loud bantering and ignored it as much as they could.

Had the lunchroom and hallways been the only places I observed teen behavior, and had I done so only at a distance, I would conclude that teens were hypersexual, wantonly promiscuous, and morally adrift. I might conclude that they had become "a tribe apart," as journalist Patricia Hersch claims in her account of teen lives.[8] On the one hand, Hersch is right that teens yearn for but have little meaningful interaction with adults, for I too found that teens were eager to pour out their hearts to a caring adult. On the other hand, journalists like Hersch are not professionally socialized to consider the representativeness of their evidence, only to gather sufficient evidence to support a catchy story line. To put it differently, if I had gone looking for "a tribe apart," I would have found evidence for it—but only among a minority of teens. Removed from the sexually charged public discourse of the high school environment, I found that most teens talk like and describe behavior like most adults.[9] That is, they want meaningful relationships with a single romantic partner, with sexual intimacy as a part of this relationship, and they are trying to figure out when and how to make this happen in their lives.

High school seniors without current romantic partners want one. Duncan Green, a white, middle-class senior, hoped a romantic relationship was in his future, possibly at college: "I'd like to maybe get a girlfriend in college—it would be nice." Kasim Douglass, a black, working-class senior at NJ High, described his "[Beth] saga"—about a frustrating on-again, off-again potential relationship with a girl he met at camp. Kasim "need[ed] a prom date" and he was "looking ahead" again with hope. Cookie Munroe, of NJ High's Girlfriends Seven, even confided, "I really don't like boys right now," but then declared, "I just want a boyfriend who doesn't play games or anything."

Meanwhile, high school seniors with romantic partners will go to great lengths to keep their partners happy. Rick Bolton, a white, upper-middle-class senior, joined the swim team: "Actually, my girlfriend *made* me swim. [Laughing.]" Sam Postman spent "basically all" of his earnings on his girlfriend. "So you've found girlfriends are expensive?" I asked. "Very expensive!" Sam responded. Tammy Biggs, a white, working-class senior at NJ High, joined a youth group at a local church that her boyfriend liked to attend. And Megan Morici (introduced in chapter 2) applied to the same university that her boyfriend attended. By the time I interviewed Megan, her boyfriend was now her ex-boyfriend and Megan regretted applying: "I was thinking about going to [Allegheny State] University. That was 'cause I was a woman and my boyfriend was there. Which was stupid." Infatuation has led many people to do things they would never do otherwise; teens are particularly susceptible to this. As Kaniesha Goode, a black, working-class senior, put it, "I met my first boyfriend and I lost my mind—I literally lost my mind!" Kaniesha has plenty of company in that experience.

Perhaps most surprising was how seriously those seniors who were involved in romantic relationships viewed their relationships. John Snow, an upper-middle-class senior, told me, "I have a girlfriend right now," and "You never know . . . I could see myself marrying her." Sam Postman told me, "It's strange to think," but he could also imagine marrying his girlfriend. Jewel Galvez, a Latina, working-class senior, and Traci Negm, a Lebanese, working-class senior at NJ High, both hoped that they would marry their current boyfriends. Both Eric Strauss, a white, middle-class senior, and Christine Darden, a white, working-class senior, thought they would marry each other (and several years later, I learned that they did). Though teens acknowledge they are young and not yet ready to make long-term commitments, most teens who were involved in romantic relationships for more than three months volunteered that they considered marriage a future possibility with their current partner.

Such ruminations were never topics of conversation among teens at NJ High. Talk of enjoying a romantic partner, of doing things to please a romantic partner, or of considering marriage as an outcome of a romantic relationship represents the private discourse of teens. These are tentative, sensitive, and emotionally vulnerable matters, and no teen with a modicum of social awareness would dare describe such matters in the coarse and competitive public discourse of high school. Unlike the gender-stereotyped and demeaning public teen discourse, private teen discourse was not only undistinguished along gender lines, it revealed a highly conventional set of relationship hopes and goals.

LONG-TERM RELATIONSHIP GOALS

High school seniors who considered marrying their current romantic partner, as remarkable as this may sound, were not all that unusual. Their relationships just gave them a head start over their peers. I could count on one hand the number of teens who were *unsure* if they would ever marry, and most envisioned marrying within the next ten years. "I hope so—I'd hate to go through life single!" was white, working-class senior Matt Roberts's immediate response. "I hope to," "Hopefully," or "Yes, definitely" were other answers to the question of being married in ten years. In fact, many of those who expected to marry within ten years also hoped to have children within that time frame, and the rest hoped to have children within ten to twenty years. Matt Roberts continued, "I foresee myself getting married. After a while, have a few kids. I don't know how many." Sandra Lombardi, a white, middle-class senior, hoped to have "one or two" children within ten years' time, "depending on when I get married." Cookie Munroe wanted to wait a little longer. "If it [having children] happens, like, when I'm 29, then OK," Cookie explained.

Even those teens whom I classify as primarily pleasure seekers (see chapter 4) expected to marry eventually, and most hoped to have kids at some point thereafter. Kato Stuart, a white, middle-class senior at NJ High, told us he would not get married within ten years just to "settle down or whatever," but will marry "when I think it's right." And if Kato did find the right person to marry, he would "probably have kids." Being married and having children, despite their declining proportions in the United States at large, are tightly woven into the future expectations and life scripts of culturally mainstream American teens. It is interesting, then, to consider the fears of moral conservatives in light of this reality, since the sexual revolution did not diminish teen Americans' desires to marry or raise children in a two-parent family. It simply removed sex from its marital restriction and made it part of the gratifications that define adulthood.[10] It is on those symbolically important gratifications that I now focus my attention.

SEX, DRUGS, AND ALCOHOL IN HIGH SCHOOL

Learning how to navigate relationships and manage gratifications are distinct but intertwined dimensions of American teen life. Separating them is useful for the purposes of analyzing and understanding them, but readers must understand that teen gratifications are managed side-by-side with teen relationships. With that caveat, I will offer three observations in this section. First, high school students know about the "beach party" that awaits those entering the first year out, and many sneak into the older teens' party. This tends to happen at two particular periods in a teen's life—immediately following puberty (eighth and ninth grades) and again when teens gain individual access to transportation and start to forge independent social lives (eleventh and twelfth grades). Second, high school students have less access to the beach party than do high school graduates. High school teens have sex less often and consume substances in smaller quantities and less frequently than many adults (or even many teens) suppose. Third, though many high school teens attempt to "surf" when they reach the beach party, most retreat to shallower waters fairly quickly. There are many individual exceptions, to be sure. But for the culturally mainstream American teens I observed and interviewed, these observations hold true surprisingly often.

Substance Usage Patterns | A number of high school seniors spoke about their "wild days" or "experimental stage" during *eighth and ninth grades*. Kristi Kramer (from chapter 1), explained:

> KRISTI: I had my little experimenting stage when I was in eighth grade.
> INTERVIEWER: Experimenting?
> KRISTI: You know, the whole, you go to little parties and you smoke a cigarette or something like that. You drink something and you're just like, "Oh, god, why did I do it?"

Kristi's description is typical: she downplays her own interest and involvement in substance use, but subsequent expressions of regret and altered behaviors indicate more substantial usage. Kristi describes "*little*" parties where she smoked "*a*" cigarette or drank "*something*," but then groans "Oh, god, why did I do it?"—indicating more extensive usage than she actually describes.

Similarly, Traci Negm emphasized how she "*only* smoked weed and drank" when she began high school. Then she added, "but I quit everything." Traci self-justified by noting that she "only" used alcohol and marijuana. But she used them consistently enough that she did not say she "tried" these substances (like many teens), but that she had to "quit" them. Raquel Johnson, a bright and sensible high school senior, revealed this about her "partying": "The end of freshman year [in high school] I realized, well, that's not cool. Because you can't just be all studious five days out of the week and then Friday and Saturday go out and party and go crazy." Most of the parties, Raquel emphasized, were "house parties." That is, parties held at someone's home with "about thirty" 13- and 14-year-olds in attendance. On several occasions, however, Raquel had friends who slipped her into actual nightclubs, where "there are people doing drugs . . . all kinds of stuff. [Laughs.] There are people having sex, like in the bathrooms, things like that. A lot goes on in clubs." Raquel, of course, did not let her parents know she was going to nightclubs at age 14 (legal admittance in New Jersey is age 21), and she told me she did not use drugs or have sex at these parties. Raquel decided to roll back her partying once she realized she could no longer party all weekend and still earn good grades. Tremaine Owens also described backing off of alcohol use after trying it in eighth and ninth grade and "sometimes" not remembering what he did: "I'm not big on drinking. Like, I don't really see the point of drinking to get wasted. . . . I've tried it, but after I've tried it, it was like, 'What's the big deal?' In the long run, you know what it's gonna do to you—it's gonna mess your liver up if you keep doing it over and over again. And sometimes you can't even remember what you did, so what's the point? There's no reward in that." Though most teens I interviewed did not explore the party scene this early, a sizable portion did,[11] enough that other teens described it as a common pattern.

The Girlfriends Seven told me all about this at lunch one Friday. "Everybody go crazy, like, in ninth grade—thinking they all grown up 'cause they in high school now," Jo declared. By crazy, Jo referred to the whole of substance use and sexual activity. Mary elaborated, "So many girls get pregnant and drop out—they just stupid!" (NJ High teens used the word *stupid* very specifically: it referred to having sexual intercourse without using contraception; thus, ninth- or tenth-grade girls who get pregnant are "stupid" because they got pregnant, not because they dropped out of school.) The

Girlfriends Seven then went on to describe three or four girls who got pregnant during ninth and tenth grades and then dropped out. All of the girls they named were black. Perhaps the Girlfriends Seven did not know of pregnancies among white girls, but my hunch, based partly on national pregnancy and abortion statistics[12] and partly on the research of others,[13] was that white girls at NJ High were more likely to avoid pregnancy by avoiding coitus or using contraception and more likely to choose abortion if they did become pregnant.

Most teens test the waters of adult gratifications after they gain independent access to transportation and develop a social life independent of their family. The precondition is transportation: teens gain access to a car, a friend with a car, or, for city dwellers, independent nighttime use of public transportation. As Rob Robertson put it, his "social life . . . took off" once his two buddies got cars. Kris Capatunio, a white, middle-class senior, told me that soon after she got her driver's license, she began drinking. Kris drank about once a week, but she stressed that she did not "get drunk a lot." (This, of course, reveals that she gets drunk *sometimes*, however often that is.) Kris also admitted, in a quiet voice, to smoking marijuana "a few times." Because Kris could go out with friends "almost every night," she had established a social life independent of her family, and thus she could join the beach party so long as she kept her grades stable and avoided coming home drunk or high.

A key reason teens give for consuming adult substances is to fit in with their *perception* of other teens' consumption. Chuck Barker put it this way: "A lot of people drink and smoke. I don't smoke, but I drink on occasion. If everybody else here is doing it, I do it." Kato Stuart stated that "at high school, kids drink anything they can get their hands on." Still, Chuck and Kato emphasized that they did not consume large quantities or drink frequently—their visits to the "beach party" were more limited and they primarily "waded" in the water. Another middle-class teen told me that she had never drunk alcohol until just before her high school graduation, when she and her friends decided they needed to "learn" how to drink to be "ready" for college. Her story illustrates a classic sociological truism: if people perceive situations as real, they become real in their consequences.[14] Because this teen believed alcohol consumption is an important part of college life (which it is, but in more moderation than most teens perceive), she altered her present behavior based on skewed perception.

I remember one lunch at NJ High, when a half-dozen teens were talking about an absent friend's antics the previous weekend. "He was *so* drunk," they giggled. When he joined the table a few minutes later, I asked him about the previous weekend. "They keep saying I was drunk, but I wasn't." He admitted he had "a couple" of beers, but he had no difficulty remembering what he did. He was just "being crazy, that's all." In the lunchroom, a senior boy who jumps up and starts mimicking a video dancer's moves is just being "crazy," but if the same thing happens at a party, he is assumed to be drunk. After spending a year observing teens at NJ High, I am confident that teens need no help from substances to become boisterous. While a couple of beers might facilitate such behavior, they are certainly not its primary cause. Peers observing another teen's antics *want* to assume drunkenness because that makes for far better gossip than accurate reports.

Perceptions and Views of Sex | Having demonstrated that teen perception of alcohol use is selective and often flawed, it takes little to imagine how much more selective and flawed are teen perceptions of other teens' sexual activities. Because sexual activities are almost always hidden from public view, teens have little basis for their conclusions about other teens beyond the public bravado, gossip, and sexual bantering of peers. Some teens take their cues from this public discourse.[15] Kris Capatunio, for example, believed "everyone makes too much of a big deal about" sex. "I always thought," Kris explained, "it wasn't really a big deal that much." She then qualified her statement, saying, "I don't think that couples really should have sex the *very* first time they meet," but "once they get to know each other and feel comfortable, I think it's OK." Kris admitted she had herself not always waited to have sex, but more recently Kris had sought to "practice what I preach, I guess" with respect to her sexual behavior. Mona Segall, a white, upper-middle-class senior, described her view of sex as simply, "I think it's absolutely fine." A good number of senior boys I got to know, about four out of ten, shared Kris's and Mona's view (a proportion that also fits with national behavior patterns, which indicate 33–38 percent of male and female high school students report one or more sexual partners in the preceding three months[16]). Sawyer Cherrington, a white, upper-middle-class senior, did not hesitate when I asked his view of sex: "I like to do it." Tremaine Owens was equally quick to answer: "I'm all for it—I'm not going to say no to it." The only qualification these teens offered was "don't be stupid about it"—which means use contraception and avoid sexually transmitted diseases.

However, more senior boys, about six out of ten, spoke privately of sex as connected to a relationship that matters. This surprised me at first, because it is the opposite of what journalistic and scholarly interpreters of

American teen culture have led readers to expect. Journalist Patricia Hersch weaves anecdotes of early and ill-considered adolescent sexual activity into every chapter of *A Tribe Apart*, concluding that "adolescence is rife with drugs, alcohol, cigarettes, sex, lying, violence. . . . This is the mainstream of adolescence today."[17] And sociologist Murray Milner begins *Freaks, Geeks, and Cool Kids* by positing that "casual sex [has] become widespread."[18] The majority of my senior boy interviewees, however, were not familiar with these books nor did they fit their overgeneralizations.

John Snow certainly did not. He was plainly hesitant about his friends' sexual activities: "I know some of my friends had sex when they were really young. . . . I know a lot of kids want to experiment and try everything, but . . . it's sort of young, I guess you could say. Because it's supposed to be about love and everything." I asked John how well his own sexual behavior aligned with his views, and John answered, "Fairly close—not on target, but close." Malik Ali, a black, working-class senior, admitted he once "thought sex was just part of a relationship," but having had sex with his girlfriend, he came to "see that it just causes problems between the two of us." Malik decided teens should wait until "they get married" or, if that is not possible (as in his case), then "wait until you've known them a while and what they were like in the past . . . so you know they're not just going with you for the sex." Rick Bolton, a white, upper-middle-class senior, was utterly serious: "It's not a game. It's nothing to mess around with. You shouldn't do it unless you both agree and . . . unless you love the person." After listening to Rick elaborating his last point at length, I asked him how well his own behavior aligned with his views. Rick answered that it did, in fact, align, though "the guys" would never believe it.

> RICK: I'm a different person when I hang around with the guys.
> INTERVIEWER: How?
> RICK: I guess like when you're with a bunch of guys you act all macho and you're like, "Oh yeah, I could get her." . . . You don't give it any thought. You're just like, "I could have sex with her," this and that. Like, you know, you're just joking around.

Rick, like many high school boys, commuted between the coarse public discourse of high school sexuality and a private discourse of intimacy and affection.

This pattern is as striking as it is sad. Senior high school boys perpetuate a coarse public discourse about sex, but privately confide that sex should be reserved for a relationship that is significant to them. At first, I found this hard to believe. I thought they were just telling me what they believed I wanted to hear. But given the details they shared with me about hoping to marry eventually and have children, given the special efforts boys in longer-term relationships described making for their romantic partners, and given the concerted efforts these boys made to form romantic relationships, I cannot see this as simply a by-product of the interviewing process.

I next considered that these teens were atypical and that perhaps my sample was not representative. Because I cannot measure my sample's representativeness statistically, this is possible. But several factors undermine this possibility. First, these boys were not "goody-two-shoes"; they used profanity, told crude jokes, drank alcohol, smoked pot, raced cars, and possessed a host of prejudices, none of which they kept from me. Second, religiosity was not overrepresented among these boys. While religious teen boys were among the six out of ten who connected sex to meaningful relationships, most teen boys assigned their religiosity to a limited and quite private compartment in their lives. Third, my field observation at NJ High gave me broad access to the entire senior class, and I requested interviews from teens who represented the full spectrum of subgroups and personalities present (see appendix). Had I heard notably different things from NJ High interviewees than I did from my other interviews, then I would have uncovered evidence for a skewed sample—but I did not. In the end, I believe this is a real phenomenon and one worth tracking during the first year out.

So what about the senior girls—how do they view sex? The same views are represented among senior girls as among senior boys, but in much different proportions. Perhaps one out of twenty of my senior girl interviewees held to the view that whenever a couple wants to have sex, and as long as they know how to avoid pregnancy and STDs, they are free to do so. Kaniesha Goode stated, "Sex is beautiful. . . . Sex to me was intended to be enjoyed. That's the bottom line." But the remaining nineteen out of twenty senior girls would not agree. The vast majority of senior girls believe sex should be reserved for a meaningful relationship. The main difference among them was what constitutes a meaningful relationship. For DeWanda Roberts, a black, working-class senior, it meant when you are "sure he likes you" and that the relationship is not based on "a lie." For Roberta Lecawiez, a white, working-class senior, it was when you "totally, totally, totally, totally, totally love the person." For others, it was somewhere in between: "It has to be a strong relationship," or "You have to really know the person and really care for each other." And for strongly religious senior girls, such as orthodox

Jews, immigrant Muslims, and evangelical Protestants, it was reserved for marriage. This means that the vast majority of senior girls must either become bidiscursive—that is, competent in the coarse bantering that is part of the public discourse of American teens (and a number of girls are)—or learn to endure a public discourse that is often demeaning to women and alien to the private discourse of most girls.

Sexual Behavior | Public teen discourse is not only the opposite of most teens' private *views*, however; it is also out of sync with most teens' reported *behavior*. About four out of ten seniors reported that they were (or had previously been) sexually active when I first interviewed them, and another one out of ten either became sexually active during the last few weeks of their senior year or subsequently revealed that they had been sexually active during high school. These figures correspond well to national statistics from the Center for Disease Control's Youth Risk Behavior Surveillance Survey.[19] Of sexually active teens, only a handful had had casual sex with another teen; most had sex with their boyfriend(s) or girlfriend(s) only. Dennis Jackson, a black, working-class senior at NJ High, explained it this way: "The only ones I had sex with were my girlfriends. . . . I just broke up with a girlfriend, like . . . four or five months ago, so since then—not active at all." Dennis did not seem too bothered by his present sexual inactivity, but some teens are. Bob Kohl, a white, upper-middle-class teen, would have liked to be sexually active, but had lacked the opportunity: "[Laughing.] I don't have sex. It's not by choice or anything. It's just . . . the situation never came up yet. . . . I mean, I'd like to. I hope that nothing bad would ever happen, like a disease or anything." Between not having a partner and his concerns about STDs, Bob had not joined the ranks of sexually active teens, as much as he would have liked to. Other teens are less eager.

Though some teens may not be opposed to sexual activity, they are not pursuing opportunities either. Jenna Leigh, a white, working-class senior, believed intimacy was a "big long road" and planned to take her time heading down it. "Like, a lot of my closer friends . . . think [of me], like, 'Oh, prude,' but . . . that's not true. I've had relationships and I can be intimate, but there's a lot of leeway and there's a big long road before you ever get to sex. . . . I'm not always going to be with this person, and so I don't want to overcommit myself into something that may emotionally burden me later." Similarly, some teens hear "horror stories" from their friends, and that is enough to convince them they should take their time before having sex. Rachel O'Leary, for example, told me, "One of my girlfriends just went out to, like, some college and had sex with some guy she just met this one day. And, like, she got torn apart, you know." Rachel did not explain whether her friend's hurt was emotional, physical, or both—nor did she need to. Rachel's point was that she was *not* going to repeat her friend's mistake. Sexually inactive teens either reject opportunities to become active because of personal views, or they lack opportunities, or both.

A teen's personal views on sex and a teen's opportunities to have sex explain much of a teen's sexual behavior. For the largest majority of teens, there must first be a romantic relationship of some importance. And such relationships are as hard to come by for high school students as they are for adults (about 25 percent of my high school interviewees told me they were currently involved in one). Then the couple requires having a time and place for sexual activity, which also come infrequently. Of those teens who were sexually active, most had sexual intercourse just a couple of times a month. Raquel Johnson described her frequency of sex this way: "It was very cool. It [sex] was just on, like, special occasions. Or if, like, we were on a special date or something like that. It wasn't like, 'Oh my gosh, it's Monday. OK, we gotta do it.' Or, 'We haven't done it in three weeks. OK, let's go.' It wasn't like that." Nick Lawrence, a white, middle-class senior at NJ High, described having sexual intercourse "occasionally," because conducive times and private places do not abound.

> NICK: I have sex but it's . . . it's occasional.
> INTERVIEWER: How often is "occasional"—a few times a month?
> NICK: Once a month, maybe. A lot of people don't understand about teen sex.
> INTERVIEWER: How so?
> NICK: They think teens are having a lot of sex, and, well, *some* are. But teens . . . need a place to have sex. . . . There's not many opportunities. (*Calling out:*) 'Uh, Mom, just keep watching television, we'll be in the bedroom.' (*Falsetto voice:*) 'OK, you kids have fun.' (*Firmly:*) It *doesn't happen* that way.

There were some teens, to be sure, who had sexual intercourse frequently. But such teens generally resided in households where their parent(s) worked evenings or weekends, which gave them more opportunity.

In sum, high school teens navigate relationships with parents, peers, and romantic partners and manage various adult gratifications, but to lesser degrees and under more constraints than teens who enter the first year out. It is akin to the difference between horses eating grass that grows though the fence into their own pasture and horses being released to the open prairie. While some horses learn to jump over the pasture's fence without detection, most are content to eat what grows through the fence, because they know that eventually they will all be released to the open prairie. I now shift my discussion to that wide open prairie.

THE FIRST YEAR OUT

Teens told me they became "more independent," "more mature," and "more grown up" during their first year out. That is, they learned how to wake themselves up, feed themselves, wear clean clothes, get where they needed to be, fulfill other miscellaneous responsibilities, and "handle problems" on their own. Susie Dane, a white, upper-middle-class, residential college student, described her experience:

> SUSIE: I'm more independent. I'm able to do things on my own a lot easier than I could have before, you know?
> INTERVIEWER: What kinds of things?
> SUSIE: Well, just living on your own, doing your own laundry, . . . feeding yourself, and just figuring out what you're going to do. Kind of setting your own agenda.

Being "more independent" also means that teens learn to relate to others better, from friends to romantic partners to parents and siblings, and to adjust to changes in their social context. Ivy Strasberger, a white, middle-class, residential college student, described it this way: "I think that . . . a big part of college is relationships, and I think that I've learned how to deal with relationships differently and better. You know, it is not always easy. You have to sometimes . . . , you have to make mistakes before you learn. But I think that I've matured in the way I handle situations and relationships." None of this happens overnight, but occurs through trial and error, mistakes and successes. Like many other teens, Eric Strauss, a commuting college student, took most of his first year out to learn to manage daily life to his own satisfaction: "I worked between fifteen and twenty hours a week both semesters, so it was difficult to try to balance time between school and work and family and friends and find a happy medium—which I really didn't do finally until the end of my second semester." Such balancing leaves most teens with little awareness of anything else. Duncan Green, a residential college student, described how he was so unaware of what was going on "outside of school" that he was shocked to learn that his all-time favorite sporting event, the summer Olympic Games, were two days away from their closing ceremonies. "I, like, totally missed them!" Duncan, so focused on daily life management, was far from the only oblivious teen during the first year out.

In this section, I will demonstrate how most teens are consumed with managing their daily life and, in particular, with navigating relationships and managing gratifications. It is a remarkable story about "horses" finally released to open prairie, who quickly corral themselves for the sake of their long-term security.

RELATIONSHIPS WITH PARENTS

Relationships with parents fade into the background of teens' lives during the first year out, growing a little awkward, and yet becoming a little more valued. This is true both for students who live on campus (hereafter, residential college students) and for those who live at home and commute to their post–high school educational institutions—be those four-year, two-year, or vocational/certificate programs (hereafter, commuting students).

Because I interviewed teens during the summer after their first year out, almost all teens were living at home and on summer break from their college or vocational programs. This moved relationships with parents back onto teen radar screens, unlike during school terms. Relationships with parents generally fade into the background during the first year out, even for commuting students. Commuting students discover that work, school, miscellaneous obligations, and social life consume most of their waking hours, and they often do little more than sleep at home. Moreover, both parents and teens convey to each other that they have reached a new stage in their relationship. Parents grant (and teens expect) more autonomy, and most parents reduce *direct* financial support of teens in symbolically significant if not measurably real ways (see chapter 4). This increased autonomy eliminates some disagreements that characterized high school students' relationships with their parents, while the reduced financial support means teens believe they need to work more hours, which reduces time for teen-parent interaction even further. With fewer disagreements and less contact, it is not surprising that the day-to-day significance of parents fades during the first year out.

At the same time that parents fade in immediate, daily relevance, however, teens often express sincere appreciation for their parents at the end of the first year out. Perhaps this is evidence for the truism "absence makes the heart grow fonder," especially among residential college students. Perhaps this is a response to the reduction in day-to-day frustrations and the opportunity that provides to obtain a longer-term perspective. Perhaps it is triggered by parental "rescues" during the first year out, such as a visit to campus for a homesick freshman or payment of an unexpected car repair. Or perhaps it is maturity that results from becoming "more independent," with teens now realizing just how much their parents previously managed for them. The possible causes are many, but the effect is quite real: many teens report greater appreciation for their parents and better relationships with their parents at the end of the first year out. Mike Plumeri, a white, upper-middle-class, residential college student, described this at length:

> I did develop a lot more of an appreciation for my parents. . . . You take things for granted when you have them all your life. And you come to school, and you learn from people, and you're away from home, and you can just step outside and kind of get to look in and see how it really was. . . . My parents did a lot for me when I was in high school. Now . . . I buy my own toothpaste and just things like that. I just have come to appreciate them more, and I realize that they love me a lot. And just because I have anger for them for some little things, it doesn't matter, you know? I've come past that.

Mike was not alone in this sentiment. Tammy Biggs, a white, working-class teen from NJ High, commuted to her four-year college. She, too, reported a better relationship with her parents, especially her mother. "I always see my parents everyday, you know. And, I mean, that's great. . . . I never had a curfew or anything, and they were very good about just letting me go, you know. I could leave whenever I wanted to; I could get home at anytime. . . . There's so much going on this year! And, like, my relationship with my parents, especially my mom, has become so much better than it's ever been." Even teens who did not express more appreciation for their parents still reported that their "fairly close" relationships with their parents stayed the same. That not a single teen interviewee described a worsening relationship with her or his parents is itself quite remarkable.

Greater appreciation and improved relationships with parents do not mean, however, that these relationships are without any problems. Many teens discover a new awkwardness in their relationships with their parents. Like Barb Miscoski, whose story opens this chapter, most teens learn to manage their daily lives and thus become less dependent on their parents—except for financial support. For example, Emily Fisher, a white, upper-middle-class, residential college student, found that "it's not always easy to listen to" her parents, as they forgot that she lived quite successfully at college without their input. A half-century ago, American teens like Emily and Barb would have been marrying and forming independent households at this age.[20] But the disappearance of stable jobs for high school graduates, combined with vastly different cultural scripts about how one becomes an adult, place later adolescents into a status beset with inconsistencies. Among these, teens find that the traditional parent-child relationship morphs into one resembling that of a patron and artist. Parents wish to remain influential in their teens' lives, just as patrons wish to influence the creative output of artists. Similarly, teens need support but seek to maximize personal autonomy, just as artists need support but seek to maintain control of the creative product or process. Still, the teen-parent relationship is among the easier relationships that teens must navigate during the first year out. Navigating relationships with peers and romantic partners requires far more attention.

RELATIONSHIPS WITH PEERS

Teens make friends, lose friends, grow closer to some friends and more distant from others, and often, in the process, gain new perspectives on themselves. The whole realm of peer relationships represents the biggest adjustment during the first year out. Dave Olsen, a white, middle-class, residential college student, described how "talking to friends I have made in my first year just let me see that I can be a little overbearing and a little stubborn in my ideas. I think in high school I had been with people so long that they just dealt with that so I couldn't even see it in myself." Dave may have been more self-aware than many male teens, but was similar to other teens in awareness of the importance of learning to navigate peer relationships. Andre Kendall, a black, working-class, residential college student, also had to learn "what time I should hang out with my friends, . . . how much time I should spend, and when I need to get back." Carol Thomas, a white, upper-middle-class, residential college student, struggled with not getting into a sorority that accepted her "best friends." Carol was working on:

CAROL: Learning how to be the bigger person in a situation. Saying "OK, fine." This didn't work out, so what can I do to change it?

INTERVIEWER: Can you give an example?

CAROL: I tried for a sorority and they said that—it was just a whole big sticky issue, like I wasn't cut, they said, but I didn't make it—I wasn't high enough. And a lot of my best friends are now in a sorority, in that pledge class and everything. And they're all saying, "Oh, we love you, you're with us next year" and everything. And it's kinda like—well, *I should have been there now*! And I wouldn't be so *angry* at them. But just make the older sisters realize, like, not "I'm better than you," but I could have been there. And you know, I'm best friends with everybody there now. I don't know. "Kill 'em with kindness," kinda. Be the bigger person.

Carol went on to say that this whole experience had helped her "realize who your real friends are." That phrase, "real friends," was used often by teens at the end of the first year out. It referred to friendships that persisted during the first year out and endured through difficult times. It was used as often by residential college students as it was by commuting students.

Commuting teens saw their friendships alter as much as residential college students'. They too saw high school friendships fade or alter; they too made new friends at their college/vocational programs and at work. (They spent twice as many hours per week at work as residential college students did; see chapter 4). The main difference was that teens residing at home had fewer casual friendships. They did not make acquaintances through residence halls or through involvement in on-campus organizations. Eric Strauss stated, "My circle of friends hasn't changed much except for the fact that it's gotten smaller 'cause I don't see nearly as many people as I used to." Knowing the possibility of feeling marginalized, Tammy Biggs made a concerted effort to befriend others at college: "So I had to put myself out more and be a lot more open. Usually I'm the shy one, but I couldn't do that, being a commuter." Consequently, Tammy established a set of casual friends during orientation week and through classes in her major, and maintained a set of closer friends, too. Kato Stuart, a commuting college student, had a circle of five friends he spent time with, three "old" friends from high school and two "new" friends from college. And Christine Darden, a commuting vocational student, did not form friendships at her photography school, but formed several important friendships through her new job as an Avon sales representative. Though commuting students may have fewer casual friends, they still have as many significant friendships to navigate as residential college students do.

RELATIONSHIPS WITH ROMANTIC PARTNERS
AND LONG-TERM RELATIONSHIP GOALS

"It's, like, always in the back of your mind, if it's not in the front—'Find a relationship. Find a relationship.'" That was what one intelligent, liberal, women's studies major told me about the importance of romantic relationships to teens during the first year out. Her voice was not the only voice I heard, but it is the one that stayed with me the most. Nothing provides more personal validation and emotional satisfaction than being caught up in the excitement of shared romance and deep affection. Those not involved in romantic relationships at the end of the first year out sound wistful, even apologetic. Rachel O'Leary, who became a residential college student, did not have a romantic partner for any portion of her first year out and sometimes wished she had one: "Sometimes I think to myself that I need a boyfriend. You know, I'm bored sometimes. I'd just like somebody to spend time with." Most teens, however, described a relationship starting, ending, or altering during their first year out. Julie Gillmore, a white, middle-class, residential college student, had two romantic relationships during her first year out. The first carried over from high school and lasted until her Christmas break. The second lasted through her spring semester then ended a couple of weeks into the summer. Julie's experience is uncommon. More common are teens who spend some of their first year in a relationship(s) and most of their first year out of a relationship.

Poppy Lopez (introduced in the first chapter) was romantically involved with one college student for two months during the fall semester and with another student for the last month of the spring semester. The latter relationship was just beginning, and, though it was not being pursued during the summer, Poppy believed, "If something's gonna happen, it'll still happen next year at school." Confounding romantic relationships during the first year is the geographic mobility of residential college students. A looming move away to college or back home leads many teens to "let go of" or bracket casual romantic relationships for which attempting "a long-distance relationship" would convey too much "seriousness." Just figuring out the status of a romantic relationship is a complicated matter for teens, a point well demonstrated by Norval Glenn and Elizabeth Marquardt in their excellent report to the Independent Women's Forum on the dating and mating patterns of college women.[21]

More than a few times, teens had a hard time answering a simple question about whether they were involved in a romantic relationship at present or during the past year. Jabari Campbell, a black, middle-class, residential college student, struggled to answer:

> JABARI: In the past year? (*Pauses.*) I don't know! Um, I hung out with a couple of girls, but that was about it.
> INTERVIEWER: Were these romantic relationships?
> JABARI: Not really. Like, I just . . . I don't know! I just, just hung out.

Joann McBride, who became a residential college student, described how she had "a couple of [relationships] that weren't real serious." Joann emphasized that they were "just college *things* . . . [that] kind of fizzled out," so she struggled to even classify them as relationships. Part of the struggle teens have in giving a simple answer to a question about their relationship status is that teens want to find romantic love without risking rejection or appearing desperate. So they often convey an attitude of nonchalance about romantic relationships and toward romantic partners (akin to the nonchalance teens express about future matters in general; see chapters 1 and 6), which reduces their vulnerability in, but also their clarity about, their relationship.

Many teens told me they learned "a lot" about themselves with respect to romantic relationships during the first year out. At times, this was because they ended a significant romantic relationship during the year, resulting in a period of reflection. John Snow, for example, broke up with his high school girlfriend, then had two subsequent relationships, for one and four months. In hindsight, he wishes he had never broken up with his high school girlfriend, who now has another boyfriend. Other teens learn to distance themselves from the immaturity of high school. Mike Plumeri, for example, described learning to not prejudge a girl who started to show romantic interest in him and to ignore the gossip of friends. "I'm going to take her for who she presents herself to be to me, you know, and I think [I've grown] just in the area of not labeling people." Mike was moving to a more mature and individual consideration of potential romantic partners. Megan Morici, who became a residential college student, was also moving to a more balanced view of romantic relationships. She described learning to keep "things" about relationships "in perspective" and not getting "upset" or "worked up" if a relationship did not pan out: "I'm eighteen years old. . . . I have so much time. . . . If it doesn't work out—there's more men. Maybe next time, you know what I mean?" In different ways, these teens have learned a little more about themselves that may help them form more successful relationships in the future. And because the vast majority of culturally mainstream teens hope to marry eventually—a hope they reaffirmed at the end of the first year out—gaining a more mature perspective on themselves and romantic relationships in general may be an important step in accomplishing those long-term life goals. Future researchers may want to investigate at what point young adults begin to alter their expectations about getting married or having children, as there was no evidence for any decline in seeking these goals during the first year out.

Maturity is not immediate, of course. And it is not always assisted by American teen moral culture, particularly at the junction of teen sexual mores and teen relationship desires. That junction is the "hookup," that is, a casual sexual encounter between two teens, which may or may not involve sexual intercourse. It is increasingly the starting point (and ending point) of teen romantic relationships during the first year out.

SEXUAL BEHAVIOR AND THE "HOOKUP"

Only a handful of high school seniors knew the term hookup, but virtually every teen did when I interviewed them at the end of the first year out. "The hookup is the starting point," one black, working-class, residential college student told me, "and relationships start or don't start from there."[22] Teens also make a number of important distinctions about hookups. Most important is the difference between coital and noncoital hookups, which is also a key distinction in the research literature.[23] Many teens restrict themselves to noncoital hookups and look down on teens who have coital hookups. "That's just nasty," one teen told me, and many with him agreed. But other important factors are level of intoxication, partner selection, not "being stupid," and subsequent reaction. Each deserves careful attention.

First, intoxication is a critical precondition for the hookup culture. Few hookups occur without some level of alcohol consumption by both parties. Intoxication is often cited by teens as the primary cause of hookups and as the reason why teens frequently avoid relationship "entanglements" following a hookup.[24] Yet teens freely choose to attend gatherings where alcohol is readily available and the potential for hookups is high, so this is a convenient excuse more than a comprehensive explanation.

Second, selection of partners involves more than willingness. Many teens look down on anonymous hookups and assert that it is better if a hookup is with an acquaintance or even a friend. There is a special phrase, in fact, to describe recurring hookups between friends who are not otherwise romantically involved: "friends with benefits." Teens consider known partners to be superior, because they assume (without evidence) that known partners are less likely to have sexually transmitted diseases than anonymous partners and because they assume known partners will know and follow the next two norms of hookups.

Third, one should "not be stupid." Officially, teens told me this means using contraception to avoid STDs and pregnancy. But contraception must be anticipated and to do so often conveys "sleaziness." Thus, more commonly, "not being stupid" means that teens avoid pregnancy by not having vaginal intercourse or by ejaculating outside of the body and avoid STDs by choosing a known partner. Though not all hookups involve oral sex, many do, and "smart" practice combines oral and hand manipulation of the sex organs. There is little gender equality in this: women are far more likely to "give" satisfaction to men than they are to "get" it or "allow" it from men.

Finally, subsequent interaction should produce "no awkwardness." That means that the next day, and in any subsequent encounters with one's hookup partner, there is no mismatch in how both parties interpret the event. Either it is "just a hookup" or it is the beginning of "something more." The worst possible reactions are when partners come to opposite views of the encounter: one hopes to start a romantic relationship, but the other does not. There is even a pejorative term one partner will use to describe the other partner's interest in a relationship: she or he (usually she) "catches feelings." If one partner "catches feelings," that means the other partner did not, and it creates the very awkwardness that teens hope to avoid.

At this point, I should explain that I did not exclude gay, lesbian, or bisexual teens. I did interview one senior who was bisexual, but despite repeated efforts to reach him for a second interview, could not do so. The best national surveys indicate 1–2 percent of the national population is gay, lesbian, or bisexual,[25] so having one bisexual teen among my pool of interviewees is proportionately accurate. Moreover, no teens at NJ High were "out," so purposive sampling was impossible. In the end, the virtual absence of gay, lesbian, and bisexual teens in this study is a sampling artifact. I did have one gay and one bisexual college student in a group interview, and both indicated that they "came out" during their first year out—making that year a significant time of public identity change for them. If this is a common pattern among gay, lesbian, and bisexual teens (and I suspect it may be), then my arguments about the use of an identity lockbox may apply only in part to such teens. Lack of research resources restricts this matter, however, to future inquiry.

Just how extensive is teen participation in the hookup phenomenon? Two studies are helpful here. The first is the previously cited study of college women by sociologists Glenn and Marquardt, and the second is by psychologist Elizabeth L. Paul and associates. Glenn and Marquardt conducted a nationally representative survey of 1,000 heterosexual college women, and Paul completed a representative sample of over 500 state college students at a residential campus. Glenn and Marquardt report 40 percent of their national college women survey respondents had experienced a hookup, 27 percent had experienced a coital hookup, and 10 percent had experienced hookups more than six times. Paul's survey of public college men and women reveals two out of ten had never had a hookup, five out of ten had noncoital hookups only, and three out of ten had coital hookups. And of students who had hookups, the average number of hookups was ten times.[26] Paul's rates are higher than those of teens nationally, as they include public college men and women and do not include students attending religious colleges or students commuting to college/vocational programs, both of whom have fewer opportunities or less interest in participating in the hookup culture. Despite the rate differences, both studies confirm that hookups are a widespread phenomenon and demonstrate how "the culture of courtship . . . that once helped young people find the pathway to marriage" has been replaced by a hookup culture that does nothing "to help young people in a critical life task, which is learning how to form and sustain mature relationships."[27]

I spoke to several teens who immersed themselves in the hookup culture. Though proportionately few, these teens are like "surfers" at the "beach party" described above—they command teen attention and dominate the scene. Sergio Sicily was one such teen. An affable, outgoing athlete and budding entrepreneur from a white, middle-class family, Sergio attended Flagship University and earned average grades his first year. But neither average grades nor a sidelining sports injury dampened Sergio's enormous enthusiasm for college life, because the highlight of Sergio's first year out was joining and living in a fraternity house. When Sergio first told me about his fraternity membership, his mother was in the next room, so he emphasized that he joined "mainly for after-school benefits." But then he lowered his voice and said that he "had a lot of good times there," repeating himself for emphasis. Some of those good times came from hanging out with his fraternity brothers, some from the fifteen to sixteen beers he would consume "mostly on the weekends" at the frat house, and some from the "twenty to twenty-five" hookups he had with "the girls who came to the parties." Sergio was stumped when I asked him about his view of sex: "I enjoy it, I guess. I dunno, it's cool. I don't have a problem with it." It was as if I had asked his view of bread. Sergio was out surfing the big waves, having "a totally awesome" first year out, and had no view that waves might be anything other than exciting opportunities.

I spoke with several other teens, male and female, who reveled in the hookup culture as Sergio did. Most teen interviewees, however, reported zero to three hookups during their first year out, for a variety of reasons. To start, some teens may report fewer hookups to an adult interviewer because they perceive it to be socially desirable. But social desirability is not the full story, nor even half of it. Some teens report few hookups because they had few opportunities. Kato Stuart, for example, a commuting college student, attended every fraternity party he could. But Kato was shy and socially awkward, and he sheepishly reported hooking up "just once—with a girl I met at a party." Other teens are deeply religious, so they reject premarital sexual activity and join organizations with like-minded teens for reassurance and distraction. These were primarily evangelical Christians, orthodox Jews, and immigrant Muslims. Still other teens describe significant commitments to their romantic partners and keep their sexual activities to those partners only. Eric Strauss explained, "I'm not one of those . . . typical college guys going to parties, you know, hooking up with every girl [they can]. . . . I have a committed, steady relationship with one person." (Partnered teens, in fact, have the most frequent sex of teens during the first year out, but it is still a weekend activity for most, after allowances for temporarily high frequencies during the early stages of a couple's sexual activity.) Finally, there are teens who do hook up but do so with the hope of forming romantic relationships (i.e., "the hookup is the *starting* point"). These teens are more selective when they hook up and more likely to pursue romantic relationships following a hookup. "The only girls I ever hooked up with ended up becoming my girlfriends," said one white, middle-class, residential college student. Or, as a female college senior told me during a focus group interview, "girls *do* hook up, but they generally do so with the hope that a relationship will follow"—to which the rest of the women in the group immediately agreed.

The hookup culture seems to galvanize teen opinion during the first year out. Partly, it is because hookups become so publicly discussed during the first year out. Partly, it is because most teens pass through a party where hookups are semivisible during the first year out. And partly, it is because teens have gained an important year of personal experience in or close observation of sexual matters. Rejection, broken hearts, and hurt feelings abound among teens during the first year out, and sex is an intensifier. Some teens respond by endorsing the hookup culture and defining sex as a physical activity requiring only basic precautions. A few women interviewees, in fact, moved in this direction during the first year out. But many other teens— women *and men*—express caution. They wade into the hookup culture because they know of no other way to begin relationships and hope, with no sense of irony, that they will find through it a meaningful relationship that will free them from such wading for a while.[28]

In the end, most teens manage their sexual gratification the same way they manage their alcohol or other substance use, preferring moderation to either excess or abstention and seeking to be fairly selective as to when, where, and with whom they will pursue gratification. Sadly, few teens realize just how many of their peers behave similarly.[29]

SURFERS, WADERS, AND SUNBATHERS

Thanks to colorful elaboration in cheesy teen movies (e.g., *Animal House*) and melodramatic novels (e.g., Tom Wolfe's *I Am Charlotte Simmons*), and reinforced by sensationalist television news accounts of fraternity pledges rushed to hospitals with alcohol poisoning, the popular image of teens during the first year out is as shocking as it is pervasive: hordes of teens packed into a house strewn with debris, shouting over the deafening music, breathing in a haze created by tobacco and marijuana smoke, taking full advantage of the readily available alcohol and drugs, and engaging in semipublic libidinous couplings of all sorts. Americans have accepted this image of teen socializing far too readily and applied it far too widely. Bacchanalian parties such as these certainly exist, and most teens will pass through a few such parties during their first year out. But what this popular image of teen parties fails to convey is not only the limited availability of such parties to many potential partiers (e.g., they do not occur at commuter colleges or most vocational programs), but also the ambivalence of most partiers to the happenings around them and the transience of most partiers within this "teen party" scene. Truth be told, those teens with access to these parties often grow bored with them, preferring instead more personal gatherings of friends or the company of significant others. The proportionately few hard-core partiers (about one out of five college freshmen[30]), then, are left with significant recruitment efforts to attract new teen guests to their recurring weekend parties.

Emily Fisher certainly liked to have fun. Her favorite times during her first year out were when she did fun stuff with "all of the girls." Like one time, when: "We went to this club in Boston, just to go dancing. All of the girls just went, and we all got dressed up and decked out and we went, and it was a lot of fun." Emily also enjoyed gatherings with just a few friends or spending time with her boyfriend. She would not attend parties, however, where "it's like a hundred people at somebody's house or some party at a frat house." Emily "hate[d]" those kind of parties. Carol Thomas, by contrast, did attend fraternity parties, as her remotely located university did not offer "much else" to do. But she never got drunk, she did not smoke marijuana or use drugs, and she remained faithful to her long-time boyfriend during her entire first year out. Tammy Biggs attended "just three" parties, but she kept herself to just three to four drinks and hooked up only once ("just kissing," she emphasized). John Snow had planned to attend parties and drink at college, but an overpowering coach convinced him and his teammates to not drink "for three months straight" during the fall varsity sport season. After the season ended, John started to consume just "a couple of drinks a week" on average. He preferred his teammates to the frat party scene, though he did get "wrecked" (i.e., drunk) with them on his birthday. He also smoked marijuana with a few teammates "during spring break." But tournament play required drug testing, as did his summer job, so John did not smoke again, "because the benefits don't outweigh the consequences." Even "partiers" like Steve Moeller and Chuck Barker, who liked to get drunk weekly, did not like "big" parties. They preferred to drink at small gatherings with just a few friends. As crowded as any fraternity row may be on the weekend, far more students are absent than attending, and of those attending, quite a few are ambivalent about the scene and manage their gratifications with care.

One of the most striking phenomena to me, however, was discovering how even those teens who gratify themselves liberally—who use substances often and heavily, who immerse themselves in the hookup culture, or who do both—also complete school, work, family, and other obligations acceptably. Though extensive substance usage or multiple sex partners carries significant risks and even addiction possibilities, most such teens avoid addiction and manage consequences (like hangovers) so as to minimize their impact. To be sure, such teens do not make the dean's list, but they do well enough to remain in good standing with their colleges or vocational programs and continue their progress toward their degree or certificate. They also manage to keep their jobs, by choosing work that fits around their partying, and they keep their parents sufficiently pleased with their progress so as not to risk withdrawal of financial support. Such managed gratification may be less about teens' abilities than it is about the declining academic rigor of average American universities, the minimal requirements employers have for low-wage employees, and the low expectations many parents have for their children (e.g., stay out of trouble, pass your classes, and come home for Mother's Day). Still, these teens have learned how to identify minimal expectations and sufficiently meet them, so that their partying can go on. Their gratification is neither instant nor delayed, just managed. (I take up this point again in chapter 5.)

In the end, an apt image of teen "partying" during the first year out is the beach party—with about one-fifth of teens out surfing (fairly well), about one-half wading ankle to knee deep, and the rest sunbathing or playing volleyball.[31] There is movement between groups—sunbathers will wade in to cool off, waders will try surfing or sunbathing, and surfers will come in for an occasional rest. It is also true that many new arrivals to the beach try to surf immediately, but experiencing its difficulty and seeing its potential dangers moves most to shallower waters or drier land fairly quickly. That teens do not realize most peers are not surfing is due to perceptual "glare," that is, a condition caused by teens primarily looking out to the ocean and consequently overestimating the number of teens surfing and underestimating the number of teens wading or sunbathing.[32] For some teens, the thrill of surfing is an unbeatable high, and they manage their schedules so as to maximize time in the waves. But for most teens, the opportunity to spend time with a few friends at the beach is plenty fun. Just making friends during the first year out is a satisfying accomplishment in its own right.[33]

ON THE ROLE OF FAMILY, FAITH, AND COMMUNITY

Teens want to have friends and want to have fun, so they put a lot of energy into managing their daily life so that they can develop relationships and enjoy time with their friends. On the whole, they succeed in doing this during the first year out. That teens prioritize everyday living should not surprise us, given how much Americans prioritize the everyday and the practical. But how teens manage their daily lives, and which aspects of everyday life teens select to receive greater or lesser attention, can be enormously influenced by teens' family, faith, and community origins.

Though families can themselves be shaped by faith and local communities, families are children's first community and influence their lives the most. During the high school years, teens who reported that their parents kept a caring but close eye on their whereabouts used substances later and less frequently, became sexually active later than other teens, and formed longer-term romantic relationships. Teens who reported overbearing parents, busy parents, or disengaged parents were more likely to have used substances or become sexually active earlier than their peers and less likely to form longer-term romantic relationships. During the first year out, teens whose parents had attended college generally seemed to have clearer expectations for, and fewer setbacks during, their first year out. Teens who rejected indulging themselves in any adult gratifications during the first year out often expressed a preference for spending time with their parents, siblings, and extended families and often "missed" their families when they lived away from them. Teens who became "surfers" during the first year out were more likely to have distant relationships with their parents, and their parents were somewhat more likely to have been divorced. But my sample is too small for firm conclusions about these latter possibilities; a future inquiry will need to examine this.[34] Overall, most teens are relatively successful in managing their daily life during their first year out because most families provide a relatively safe and supportive environment in which teens can begin to learn such skills. If success begets success, then relative success must beget relative success.

Faith communities, or simply the notion of religion, affected how teens navigated relationships and managed gratifications in a number of important ways. To teens who immersed themselves in adult gratifications, religion was sometimes cited as the cause of people's hang-ups about sexual activity or substance use. Mona Segall, for example, offered a version of the secularization thesis to explain societal views of sex: "A lot of times, like, throughout history, it [sex] was classified as a sin kind of thing. But really . . . it was just because of the time and the way that people's minds were. . . . As time progressed, their ideas changed. It became more accepted, and now I think it's part of our everyday life." Such teens reject religion, partly for these reasons, and they hope it will fade or disappear from society so as to make everyone's enjoyment of sex and substances easier and more frequent. At the other end of the continuum, one finds teens who refuse all adult gratifications because they view relationships and gratifications through the lens of faith. These teens expressed and sought to live in keeping with traditional religious principles and mores. Andre Kendall believed sex "is created by God and made for marriage, and you shouldn't be doing it outside of marriage at all." Andre had never had sex, did not drink, and had never used marijuana or other drugs. While some strongly religious teens drink alcohol in moderation, virtually all strongly religious teens avoid drunkenness, drug use, and premarital sex. Semi- and nonreligious teens are often unaware of how many of their peers do not gratify themselves because of their religious faith. This is partly because strongly religious teens often socialize with like-minded peers, partly because strongly religious teens generally keep their religious views private in nonreligious contexts, and partly because of the general perceptual problem teens have with respect to their peers' actual behavior. But, in fact, some 30 percent of American teens take religious faith very seriously, and teen faith is strongly associated with lower rates of risky behavior.[35]

The largest share of American teens falls, of course, in between: semireligious teens who indicate an affiliation with a faith community and who voice opinions that are in keeping with popular American moral culture. That is, they desire long-term monogamous partners and domesticity, believe in loyalty to family and friends, and make allowance for some "good ole fun" now: noncoital hookups occasionally, coitus generally reserved for more meaningful relationships, alcohol in moderation (from social drinkers to "managed" heavy drinkers), and other substances rarely to never. This is a wide category, as it includes both Barb Miscoski and Sergio Sicily. Both teens value religion and attend church semiregularly, both hope to marry and have children, and both enjoy a measure of sex and alcohol; the primary difference is in the amount they measure. Some of that difference is surely due to the sexual double standard, and some of it is due to the differing social contexts and networks in which Barb and Sergio are located and have chosen to locate themselves. There is little direct influence of religion on them, just generic reinforcement of popular American moral norms surrounding family, friends, loyalty, and general diligence.

Local communities affect teens in various ways with respect to navigating relationships and managing gratifications. Teens from more affluent communities are more likely to become residential college students and less likely to be employed for as many hours as teens from less affluent communities. (I develop this point in chapter 4.) Thus, affluence increases the time that affluent teens can devote to navigating relationships and managing gratifications, and it helps to explain why a higher proportion of those most immersed in managing gratifications (i.e., "surfers") seem to come from more affluent communities. Teens from some minority communities indicate relatively less interest in the gratifications of alcohol or marijuana and relatively more interest in sexual gratifications. Tremaine Owens described drinking parties and dancing parties, with the former being a "white guys' party" and the latter being a "black party." Tremaine preferred to attend

> dancing parties . . . [where] I'm trying to meet girls and just have fun with my friends. A drinking party—me and my friend, we define that as a white guy's party. I been to a couple of colleges and they say, "we're going to a party," and it was just a bunch of white guys drinking. That's not fun. . . . I'm just trying to enjoy myself, and drinking is not enjoying myself. As opposed to, like, a black party, where it's just packed, and a lot of music, no lights, and people dancing.

Other black teens described dancing as their primary activity at parties, while many white teens used the term *partying* synonymously with drinking and smoking pot, supporting Tremaine's classification. Black interviewees also reported sexual intercourse somewhat younger and somewhat more often than white teens, which fits with national survey data.[36] These are tentative rather than certain findings, but they suggest there may be important racial differences in gratification preferences and management patterns, which future researchers would do well to consider.

In sum, learning to successfully navigate relationships and manage gratifications is the common task, primary focus, and major accomplishment of culturally mainstream American teens during the first year out. What strikes me is how, despite diverse possibilities now available, most teens seek and form relatively conventional relationships and generally moderate their use of new adult freedoms. That is, most culturally mainstream teens seek and sometimes find a romantic partner with whom they can form a meaningful relationship and generally consume fewer than six alcoholic drinks in a night.

Of course, teens complete other tasks and spend time on other matters during the first year out, some of which they recognize and some of which they do not. These include the critical life arenas of leisure, money, and work, to which I turn my attention in chapter 4.

FOUR

Working for Money, Spending for Fun

Eric Strauss was the kind of young man that many parents boast about. A good student from a white, middle-class family, Eric was responsible, thoughtful, and hard working. Eric first started working the summer after ninth grade, and he had "been working steadily ever since." Like many high school seniors, Eric told me he "put away" the money he earned from working thirty hours a week, but "a lot of it went into the car . . . because I was working full time and I needed a car during the summer." Eric was proud that he bought his sporty, recent-model car entirely on his own and proud of his capacity to pay his own car insurance, his own phone bill, and his cell phone bill, and to "pay for a lot of my own clothing." His parents did give him $30 a week "for gas and food," but Eric paid for car repairs himself, and he also handled all of his entertainment expenses himself. The latter were considerable, because Eric had a steady girlfriend, and they liked to go out to dinner, play pool, go to the movies, play miniature golf, or spend a day in the city. Eric was proud of the $600 savings he maintained in his bank account, as a cushion for unexpected car repairs. "I don't have to work the thirty hours a week I work," he acknowledged, but he liked "the advantage of having the extra money that I do to allow me to enjoy myself. . . . You know, buy myself a pair of jeans if I need to, or see a shirt that I like and buy it, . . . buy a CD if that's what I want to do." In short, Eric worked to maintain a particular standard of teen living—to wear preferred clothes, listen to his own music, drive his own car, and purchase entertainment for his girlfriend and himself. Though maintaining this lifestyle required a lot of hours at work and minimized time for leisure, Eric had not let up in the slightest when I reinterviewed him a year later.

THE AMERICAN TEEN LIFESTYLE

How typical is Eric? Well, upper-middle-class moms and dads absorb a sizable portion of their teen's expenses, especially car expenses, so these teens live similarly to Eric with fewer hours of paid employment per week. Working-class teens, by contrast, drive less expensive cars or spend less on entertainment, and so do some middle-class teens. But most teens, including Eric, do not question this high standard of living. It is part of what sociologist Peter Berger calls the "taken for grantedness" of everyday (teen) life. Upper-middle-class teens set the standards, taking their cues from the impossible standards of television and magazines. The son of a Fortune 500 executive I interviewed, Mike Plumeri, was explicit: "I have a high standard of living, I guess you could say, because I grew up with a lot." Middle-class teens then strive to reach the living standards that affluent peers like Mike set, while working-class teens will sacrifice to meet the most critical standards, such as clothing standards or car ownership.

The pressure to conform to the American standard of teen living can be intense, and teens will go to great lengths to look like they can afford the same things everyone else does. I vividly recall an incident I observed during a lunch at NJ High. It involved Monica, a social outcast for three reasons: she was obese, she seemed to have bipolar disorder, and she was considered "poor" because she lived in a working-class neighborhood bordering Small City.

> Monica was sitting with Tracy at lunch. [Tracy is a kind-hearted, widely accepted girl who has been friends with Monica since grade school.] After I sat down with them today, four of Tracy's friends joined us. Soon, Tracy's friends started talking about—what else?—the prom: who was going with whom, where they found shoes, whose earrings they were going to borrow, *ad nauseum*. Suddenly, Monica asked Tracy—"Hey, wanna rent a limo together?" It was an awkward and ill-timed question. A couple of Tracy's friends rolled their eyes and gave disapproving looks. One muttered, not that softly, "Oh, god!" and the four made little effort to mask their giggles.

Tracy, looking very awkward, said limousines cost "a lot of money" and that Tracy's boyfriend wanted to drive anyway. Tracy's four friends quickly generated some excuse to leave the table, and Monica stared at her scoop of mashed potatoes. I felt awful, knowing this was a painful moment for Monica and an awkward one for Tracy, but not knowing what to say next. Tracy, thank goodness, broke the silence by asking Monica if she had decided to go to the prom after all. "I dunno," Monica replied. "But if I do go, I'm gonna ride in a limo." It was then clear that Monica had wanted to impress these other girls with the idea that she was going to the prom (i.e., had a date, etc.), and could afford a limo, too. It was a sad encounter to witness, and I am once again grateful that my high school years lie far behind me. (Field Notes, NJ High, February 2001)

Though the cost of proms can quickly exceed $1,000,[1] Monica wanted her classmates to believe that she could afford to go to the prom in high style (she subsequently chose not to attend). The desire to conform to the American teen lifestyle, even when located on its periphery, is powerful indeed.

The prom is, to be sure, a particular moment of teen extravagance. But when I tallied the ongoing costs of the American teen lifestyle, I was stunned. The American teen lifestyle requires cars, clothes, meals, snacks, entertainment, and technology, and the teens I observed or interviewed for this project spent the following sums *weekly*: car expenses (payment and insurance), $50–100; gas, $10–20; clothing, $10–80; meals/snacks, $20–60; personal items, $0–10; entertainment (including age-restricted or illegal substances), $10–50; technology, including cell phone, $10–30; for a weekly total of $110 to $350. Calculated monthly, it costs between $495 and $1,575 each month, or $1,035 on average, for a teen to maintain the American teen lifestyle. (Friends with teenage children confirmed my estimates.) Note that this is only the cost of the teen lifestyle itself—the car, clothes, food, entertainment, and technology. It does not include parent-funded living costs such as housing, groceries, utilities, education, health care, and the like. Seeing these sums, one can readily understand why parents are so willing to let their children start working. One can also understand why it is that teens have so little to show for their hours of work, except for their cars (a depreciating asset that may be worth less than what they owe), a closet full of rarely worn clothes, and a stack of receipts.

How did this happen? It happened gradually, of course, for each teen as she or he ages and for successive teen cohorts as standards rise. In the rest of this chapter, I will describe how teens (1) develop clear preferences for leisure (of which consumptive leisure preferences are most prevalent) sometime prior to their senior year of high school; (2) obtain support from their parents to start working, with the official goal of saving for college and an afterthought about earning "a little spending money"; (3) select jobs that above all are conveniently located and offer desirable work hours, but which do not introduce them to career fields of interest or develop future work skills; (4) spend virtually all of their earnings (and often take on debt) to maintain the American teen lifestyle; (5) define good money management as *having* money to spend and *knowing how* it was spent; (6) become the restless consumers our American economy craves; and (7) gain early admittance to the work-and-spend cycle of American adults.

Scholars are divided over the value of teen work. In the 1980s, researchers questioned the value of rising rates of teen employment. Psychologists Ellen Greenberger and Laurence Steinberg, for example, asserted that teen employment "undermines" teen education and has "negative consequences for their [psychological] development."[2] Moreover, because teen work is often simplistic and repetitive, Greenberger and Steinberg assert, such employment promotes a cynical attitude toward work and fosters materialism. On the latter point, social psychologist Jerald Bachman concurs. He reports that the increase in teen earnings brings about "premature affluence," that is, a high level of discretionary spending due to minimal fixed expenses. But because teens cannot sustain a high rate of discretionary spending during early adulthood, Bachman argues, premature affluence produces the well-documented dissatisfaction with post–high school standards of living and may even delay American youth in becoming financially independent and leaving home.[3]

More recent research both confirms and qualifies this earlier scholarship. Sociologist Murray Milner, for example, argues that American high schools have become an arena of intense status competition through consumerism, driving the rise not only in teen employment but in teen shoplifting, too.[4] Sociologist Jeylen Mortimer, however, offers a more nuanced and optimistic picture. She agrees with earlier research that intense involvement in employment can be harmful to youth, yet notes how disadvantaged youth who choose early and extensive employment activity do experience a short-term economic boost for the first few years after high school (though they are subsequently outpaced by college graduates). More preferable to Mortimer is low-to-moderate employment of teens, which helped her Minnesota teen sample "acquire valuable money-management skills," "human capital," "social capital," and time-management skills. The chief problem, Mortimer maintains, is that schools do too little to guide teens in their employment choices or to "supervise" teen employment (as in paid internships), and this particularly affects disadvantaged youth.[5] If this were to change, Mortimer suggests, teens would learn more from their work experiences and some of the negative consequences of teen employment (including apathetic attitudes toward work) would be lessened. Sociologists Schneider and Stevenson, in their study of high school students, make a similar argument about the need for greater parent and teacher guidance of teen work and career plans.[6]

I partly concur with, and partly diverge from, the scholars above. While I did not observe any teens whose psychological development appeared to be negatively affected by their employment, I found plenty whose employment did nothing to help them learn about career fields, plenty who saw work as little more than a necessary nuisance, and plenty whose earnings did little to impart "the value of a dollar." What the teen employment I observed largely did was fund the American teen lifestyle, shift its costs from parents to teens, sacrifice irreplaceable teen hours for quickly forgotten consumer goods and services, and insert teens into the relentless American cycle of work-and-spend.[7] And I am dubious, for reasons described below, that increased "guidance" or "supervision" of teen work by adults would do much to alter how teens generally approach work. I will admit that teen employment facilitates the successful entrance of culturally mainstream teens into America's ever-expanding and highly consumptive economy—if success is measured by teens demonstrating attitudes and behaviors similar to those of American adults. But teen employment does little to help American teens identify meaningful future pathways, understand their economic interdependence with others, or evaluate the deeper, longer-term purposes of their work, leisure, and financial activities. There are exceptions to this pattern, but not many. It is a powerful process precisely because few teens recognize or question it. And the leisure preferences that teens develop within the context of their peer friendships, I suggest, are critical to the whole process.

LEISURE

Teens do not use the term *leisure*. So teens would look at me quizzically when I asked, "How do you like to spend your leisure time?" I would then explain that I wanted to know how they preferred to spend their time outside of school and work. "Oh, you mean free time." Though I would allow teens to make this equivalency, free time is not the same as leisure time. *Free time* is a phrase lifted from institutionalized schedules, such as those at youth camps or school, to describe a block of *less* structured time in an otherwise tightly structured day. *Leisure time* refers to those hours over which one chooses activity or inactivity freely. American teens, in fact, have a lot of leisure time. Beyond eating, sleeping, and school, most teens are free to choose how they spend their weekday and weekend hours. But this is not how teens think about their time. Most teens do not recognize that they choose to work, play sports, perform in artistic groups, or engage in school activities and that by making these choices, they simultaneously choose to reduce availability for other pursuits. Rather, teens view sports, activities, and work as obligations and view "free time" as the hours left over. Kasim Douglass, a black, middle-class youth from NJ High, described it this way: "I don't really have, like, free time during the week. I sleep, [play varsity] baseball, and [go to] school. I talk on the phone. That would be about it." The effect is significant: Kasim not only resented baseball practice, he also "forgot" that it was his choice to play varsity baseball. Kasim's forgetfulness is not unique, however. Like many other teens he became culturally blinded to the major effect his own leisure preferences had in constraining his weekly schedule.

Though preferences are sometimes thought to be individual matters, teens are members of specific social networks that rank leisure activities quite differently, and these networks affect the forms of leisure their members prefer. The teens I observed and interviewed demonstrated clear preferences for one of three leisure "clusters."[8] There are teens who prefer quiet leisure activities, such as reading or drawing; teens who prefer active leisure activities, such as sports or drama; and teens who prefer consumptive leisure activities, such as shopping or eating out. Which cluster teens prefer strongly affects how teens use their time, spend their money, and establish patterns of behavior.

QUIET LEISURE

A few of my teen respondents preferred quieter leisure activities. They liked to read, watch television, draw, sleep, exercise, or get together with a friend to watch television or play cards. These were rather shy teens, though not all were. They were usually employed, like most teens, but worked fewer hours than teens who preferred consumptive leisure activities. Teens who preferred quiet leisure activities did enjoy shared activities from time to time. Thus, Alicia Right, a white, middle-class youth, said she "used to go with a bunch of friends and we [would] go biking a lot," but mostly she "likes doing things on my own . . . like reading." Traci Negm, an NJ High teen, liked to "draw a lot—like, I sketch. Or I hang out with my boyfriend or just sleep. . . . I do watch a lot of TV, actually. Or I could be, like, listening to music." One thing I never heard from these teens was, "There's nothing to do around here." Teens who prefer quiet leisure readily fill their free time with another book, another television show, a different radio station, another nap, or another visit with a friend. They do not depend on a steady stream of money or a changing array of activities to keep their leisure time enjoyable.

ACTIVE LEISURE

A sizable share of teen respondents, perhaps one in four, said they preferred active leisure activities. Sports were most common, but there were also teens who liked theater, music, and dance, or who enjoyed clubs or organized activities at school, church, or in the local community. Though varsity athletes concentrated on "the season," most teen athletes enjoyed a wide range of sports and would readily play a pickup game with friends or acquaintances. Teen athletes often have a competitive streak that spills over to video games, pool, ping-pong, or just "horsing around." Jenna Leigh, a white, working-class youth, described her leisure preferences as "a lot of, like, outside sporting activities and stuff. On days off, sometimes, I have some friends and [we] go over and play ultimate Frisbee. I'll go over to [the park] and we'll play volleyball out there on the courts. . . . I'm a very naturey, outdoorsy kind of person. Running around doing stuff makes me feel good." Occasionally, when teen athletes are physically exhausted, they will watch television to relax, but not for long. They are too restless to sit still for long stretches of television programming.

Other teens prefer active leisure activities that involve the performing arts. Budding musicians form bands with friends or just hang out playing music. Other teens enjoy dance or drama, spending long hours in practice and otherwise occupying themselves with a variety of arts-related activities. One such teen, Anna Davis, loved both to dance and to teach dance. This white, upper-middle-class teen was at her studio "six days a week" taking lessons, dancing on a competition team, and teaching lessons to younger kids. When not at the studio, Anna liked to sleep "or go to concerts. . . . I have a lot of friends who are in local bands, so I go to see them almost every weekend." Another such teen, Nick Lawrence, enjoyed both music and graphic arts. He played trumpet in the school band and did a lot of extra work for his art class. Nick also had his own band: "I play guitar in my band—actually acoustic guitar. . . . We pretty much just get together and jam whenever we can. . . . We have our own original stuff." Though a preference for performing arts can result in significant consumption of tickets, some teens can be quite savvy about finding free performances to quench their thirst for live entertainment.

Because sports or the arts often demand extensive time commitments, teens who prefer these activities are less likely to work for pay, and when they work, they seem more likely to choose interest-related activities (such as working as a timekeeper for another sport) that require fewer hours. Teen athletes and artists prefer to keep busy by supplementing their primary sport or artistic activities with other school, religious, or community activities. For example, helping with the school yearbook is an easy choice for a teen already active in school performing groups, and popular athletes are readily elected to student government. Other sport-loving teens volunteer with local recreational leagues as scorekeepers, referees, or assistant coaches. And some find themselves involved in church youth groups and related religious activities, though many high school seniors had disengaged from these groups by the time I interviewed them.

It struck me how the frequent observation that 80 percent of an organization's work gets completed by 20 percent of its members holds true even among teens. At NJ High, the same core group of teens was active in virtually every event, performance, or game. Teens involved in the annual musical sell baked goods at the basketball game, while varsity captains sell tickets at the musical. Such breadth of involvement is refreshing, as it is good when teens enjoy a range of activities, and it can impart a sense of community that is often absent from suburban life. But the passivity of the majority of NJ High teens was troubling. Not that every teen ought to be involved at school—there are downsides to both organized schooling and student culture that should not be ignored.[9] But few teens are active *outside* of school who are not also active *inside* of school. Most teens are either involved in multiple activities or involved in none. And neither group of teens cares much for the other. Uninvolved NJ High seniors disliked the "stuck-up crowd" and "athlete/pretty girl cliques," while involved NJ High seniors referred to their counterparts as "rude," "stupid," and "trash."

CONSUMPTIVE LEISURE

The majority of teen respondents did not prefer either active or quiet leisure. About two out of three said they preferred consumptive leisure activities, that is, leisure that requires paid consumption of goods or services. Shopping was a popular leisure activity, and so were eating out, going to the movies, playing miniature golf, bowling, going to video arcades, attending stadium concerts, hosting "parties," clubbing, and going on day trips (to theme parks, beaches, or cities). Kris Capatunio, a white, middle-class female, said:

> KRIS: I usually spend [my leisure time] with friends. I go out almost every night, even if I don't do anything big. I just like to spend time with my friends outside of my house and do something everyday.
> INTERVIEWER: What specific types of things do you do with your friends?
> KRIS: We could just go out to a restaurant, go see a movie, rent a movie, go to somebody's house, go to a club, go walk around [Big East City], or something.

Steve Moeller, a white, middle-class youth from NJ High, put it succinctly: "I like to shop and go out to eat." Note how Steve's and Kris's leisure choices require businesses that sell desired goods or services. These teens depend on external sources for leisure satisfaction. They do not satisfy their leisure desires individually or interpersonally. Local leisure options are satisfactory early on. A local mall, a few restaurants, and the movie theater provide ample leisure opportunities, especially for teens without cars. But once teen get cars, local options "get old" and "boring." I often heard teens who preferred consumptive leisure activities lament "there's nothing to do around here." John Snow, a white, upper-middle-class youth, told me, "It gets very repetitive, the things we do. Sometimes it's boring. Sometimes you just sit on the phone: 'What do you want to do?' 'I dunno, what do you want to do?'" Joann McBride, a white, upper-middle-class senior, explained that she liked to be busy: "I get bored very easily. I don't like sitting around doing nothing. . . . I have to be on the go constantly. When I'm not doing anything, I feel like I'm missing out on something. I feel like there's something I could be doing, that I could be having fun at, that I'm just not." For teens who rely upon external leisure providers, the pool of available options must continually expand. Trips to the beach or away for the weekend are desired once local leisure options no longer satisfy. But even those grow dull. Keith LeCourtier, a white, upper-middle-class youth who summered at his parents' beach house, said he was planning to go away for a week with a friend—so he could "have a little fun this summer." Apparently, spending the summer at the beach had become a burden for Keith. "Fun" lies just over the horizon, and many teens just never seem to get to it.

Some teens so depended upon external providers for leisure fulfillment that they could not conjure up a vision of desired leisure themselves, other than wanting "lots of stuff to do." Kato Stuart, a white, middle-class senior at NJ High, for example, struggled in this way:

> KATO: We always complain there's nothing to do around here, and my dad asked me, 'Well, what do you want to do?' And I don't even *know.*
> INTERVIEWER: If you were near a bigger city, would there be things for you to do there?
> KATO: Uh, yeah, I guess probably.

A culture that creates restless leisure consumers like Kato, Joann, John, Steve, and Kris is certainly serving its economy well. I observe, however, that most restless consumers do not have meaningful connections to the communities that nurtured them and do not express much satisfaction with their leisure after-the-fact.

NO TIME LEFT

The desire for consumptive leisure, with its corresponding appetite for income, soon dominates teen schedules. There are teens, for instance, who once enjoyed creative activities but whose growing desire for consumptive leisure and corresponding work demands mean they no longer have time for them. Christine Darden, a white, working-class senior, described how she "likes to sculpt, although I haven't been able to do that much lately because that costs money to buy supplies and that type of thing" (though she could readily afford such supplies when earning less money as a babysitter). Another teen, Kris Capatunio, actually equated leisure with spending. Kris told me she would not want any more leisure time, because her leisure was already too expensive: "I wouldn't have any money if I had more leisure time." But then Kris added that, if she did gain more leisure time, "I would probably spend more time designing things, because I have not been drawing very much lately. I would sew more things." Eric Strauss stopped playing the trumpet, because "I couldn't afford to put in the time, . . . because I had to work [to pay] car insurance."

I also spoke with gregarious teens who enjoyed talking with their friends, but who found that neither they nor their friends had much time to do so. Julie Gillmore, a white, middle-class senior, complained, "Everyone seems, like, really involved in their own business. . . . Everyone seems very busy." And Nick Lawrence, the budding artist and musician, observed, "A lot of people I know work too much. My friends work like dogs, like no time for anything. They're wasting away their time, and this is high school! Have some fun!" Though teens lament the busyness of their own lives and those of their friends, they do not convert that lament into changed behavior. Mona Segall, a white, upper-middle-class senior, felt she could not slow down. When I asked Mona whether America would be a better place if everyone had a little more leisure time, Mona replied, "I don't think the American people *can* be given leisure time, you know. I mean, like, it's a rat race, and it's something you have to do. It's like a cycle. You can't stop it. You have to just keep going on and on, and if you stop, if you took a break or something, it would cause problems. It would bash us." Even teens who gain an outsider's perspective on American "busyness" find they cannot conceive of altering their own behavior patterns. Jill Fairlawn, a white, middle-class senior, recounted this story: "I went to [Europe] this past summer, and I stayed with a family for three weeks while I was there. And they keep asking me, because I would rush from place to place—because it's just customary for Americans to be rushing from place to place. And they just didn't understand why. How I could do it and why I didn't go crazy from doing it? And I was trying to explain to them that that's the culture that I'm in, and they just couldn't understand it." These statements confirm the "taken-for-grantedness" of everyday (teen) life and the unquestioned acceptance of the American teen lifestyle. Rather than slow down their own lives, or reduce their own consumption, teens sacrifice drawing, sewing, playing trumpet, or shared conversations so that they can devote more time to earning money and purchasing leisure.

LEISURE EXCEPTIONS

A few teens completely orient their lives around maximizing pleasure and minimizing work. These teens are "pleasure seekers," and they represent an extreme version of consumptive leisure preferences. Pleasure seekers combine a strenuous avoidance of hard work with a focus on leisure activities.

Male pleasure seekers at NJ High, such as Steve Moeller and Tremaine Owens, focused on "hanging out" with their drinking and partying buddies, while female pleasure seekers at NJ High, such as Minki Rich, spent enormous sums of money on their wardrobe, appearance, and entertainment. Though they have occasional romantic partners, their relationships are particularly short-lived (even relative to the brevity of many high school romances). It seems as if they select girlfriends or boyfriends for specific purposes: a date for the prom or some other important event, or simply for sex.

Chuck Barker, a senior at NJ High, did not hide his dislike of work nor his desire to goof around with his drinking buddies and have sex with girls. Sexually active himself, Chuck believed it was "OK" for even eighth-graders (i.e., 13-year-olds) to be sexually active, as long as they are "informed about what could go wrong." Chuck had had several girlfriends, one lasting a few months and the rest lasting only a few weeks. He spent most of his time with his drinking buddies—playing pool, cards, or video games, going bowling, or just "hanging out"—but complained, "There's not much to do around here." On two occasions, the police had been to Chuck's house, once because he sped away from an officer who was attempting to pull Chuck and his friend over for street racing and a second time for running a stop sign at 2:00 a.m. near a local college's fraternity row. Both times, his parents "believed my story," and his mother "knows somebody" who kept "points off" of Chuck's driving record. Chuck laughed freely as he told these stories, rolling his eyes as he described how his parent's believed him, inviting me to join his incredulity at his "luck." From my perch as a field researcher, Chuck stood out as a clear leader of a cohort of pleasure-seeking boys, brighter than his buddies and sly enough to deceive most adults who knew him. He played the teen pleasure-seeker game perfectly: appearing to conform to adult standards but primarily pursuing pleasure.

At the opposite end of the work/play continuum from Chuck stand a very different cohort of teens. These teens so focus their lives on school and work that they have virtually no time for leisure. I call these teens "strivers." Often working-class, but sometimes from newly middle-class homes, these teens are on a mission to move up in this world, and they do not have any time for "leisure." Jewel Galvez, a working-class, Latina youth, described how she spent her time:

> JEWEL: I always put work at the same level as school. I feel that that is really important. Work is really important to me. . . . [It] really impresses people that I have my own car and buy everything myself. That really impresses

people, and I like that. And when people realize that I'm a hard worker, I want that to be my characteristic. . . .

INTERVIEWER: How do you spend your leisure time?

JEWEL: Leisure time? [Long pause.] . . . Uh, cleaning my room. [We both laugh.]

INTERVIEWER: You like to be clean?

JEWEL: Yeah!

INTERVIEWER: You, like, actually *clean* stuff?

JEWEL: Organizing. I organize the same things, and I sell [Mary Kay], and I just read about cosmetics. I like to sell. I just like learning new things on how to keep yourself healthy or looking healthy. Just reading, . . . and I'm always organizing my papers.

Another teen striver I encountered was the salutatorian of NJ High. The daughter of working-class Ghanaian immigrants, Rashida was involved in a half-dozen school activities as well as a time-intensive internship at a local pharmaceutical company. Twice she canceled interviews with me because of other obligations. Rashida simply had *no* free time; her waking hours were consumed by school, school activities, schoolwork, internship hours, family responsibilities, and religious obligations. Very polite, but utterly serious, Rashida's diligence paid off with a full scholarship to a seven-year dentistry program. But with more than seven years of intensive work ahead of her, Rashida would have precious little time for leisure for a long time. Indeed, it seemed as if Rashida did not even have time to laugh.

That the teen strivers I met were all female, while the pleasure seekers were primarily male, suggests two possible interpretations. One interpretation is that this is a gendered phenomenon, that American culture is producing more young women who are serious about their education and career and more young men who resist the same. There are authors who suggest precisely this point,[10] but my data do not allow me to evaluate this possibility systematically. Another interpretation is that this is a developmental phenomenon; that is, high school boys mature more slowly and high school girls more quickly. Indeed, the high school boys I observed and interviewed were, on average, less mature than the high school girls were. But a year later, none of the pleasure seekers showed signs of greater maturity, and none of the strivers showed signs of letting up, which suggests a maturational interpretation is not tenable. Jewel Galvez, for example, was as devoted to her work and her studies at the end of her freshman year as she was in high school. She told me: "I don't like to relax. I'm not really a relaxing person unless I'm really tired. I just like working, and when I'm working I feel like I'm accomplishing something, . . . like I'm getting ahead. I'm working hard, but I'm getting ahead." Jewel was young and energetic, and her eighteen-hour days, seven days a week had not notably affected her health. But she may have been abusing her youthful body's resilience just as much as teens who abuse substances. Strivers like Jewel look down on partying peers, failing to recognize that their own relentless drive to achieve can be equally detrimental to health, relationships, and long-term happiness. Most teens, however, are in no danger of overworking themselves, as is evident next.

WORK

I could count on one hand the seniors at NJ High without jobs and would not need to use any fingers to count follow-up interviewees without jobs. Paid employment is as common among high school seniors as blue jeans and T-shirts. And it is universal at the end of the first year out. Teens will tell you that they work for a variety of reasons. They work because they need money, because they need to pay for clothes or college or cars. They work because they do not want to depend on mom and dad for cash handouts. They even work because they are "bored," as Rachel O'Leary, a white, upper-middle-class senior, told me: "I didn't have much to do anymore because I was done with all my sports and I was, like, starting to get bored in the evenings. I just decided, like, I could be making money." Almost all of the teens I interviewed had worked for several years prior to their senior year. A paper route or yard work was a frequent start for boys, while babysitting was a common choice for girls. By the senior year of high school, work choices were less gendered: retail sales, food service, and clerical positions were common choices for all high school seniors (though young women worked in clothing stores somewhat more frequently). During the school year, students at NJ High worked ten to twenty hours per week at local grocery stores, ice cream shops, bakeries, bagel shops, cell phone stores, music stores, various offices, clothing stores, home decor stores, mall boutiques, fast food restaurants, local restaurants, and chain restaurants. Many students continued at the same employers during the summer, expanding their hours to full-time, while other students took on second jobs or accepted summer jobs as day camp counselors or lifeguards.

It was interesting to hear how teens found employment. Location and hours were by far the most important factors. More often than not, teens were employed at the strip mall nearest to their homes, at whatever business was hiring when the teens sought employment. Megan Morici (introduced in chapter 2), for example, disavowed any role in selecting places of employment: "I just walked around and looked for 'help wanted' signs. It's not like I chose anything. Just whoever would hire me." If teens liked the hours, liked their boss, tolerated the work, and could socialize with co-workers and customers, they would stay—sometimes for several years. If any of these elements was missing, they would move on—to the store next door or the strip mall across the street. Location was naturally important to teens who lacked cars of their own, but it was also quite important to teens with cars. There are a several reasons why this is so. First, parents play an important role in approving their children's first jobs, and nearby businesses are known, safe, and verifiable. Second, teens prefer employers whose products or services they know and, ideally, enjoy (e.g., ice cream shops). Third, most teens view jobs as a "necessary nuisance," and a nearby job is less of a nuisance than a more distant one. It is obvious that most teens seek little more from a job than minimal inconvenience, tolerable working conditions, and a paycheck.

Tolerating work as a necessary nuisance can be found not just among teens; it is common among parents, too. Work is often viewed, except among those in the most privileged professions (like mine),[11] as means to a lifestyle end. Recent researchers overlook crucial cultural factors when they criticize parents, teachers, and other school personnel for not doing more to guide teens toward work choices that would develop their career interests and foster better "life planning." While I share these researchers' disappointment over the way most teens select workplaces, I disagree that parents, teachers, or other school personnel are the culprits. To the degree that Americans as a whole treat work as a means to a paycheck, and their paychecks as a means to an overconsumptive lifestyle, Americans *as a whole* are responsible. Most adults (including school personnel) put up with work and dream about early retirement or winning the lottery so they can say goodbye to their working days. It is unreasonable to expect parents or school personnel to convincingly convey a view of work that is alien to their own experiences.

Megan Morici was typical of many teens I interviewed. She was already on her fourth job, as a waitress in a local tavern (even though it is illegal for teens to serve alcohol in Megan's state), when I interviewed her the first time. This fourth job seemed to suit Megan well, because she was outgoing and enjoyed talking with the tavern "regulars" as well as meeting

new people. Other teens who used Megan's job-search strategy of applying at every nearby business with a "help wanted" sign most often ended
up, however, working at uninteresting and repetitive jobs that they did
not enjoy. Kato Stuart was on his second job when I first interviewed him.
He landed his first job with the help of his father, running copy machines
for his father's employer. Kato chose his second employer, a local discount
store, "because I know they're always hiring and I could probably get a job,
so I wouldn't have to be searching for a while." For Kato, the convenience
of a short job search, rather than consideration of the type of work, drove
his decision-making process. Both jobs were "boring," Kato told me, and
made him "feel like a machine sometimes." Yet when I reinterviewed Kato,
I learned that he was starting his third summer at the copy center and that
he stayed at the discount store for almost two years. I asked Kato why he
did not look for jobs he might enjoy more. He answered, in the clipped way
19-year-old young men often do, that he "just figured, you *have* to do it [i.e.,
put up with boring work] to get money." At 19, Kato resigned himself to the
idea that work was something to be endured, not something to be enjoyed.
Not all teens so resign themselves, but given the methods most use to find
work, many seemed headed in that direction.

GOOD JOBS

Despite jobs that assign repetitive and boring work, many teens say they
have good jobs and find their hours go by quickly. They cite three reasons
why: a "good" boss, friendly coworkers, and the opportunity to interact with
others. A good boss is relaxed about the rules, accommodates teen schedules, allows teens to socialize ("have fun") with coworkers or customers,
provides employees with special "treats" (e.g., provides a meal, lets employees out a little early), shows appreciation for the employee's work (ideally,
through pay raises), works alongside the employees, and makes sure everyone does their fair share of work. Friendly coworkers are as important as a
good boss and can sometimes offset a not-so-good boss. Preferred coworkers are other teens, because they help make uninteresting work go by more
quickly. One teen told me, "When there is no customers in the store, we'll
throw bouncy balls around and stuff like that." Teens also stay at their jobs
longer when they have friendly coworkers, and longest when they have
friendly coworkers combined with a good boss.

Yet, as important as the boss and coworkers are, many teens say the best
part of their jobs is getting to interact with "lots of different people." These

people might be customers at a store, kids at a day camp, swimmers at a pool, other workers at a large employer, or diners at a restaurant. Teens give a number of reasons why, to their surprise, they come to enjoy interacting with people most at their jobs. First, working with people is generally more interesting than the repetitive tasks teens perform otherwise. Even in routine business encounters, such as with a cashier, the variation of people and their situations makes the job a bit livelier. Second, teens like to be appreciated. For example, lifeguards are thanked for helping a child swim and waiters are thanked for good service. Third, teens find satisfaction in successful, independent interactions with others (i.e., where they are viewed as responsible individuals and not as children who need assistance from family or teachers). Kaniesha Goode, a black, working-class teen, worked at a mall clothing store. She told me that she enjoyed "making people feel good" by helping them select clothes: "People come in and tell me their lives . . . : 'I've lost 300 pounds and I need a whole wardrobe.' . . . [Or another] woman came in and said, 'Gosh, I don't have no more boobs—I need you to pick out a bra for me!'" Kaniesha took this job for financial reasons only, but discovered that interacting with people can be personally rewarding, at least sometimes. "It's *work*, you know; it's not that I'm playing. It's *work*, . . . but I enjoy the people that I work with." In other words, Kaniesha, like most teens, would not volunteer to do her job, but she did find it to be a generally tolerable source of income.

WORK EXCEPTIONS

There are exceptions to the above patterns. There are a few teens who consider their long-term interests and seek jobs accordingly, who find their work inherently interesting, and who take pride in gaining new work skills. There are black teens who work diligently to honor the sacrifices so many blacks made to secure the right to work. There are teens who do not enjoy working with other teens, who prefer to work alone and focus on their assignment. And there are pleasure seekers who boast about doing minimal amounts of work for high pay.

Carol Thomas, a white, upper-middle-class youth, was unusual in that she did not cite money or convenience as reasons for working. She took her first job, teaching art at a summer camp, because she had been a camper there herself and loved the place. Carol's second job was as a day-camp counselor, which she took because "it was fun. . . . As a counselor you don't get very good financial rewards, but . . . the money wasn't all that important when you knew you did something good for someone." Carol selected jobs based on her values—reciprocity toward a camp that she loved as a child and desire to help kids learn new skills at a day camp. Like other teens, Carol wanted to "have fun" at her jobs, but, unlike other teens, Carol did not give much consideration to income. This was partially because her parents gave her an allowance to use for spending money (though that is relatively common among middle- and upper-middle-class families), but mostly because Carol did not like to spend money and would rather save it for the future. When I reinterviewed Carol after her freshman year, she was still saving money—even bringing money home from college that she had set aside for spending there. What Carol's story illustrates is that her lower desire to live the American teen lifestyle translated into jobs chosen for reasons other than salary and convenience.

Andre Kendall, a black, working-class senior at NJ High, was relentless about working hard. Andre worked diligently because he saw "the struggle that my parents had gone though . . . and the struggle that blacks are going through, period" to make economic freedom available.

> Anybody that has a business now, any adult black that's, like, say, over forty, that has a business, they went through these tough times, even before I was alive. And now in this day, it's not as much segregation, and you know, I have the same resources as everybody else in America. If they can do all that in that time, I should be able to do ten times more. So it gives me more of a . . . I kind of feel responsibility for the black man, and I just don't want my children to have to suffer too much.

Andre was also a devout Baptist, and he reinforced his desire to honor his parents and his parent's generation with religious values about diligence. I suspect the two businesses that employed him, a janitorial service and a telemarketing firm, did not have many employees who were as diligent about such undesirable work as Andre.

At the other end of the spectrum from Andre and Carol are the pleasure seekers, who seek easy money above all. Two pleasure seekers at NJ High, white, middle-class Steve Moeller and black, middle-class Tremaine Owens, played the lottery regularly and outlined elaborate spending plans if they ever "hit it big." Until then, Steve worked as a city parking lot cashier, because he could talk for hours with the other cashiers and did not have to do much work. In fact, Steve aspired to be a full-time cashier, because such positions were unionized and earned "seventeen dollars an hour!" But the city refused to hire more full-time cashiers and remained firm on that policy when I reinterviewed Steve, so Steve settled for the $8.00 an hour that part-time cashiers earned. Tremaine worked at a sneaker store in the mall and worked one summer in a local office building (until being dismissed). Tremaine was blunt about not liking to work: "The only thing that, like, makes me work anywhere is how much I get paid an hour . . . and that's it." Steve and Tremaine prided themselves on doing the least work possible to keep their paychecks coming. While Steve and Tremaine do not represent a majority of teens, they do represent an observable, pleasure-seeking cohort that exists among even culturally mainstream teens.

SEEKING FINANCIAL SELF-RELIANCE

To be fair, the large majority of my teen respondents wanted to become financially self-reliant, and their work demonstrates an early expression of that value. Most of these working teens described putting in a reasonably good effort at their jobs, not for the intrinsic value of the job, but because they wished to please their boss and not make their coworkers resentful. Most working teens also seek to honor their agreement to work in exchange for a weekly paycheck. For Susie Dane, a white, upper-middle-class youth, remembering her paycheck was an important motivation: "Sometimes when I don't feel like working, I think about the fact that I am getting paid. So I think that that's a motivator—big time." This is a laudable characteristic, and it suggests that American culture's socialization processes generate a large proportion of relatively diligent workers. To this extent, I concur with sociologist Jeylan Mortimer that *moderate* amounts of teen employment can be beneficial for teens.[12] But I diverge from her sunnier assessment when I evaluate teen employment in light of teen spending.[13] I found no working teens who considered whether the goods and services they purchase so readily are worth the hours they sacrifice. Some might argue that this is just teen naïveté and that, with more time in the labor force, these teens will come to appreciate "the value of a dollar." But I found the strongest association was *not* between working and saving, nor was it between working and spending wisely, but between working and spending, period. Those teens with the least money seemed to be the best managers of it, while those with the longest work histories seemed to have the least to show for it—contra sociologist Mortimer's Minnesota teens—even after one accounts for differences in social class. Seeing how teens use money was eye-opening for me.

MONEY

Marketers covet American teen dollars, for a number of good reasons. Teens are more willing to consider new products than older consumers. Teens follow consumer trends closely, from fashion to cars to technology. Teens in the United States have a lot of dollars to spend, and most of these dollars are discretionary. And teens spend almost every dollar they have (if not immediately, then within a few months).[14] Marketers are wise. They know the value of a teen dollar. Fewer teens seem to; even those who spend their own earnings.

Mona Segall lived in a rural community exploding with "big box" retailers and upscale housing developments. Mona admitted, "I spend money like it's water," because she "needs new things" and "likes to wear new things." Whenever Mona got into a financial tight spot, which was fairly often, Mona called her father, who always sent her the money she wanted. After three years of working, Mona had accumulated no savings, but she intended to start saving soon, because "I want to get a credit card and I think you have to have credit, you know, in order to get a credit card." It is just "so hard" to save money, Mona giggled, when "there is so much out there to buy!"

Mona was more extreme than most teens, but not by much. Most teens will tell you how they put all, or most, of their earnings into their bank accounts. But teen bank accounts have revolving doors. Rachel O'Leary explained: "I mean, I've always tried to save. Like, I take my paycheck and put it right in the bank, then I'll be at the bank, like, a couple days later taking money out. I can't imagine how many hundred dollars I spent on the prom this year." Rachel described the one form of saving most teens manage, short-term saving for a critical expense in the American teen lifestyle, like the prom or a car. Lowanda Smith, in her colorful way, described her finances:

> LOWANDA: I don't have a dime in the bank account, and it's pitiful 'cause I've been working there for two years. I have like $7 in the bank account. Ask me what I did with it? I don't know! (*Pauses, then excitedly.*) I put $600 down on my car!
> INTERVIEWER: How did you manage that?
> LOWANDA: Determination!

Many other teens, with complete sincerity, told this college professor that they work so that they can "save for college." Such claims must impress parents, overwhelmed as they must be about the cost of sending their children to college. Parents then permit teens to begin working, so teens can save money for college and, as one parent told me, "maybe use a little bit to pay for things she needs now." But when I asked employed teens how much money they had put aside for college thus far, only a handful reported savings of more than a few hundred dollars. Dennis Jackson, a black, working-class senior from NJ High, spent his earnings as follows:

> DENNIS: Either I spend it on clothing, or I put it in the bank. Or I spend it on my car.
> INTERVIEWER: What is the most that you had saved at one point?
> DENNIS: I would say $900. . . . That's, like, gone [now]; it didn't take too long to finish that off.

As sincere as working teens may be about saving money, their desire to live the American teen lifestyle in effect coats the insides of their wallets with Teflon, keeping money from sticking there.

Many teens get jobs months before they are allowed to drive. But waiting for Mom or Dad to drive you to and from work "gets old," riding a bike to and from work is "no fun" when it is raining, too hot, or too cold, and virtually any distance is just "too far" to walk ("I walked there once. It took, like, forever!"—actual distance: 1.4 miles). Ivy Strasberger, a white, middle-class senior, described how her initial plans to save got modified:

> I was saving it up for college or for a car, and ended up putting it towards a car the beginning of my senior year; and then my senior year I didn't really save much. I don't even know, like, money goes so quickly. . . . Like taking care of my car was a big thing, having gas and insurance and when things went wrong. But also just like, I don't know, like silly things. Like, you go to the store and you buy a cup of coffee and a pack of gum, and you do that every day. . . . Also, I really like to shop, so if I had money I would always want to go shopping and buy clothes. Yeah, I love clothes.

Money that Ivy intended for college savings got diverted to a car, which in turn must be fueled, maintained, and insured. Ivy's car then provided easy transportation to a host of new opportunities to spend money, which further fueled her desires to do so. And Ivy is no teenage exception.

Americans love cars, but teen Americans may love them the most. That is because car ownership often represents the last hurdle between teens and their perception of full adulthood. Other rites of adulthood, like consuming alcohol or having sex, are available to teens well before their senior year of high school. But obtaining a driver's license, getting car insurance, and buying a car are clearly age-restricted. Hence, NJ High teens talked a lot about cars. Those who had cars made sure everyone else knew it. High school boys were especially likely to do this, but the high school girls made their car ownership known too. Seniors talked about the cars they planned to buy or about their plans to add stereos or other items to the cars they owned. I heard a few boys jealously "trash talking" the cars that their peers bragged about, sometimes using ethnic slurs, such as "Jap crap" to describe a Nissan. But no teen ever questioned the value of driving or owning a car in general; a teen (in suburbia at least) wants a car like a puppy wants love.

Teens with cars must earn money. Even upper-middle-class parents who provide cars or insurance for their teen children often require teens to pay for their own gasoline and to assume the costs of their own entertainment (which were previously underwritten by their parents), thus forcing these teens to earn money, too. For some teens, car expenses consume virtually all of their take-home pay. Jill Fairlawn was one such teen: "Well, I have a really bad car, and my car always needs money, so I need to keep working so I can keep paying my parents back for getting my car fixed." For other teens, car expenses are the top item on a long list of teen expenditures, such as clothes, phone bills, meals, snacks, and entertainment. Duncan Green, a white, upper-middle-class teen, used his money for "insurance and going towards the car. I bought a new guitar recently, so it went to that. Like at school we go out for lunch everyday, you know, and so here and there, you know. And gas for the car. I like going to music concerts, so it pays for that. So it, like . . . whatever I do for recreation or entertainment-wise . . . the money goes to that. I pay for all that stuff." Even teens without cars spend a lot of money maintaining the American teen lifestyle. Rob Robertson (introduced in chapter 1) earned just $30 a week as a Little League umpire. But when his buddy Rich got a car, Rob said, "my social life took off." He no longer had a parent-drop-off-and-pick-up-at-the-movies kind of social life. Instead, he could enjoy a full evening that began at the movies, then included a bite to eat, then a stop off at somebody's party, "and by that time . . . [you've] spent more money in the course of a night." Rob admitted that he was bothered by not having as much money as his friends had, but compensated by being a skillful "moocher." And perhaps because Rob was a popular athlete, Rich willingly "loaned" him money in exchange for his company.

MONEY MANAGEMENT

An expanding social life forced Rob Robertson to become a good manager of his money, and of his lack of it, too. Most teens say they need to become better money managers, because they do not have enough money and cannot track where their money goes. Shatoya Barkley, one of the Girlfriends Seven at NJ High, confessed, "I have no idea what I do with my money." What she and most teens consider "good" money management is *having* money to spend and *knowing how* it was spent. When asked, "Are you a good manager of your money?" Poppy Lopez (introduced in chapter 1) replied,

> POPPY: Very much.
> INTERVIEWER: Why?
> POPPY: Well, I used to be very stingy, but now when I have it, I'll spend it or buy something.

Jill Fairlawn explained that she was a good money manager because "I hardly ever have problems with money. . . . I hardly ever have to ask my parents for money." Still other teens point to their shopping skills as evidence of their good money management. Ken Drake, a white, middle-class senior who likes electronics, pointed to the computer in his room and explained how he "purchases sales when buying big things [like] computers. . . . I found this for $300 bucks—it was wholesale price!" A white, upper-middle-class senior, Tami Scott, claimed that she was a good money manager because "I tend to bargain shop, and I am aware of what I buy, unlike my sister." While these may be characteristics of a good consumer, they do not define good money management, at least not how personal finance experts would describe it.

TYPES OF MONEY

American culture did not come to possess such an expensive teen lifestyle overnight. Various economic and historical factors brought us to this point. I suggest, though, that the way teens conceptualize, or think about, their money itself plays an important role. Sociologist Viviana Zelizer has helped us realize that money is not a neutral tool of economic exchange, but one that has distinct social meanings. Life insurance proceeds are treated differently than wages, women's "pin money" is different than their grocery money, "blood money" is different than church offerings, and so on.[15] The teens I interviewed conceptualized their money in different ways. There was birthday and Christmas money, money from Mom and Dad, money from divorced fathers who did not have custody of their children, college savings, money from work, and, most important of all, "spending money." Spending money has one and only one purpose—to be spent for personal enjoyment. Spending money may be apportioned, for example, as gas money (or as car savings for those without cars). But its ultimate purpose remains the same. The key to understanding teen money use is understanding spending money.

American youth have a long history with spending money. Young children receive it for the first time as a gift, for whatever toy they might want, and parents enjoy teaching children how to buy an item at a store. Grade school kids get spending money to use on vacation or during a school field trip. (I can vividly remember jamming myself into museum gift shops with my classmates, as we all tried to decide how to spend the few dollars our parents gave us.) Young teens get spending money to use during some activity with their friends, such as a day trip, movie outing, or shopping. From birth to puberty, most of the money American teens receive is preclassified as spending money—and that is exactly how these budding consumers use it. Parents do try, of course, to teach the virtue of saving money, by opening savings accounts with their children or requiring children to "save up" for some desired item (e.g., a bike). These activities are mostly symbolic, however. Few adult Americans save more than modest amounts themselves,[16] and even fewer teens have more than token sums set aside "for college." What most teens do successfully is apportion spending money: car "savings," insurance money, gas money, phone money, prom money, and so on.

Though spending money may be the dominant type of money, some teens have other types of money that are very important to them. Lisa Smith, a white, working-class senior at NJ High, was rather conservative about spending her own money (i.e., wages), but had different standards for her divorced, noncustodial father's money. "I can resist buying a lot of stuff when I'm spending my own money," Lisa reported, but "when I'm spending my Dad's money, I'm all over the place!" Similarly, Mona Segall extracted money from her noncustodial father to rescue her from the financial difficulties she created by overspending. Though labeled "Dad's money," it was used far more liberally than money from custodial fathers. Money from resident parents is most often *designated* spending money. Most parents prefer to give money for designated purposes, for example, "sneaker money," "lunch money," or "trip money." Teens know they must use such money for its designated purpose or risk being cut off. By designating money, parents send the message that they will pay for specific expenses but not for the entire cost of the American teen lifestyle.

Another interesting way some teens label their money is with the term *real*. *Real money* refers to money earned from a future, full-time, adult job—not the part-time jobs that teens hold now. "Real" (or "regular," "serious") credit cards are MasterCard and Visa, not the store credit cards that teens use. Minki Rich told me: "The money that I make from [my job], like, I really don't need it for any *real* expenses. Like, it's just sort of my money to play around with. . . . Like when I get older, and I'm making at, like, a *real* job, and I'm making, like, *real* money, I'm gonna manage it better." Two other seniors at NJ High made these distinctions. Shatoya Barkley explained that she has "*store* credit cards . . . not a *serious* credit card." And white, working-class senior Tammy Biggs said: "I don't have a *regular* credit card. I have a credit card, two credit cards, . . . to The Limited and to Victoria's Secret." By so distinguishing between their current wages and future ("real") wages, and between current credit cards and future ("regular") cards, these teens justified liberal spending of present money and future money, too. And for teens in general, once a sum of money is designated as spending money, its fate is complete. Though teens vary in consumer choices and general value-consciousness, they do not vary in spending their spending money.

GIVING?

Asking teens about giving away money produced interesting responses. Many teens were incredulous when asked, "Do you ever give any money away?" Eyes opened wide, jaws dropped open, and teens said, "Huh?" "Say what?!" "To who?!" "What do you mean?!" I would explain that I wanted to know about giving to charitable or religious organizations, or to individuals. Some of these teens then answered no and provided no elaboration. Lisa Smith did elaborate: "No. [Laughing.] I'm *greedy* with my money!" Others stumbled about, describing how they let friends "borrow" a dollar or two to buy food. Still others described dropping coins in collection cans near cash registers, like Cookie Munroe of NJ High's Girlfriends Seven, "If I see, like, if I'm in the store and they have the cans or something, I always put money in—I try to do that." Most teens described token giving, if any at all.

Yet there were two atypical responses to the giving question, made by two identifiable groups of teens. The first came from highly religious, often evangelical, youth, who regularly gave money to their churches and to other charitable organizations. Duncan Green told me: "My paychecks all go into the bank, and then 10 percent I tithe at the church. Yeah. Whatever I get, that's automatic. You know, whatever I get, it's because he [God] gave me the ability to work hard, and I'm grateful for that. So I just give that back to him, you know, I give to church." And Tadia Williams, of the Girlfriends Seven, also mentioned giving "tithes," which is the biblical term for a one-tenth portion. "I try to do tithes when I have it. I think I might have followed my tithe maybe once, and that's not a good thing. But I try, and I do offer it in the church." Such teens feel a strong obligation to give to church and feel a sense of guilt when giving less than a tithe. But Amy Lawson, a future social worker from an upper-middle-class, evangelical family, described a different perspective on giving. "There's definitely a joy in giving. And I learned a lot about it from my grandparents. That it wasn't mine to begin with, so why not give some of it away? . . . If I have [spent money unnecessarily] it would be on clothes. But if I do spend it on clothes, I try to give at least that much away—take it out of my closet and give it to Goodwill. 'Cause I don't really need that much." Amy's perspective on money and giving was exceptional not only among youth in general, but also among religious youth. Many religiously active youth gave money to their places of worship, and some spoke of trying to give 10 percent. But only Amy associated giving with joy and connected her own spending patterns with the needs of the poor.

The second atypical response to the giving question came from working-class teens, blacks in particular, who often gave money to their parents or siblings to help pay family expenses. Shatoya Barkley occasionally gave money to her mother for groceries: "I give away money sometimes—[to] my mother, if she is grocery shoppin' or something." Kaniesha Goode said:

> KANIESHA: I've given money basically to help pay the bills.
> INTERVIEWER: For the household?
> KANIESHA: Yeah. My brother's prom, junior/senior prom, was a couple weeks ago—helped pay for that. Phone bill. Money for my mother to pay bills. Sister's . . . some of her tuition for summer camp this summer. So just . . . I haven't done anything for myself! (*Laughing.*)

And Kristi Kramer (introduced in chapter 1) occasionally gave money "to my parents, just if they need it, if things are tight. If I have it, I don't mind giving it to them." Working-class families live paycheck-to-paycheck, with little room for unexpected expenses, big or small. Most of the black, working-class teens, a couple of black, newly middle-class teens, and a couple of white, working-class teens described giving or loaning money to their parents. Though my findings need systematic replication, several potential interpretations suggest themselves. First, it may be a cultural norm for black teens to share earnings within their families.[17] Second, it may be that working-class, black, teen families have less stable financial situations than their white counterparts.[18] Third, it may be that teens in single-parent households are more likely to share earnings and that I just happened to interview more black teens from single-parent families than I did white teens. All three are reasonable possibilities and merit future investigation.

FINANCIAL EXCEPTIONS

There are a few teens who have good money management skills, who save quite successfully for college and even beyond. There are also teens who do not like to spend money and do not get caught up in the costly American teen lifestyle that their peers do. What makes these teens exceptional are the following characteristics: they come from middle- or upper-middle-class families; they live in two-parent families; they have financially disciplined parents who have passed on money management skills; they are active in school or voluntary activities, sports in particular; they enjoy spending time with their families; and they prefer forms of entertainment that are less expensive. Not every financially exceptional teen possesses all of these characteristics, but most possess at least four.

Moesha Anderson was one such exception. Moesha had never held a regular job, which was partly how she had time to be involved in more than a dozen different activities, including sport teams and student government. When Moesha was not occupied at school, she enjoyed spending evenings at home watching TV with her family. Moesha said, "I have no need for money," partly because her mother earned a comfortable salary as a speech therapist, but mostly because Moesha's entertainment consisted of school sports, extracurricular activities, watching TV with her family, and hanging out at friends' homes. Moesha said she was "definitely" a good manager of her money, because "it's really easy for me to save." She saved "three-quarters" of any money she received (e.g., birthday gift money), putting it into a savings account that she did not touch, and putting the rest in a drawer at home. Part of what helped Moesha was how she classified this drawer money. She called it "emergency" money, which was only reclassified when she needed to buy a gift or, occasionally, go to the movies with her friends. Amazingly, Moesha had $100 of emergency cash hidden in her dresser, more than many employed teens accumulated after two or even three years of paid employment.

Rob Robertson and Carol Thomas were also exceptional. Rob would "mooch" from his friends to support his social life, so he could save most of the $30 he earned weekly as a Little League umpire. Rob said, "Another family value, especially from my Dad, is to save your money." Rob's parents, both with graduate degrees, wanted Rob to focus on his schoolwork first, and then on athletics and community service. Thus, Rob did not have a car of his own, and his parents paid the additional car insurance so Rob did not have to get "a real job." For entertainment, Rob enjoyed going out with his friends on occasional weekend nights, but he also liked to lift weights, play pickup basketball, and have friends over to play ping-pong or video games. Carol, unlike Moesha and Rob, received an allowance and worked only during the summers. But Carol was disciplined about saving her summer pay for "college spending money." She said she used her allowance to buy "some clothes," or when "I know I'm going to do something, I just try to save my allowance as long as I can." Carol was a varsity athlete, so during her two sport seasons, she had little time for entertainment. But even when she had more time available, Carol preferred to spend her weekday evenings at home with her little brother, mother, and father. On the weekends, Carol hung out with friends, sometimes going shopping or to the movies, but mostly preferred just "being with friends."

For pure ability to manage and accumulate money, no teen came close to Sergio Sicily, a white, middle-class youth. At our first interview, Sergio had almost $14,000 in savings and planned to pursue a career "dealing with money." His savings came from working five summers making pizzas at a beachfront restaurant. Sergio explained, "I'm not a big money spender. I don't buy a lot of things for myself." So he kept most of his savings in certificates of deposit, where he earned a better rate of interest. Sergio's "father figure" worked as a mechanic and his mother owned and operated a candy store, but Sergio did not get money from his parents. Sergio had planned to use some savings to buy a car, but said he "lucked out" when his mother gave him her old station wagon, rather than trade it in for $800. Though many teens would sooner walk than drive their mother's old station wagon, Sergio was unfazed. As for leisure activities, Sergio liked sports. When he was not playing varsity football or baseball at school, he played pickup games of football or basketball with friends and worked out five days a week at the gym. "Once in a while I like to go . . . to the movies," he said, but Sergio preferred playing sports to just about anything else.

Leisure preferences, then, make an enormous difference in the amount of money teens seek to earn and spend. Although being with friends is the favorite activity of virtually every teen, friendship groups have distinct leisure preferences. Those preferences either constrain or liberate a teen's time and money.

THE FIRST YEAR OUT

Leisure preferences have a strong carryover during the first year out, making a teen's leisure adjustment primarily one of schedule and context. And because teens are accustomed to finding convenient jobs and working for pay, the world of work presents another straightforward adjustment for teens during the first year out. Once the time constraints of high school schedules are lifted, however, social class differences in teen labor emerge clearly. Money adjustments are the most significant to teens during the first year out, as teens are made increasingly responsible for their own financial matters. A closer look at leisure, work, and money reveals a number of interesting patterns.

LEISURE AND THE FIRST YEAR OUT

Teens who preferred quiet, active, or consumptive leisure as high school seniors carried those preferences over during their first year out, which is consistent with quantitative research into teen leisure behavior following high school.[19] High school seniors active in sports, performing arts, or other school activities remained active as college freshmen. The same holds for teens who preferred quiet forms of leisure and those who preferred consumptive forms of leisure. The main adjustment for all of these teens was their new freedom to pursue leisure at any hour of the day, any day of the week. The high school schedule no longer restricted time for leisure activities. A high school schedule of 7:30 a.m. to 3:00 p.m. not only eliminates leisure activities during those hours, it also imposes sleep and meal schedules to a significant degree. After high school graduation, teens can choose schedules for work, class, mealtime, sleep, and leisure, and balancing their leisure with their other obligations can be a difficult adjustment for some teens.

Outgoing, active teens who attended four-year residential colleges seemed to have the most difficult adjustment. These teens discovered college offers an exponential increase in activities, and they found it hard to resist the many possibilities. Only after they received their first-semester grades did many of these teens realize they had overcommitted themselves.[20] Even Andre Kendall, who was unusually self-disciplined as a high school senior, had difficulty during his first semester:

> I'm learning time management, learning self-discipline better. Before, I had some self-discipline, but it was a lot because of my parents. Now I have to maintain it on my own. You know, as far as even getting up in the morning sometimes. . . . [I] missed quite a few classes—I didn't get up on time. . . . I didn't do too good with my schoolwork, but I'm getting better with that. . . . I need to put my studies first. I got involved in a lot of clubs and organizations at school, and I was trying to put so much time in different places it kinda took away from my schoolwork.

Andre cut back his involvement in several student clubs and focused more on his classes during his second semester. That helped him improve his grades during the second semester, but not as much as he had hoped, so he indicated he would make his classes an even higher priority during his sophomore year.

Julie Gillmore, a varsity volleyball player, had less of a problem with overinvolvement. Still, she described learning how to balance time for friends with time for studying: "You can't study the night before a test. I tried and it didn't work. [Now] I will start studying a week before, and I do a study guide." Freshmen varsity athletes, on the whole, seemed to have fewer problems with overcommitment. This advantage stems from three sources: athletic schedules consume a large number of student hours, NCAA minimum grade requirements force players to put a basic effort into their classes, and coaches often take a highly directive role with their players, especially new freshmen. The college athlete's advantage is also attitudinal: they enter college with the mindset that their time is restricted and thus more easily ignore competing activities.

Freshmen who preferred reading as a leisure activity often reported smooth transitions into college. While they had little time for leisure reading during the semester, they generally enjoyed their class reading and spent a lot of time doing it. So long as freshmen with quiet leisure preferences found at least one good friend with similar interests, they seemed quite happy. Alicia Right, for example, loved her classes, earned good grades, and reported having a very good freshman year. The main challenge for residential college students with quiet leisure preferences was making friends. Alicia did so successfully, but Reggie Kraft, a black, middle-class, residential college freshman, did not. Reggie never connected at more than a superficial level with his classmates, and a difficult roommate only exacerbated matters. Reggie opted to transfer to another college for his sophomore year. If he succeeded in making a couple of good friends there, then I suspect his sophomore year went much better.

Most freshmen, however, enter college with well-developed preferences for consumptive leisure, and they seem to enjoy themselves the most. That is because college life is the perfect antidote to the complaint "there's nothing to do around here." At any given hour, on any given day, a residential college student can find friends to "go do something with." College students would have to work hard to be "bored." Most campuses offer a wide range of leisure activities (snack shops, shows, billiards, movies, cafés, concerts, spectator sports, trips), and few campuses are not close to a town or city that offers even more leisure options. Many of these teens, who rarely attend academically intense colleges, reported going out with friends every night.

Given the unusual availability of peers and leisure time during college, these teens will likely view their college years as "the best years of their lives." Once postcollege obligations restrict the time and money available for consumptive leisure activities, these college graduates will likely develop a strong nostalgia for their college years. Though nostalgia is not exclusive to those who prefer consumptive leisure activities, those who depend on external leisure providers and the wide availability of friends for leisure may find their nostalgia is particularly intense.

WORK AND THE FIRST YEAR OUT

Early in Milton Bradley's The Game of Life (an American cultural artifact in its own right), players finish high school and choose between two paths: the shorter path of "work" or the longer path of "college." Those choosing work skip tuition bills and speed their progress in the game of life, while those choosing college delay their journey. To a recent high school graduate, however, the design of The Game of Life has to be baffling—for teens do not choose work or college, they choose both. It is only the ratio of work to college that varies. Freshmen enrolled in four-year college programs work an average of ten to fifteen hours per week during the school term, while those enrolled in two-year college programs or technical programs work twenty to thirty hours (or more) per week.[21] Freshmen with particularly time-intensive programs, such as varsity athletes or premed students, usually work fewer hours than their classmates do. They often compensate for the loss of wages by working more hours during the summer and college breaks and by reducing their spending (a by-product of reduced leisure time). Some colleges also restrict freshmen from having cars and restrict financial aid recipients from working, which limits paid employment among freshman. But by and large, freshmen work the hours typical of their peers by the end of their first year of college.

Initially, many freshmen avoid paid employment by drawing from their college savings. For some freshmen, this represents the longest break they have had from paid employment in three to four years. The length of this work gap varies from student to student, based mostly on the social class of the freshman. Raquel Johnson, for example, got a job her first semester when she "realized that the money was running out before the week was running out." Raquel wound up employed at a nearby office supplies store, doing a job that was "considered part-time, but I worked seven hours a day," four days a week. Another freshman, Dave Olsen, a white, middle-class teen, drew from his college savings for several months, supplementing those funds by working long days at his hometown employer during extended weekends and school breaks, and eventually working as an intramural sports referee at college.

Upper-middle-class freshman John Snow did not work during his freshman year. John played two varsity sports, so he could not have held a job during his sport seasons even if he had wanted to. John compensated by working full-time during the summers and saving a significant portion of his summer earnings. The latter went further because John's parents underwrote many of his college living expenses and because John preferred sports to more consumptive leisure activities. Another upper-middle-class freshman, Paul Stephens, could have "gotten by" without working his freshman year. But Paul took a job in a chain restaurant soon after starting college, because he liked the money, the schedule, the free food, and the "cool people there." Paul was not a model employee, however. He was fired for calling in sick when not ill, but found another job quickly. "I'm supposed to be paying off my car insurance," Paul reported, but "my parents have money and I'm not very materialistic." So Paul used his money to fund his friends' entertainment costs: "I'll be, like, 'Dude, I got ya, I'll spot ya.'" Paul, like John, enjoyed having a certain level of spending money at college and, accordingly, chose to work.

Working-class freshmen do not have as many work options as their more affluent peers. The most fortunate of this class make it to four-year college programs, but often live at home and continue in their precollege job(s). That was Tammy Biggs's experience. Compared to other working-class teens, Tammy was quite fortunate. She had a good academic record, gained admission to a highly selective state college, and even received a small scholarship. But Tammy's perspective was shaped by comparisons to her middle- and upper-middle-class high school classmates, who were not restricted to living at home and attending state colleges. Thus, she resented her parents for not being able to afford on-campus room and board, she resented having to work so many hours weekly, and she even resented (secretly) the affluence of her best friend—"she doesn't work, she doesn't have to pay car insurance, she doesn't have to pay anything, and her parents *give* her their credit card—enough said!"

More typically, working-class freshmen enrolled at their local community college and continued to work thirty-five to forty-five hours per week. Some wound up at community colleges because, as a few put it, their "financial aid fell through"; that is, they discovered they were ineligible for more than educational loans, or they learned that neither they nor their parents could afford to pay what the financial aid office decided they ought to pay, or both. Others enrolled in community colleges directly. Once enrolled, community college freshmen discovered that the academic demands of their classes were not especially high ("It's thirteenth grade!"— see chapter 5), and thus quite compatible with a full-time work schedule. Kristi Kramer and Shatoya Barkley both attended community college full-time, and both worked between thirty-five and forty-five hours per week. Though both young women lived at home, their tuition, textbooks, car, clothes, meals, and entertainment expenses were their own responsibility. Such expenses did not make saving money easy—nor did Kristi's and Shatoya's spending patterns—so neither freshman could foresee any let up in their work hours.

Attrition from community colleges is often high, however, and several interviewees had either dropped out or were on a clear trajectory to do so. Christine Darden wanted to become a kindergarten teacher when I first interviewed her. But working as a preschool aide, combined with "boring classes" at her community college, led Christine to drop out of college and enroll in a for-profit photography school. When I reinterviewed her, photography consumed many of Christine's waking hours, and her work as an Avon representative consumed the rest. Christine described herself as "very happy" with her new career path, but not all community college dropouts make the transition as successfully as she did.[22]

These interviews clearly reveal social class differences—differences that were previously masked by the schedule of high school. Upper-middle-class freshmen choose rather freely the duration and hours of work to suit their desired lifestyle; middle-class freshmen feel compelled to work so they can stay within the norms of American teen life; and working-class freshmen *must* work to pay certain mandatory expenses (e.g., college fees) and feel compelled to work so they can stay within the lower bounds of the American teen lifestyle. Teens are oblivious to these differences, however.

In sum, working presents few concerns to teens during the post–high school year. The product of their working—money—is a wholly different matter.

MONEY AND THE FIRST YEAR OUT

Many teens cited financial issues as a major area of adjustment during the first year out. Financial matters make real the change in teens' lives following high school graduation. For teens who move onto residential campuses, there are a myriad of financial issues, from laundry money to checking accounts to financial aid. College freshmen also discover that their school's billing offices regard them as financially responsible adults, requiring these teens to sign loan notes, cosign aid checks, and file paperwork promptly. Post–high school teens discover both financial freedoms (e.g., opening a credit card account) and responsibilities (e.g., paying the credit card bill) that symbolize their status as young adults.

To more seasoned adults, financial matters are ordinary activities, no more interesting than the commute to work. But for young adults, learning to handle these matters has a nervous excitement to it not unlike learning how to drive. And like learning to drive, the increase in financial responsibilities during the first year out is a rite of passage. A number of teens described, without prompting, how they learned to handle financial matters during their post–high school year. Lowanda Smith observed, "You're an adult once you go [away] to school, so I've learned to handle my business." She explained that the financial aid staff "wants to speak to *you*, the student," and "I have to be the one to go up to the financial department and say, 'This is my student loan, did it come through?'" A number of other teens pointed to handling their own financial matters as evidence of how they changed during their first year out. Malik Ali, a black, working-class teen, answered:

MALIK: I'm a lot different.

INTERVIEWER: In what ways?

MALIK: Handling money. I mean, basically, doing what I have to do. . . . It's more on you to do what you got to do. . . .

INTERVIEWER: What do you mean?

MALIK: Budgeting money, getting money. I was on a scholarship at [my university], so I couldn't get a job, so I had to wait for my mom to send me money—and that's kind of hard.

Nick Lawrence, the NJ High teen who liked art and music, attended a four-year fine arts college. He also pointed to taking responsibility for more of his financial matters as a chief way that he changed:

I moved in with Dad because it was the most affordable alternative we had. 'Cause I don't have a whole lot of money to work with for college. . . . [But now] I got a good job—I'm in at [Chain Steak House]. . . . Everything's just clicked, and I feel like I've built up my own thing now. Like, I've got my own thing going on; I don't feel like I'm as dependent, anymore—other than Dad's paying for school. But I feel like I'm starting to make my own arrangements with things. It's been a good transition I think.

Even doing laundry gets cited by many teens as a sign of their new independence, financially and domestically. Raquel Johnson described how she got a job (in part) so that she could afford to do her laundry: "Little things, like not having money to put on my laundry card. What are you gonna do, call home and be like, 'Mommy, wire me some money'? 'Cause they send money every week anyway, but when that runs out . . . and if I didn't have a job, then . . . It's like, 'Oh, well then, you just can't do laundry this week,' or things like that. You have to budget." Being able to handle financial matters, from the simple yet symbolic washing of one's own laundry to the significant signing of one's own loan notes, signifies to teens that they have indeed made important steps toward independence and adulthood.

Teens are not, of course, the only financial players during the first year out. Parents alter their own financial roles during this period, choosing to scale back financial support in a variety of ways. Kim Faust was a white, middle-class teen whose mother had recently divorced. Kim's mother, feeling the financial setback of her divorce acutely, barely managed to afford her share of the tuition, room, and board expenses at Kim's private college.

So Kim had to spend her entire college savings on back-to-school items. "I spent it on stuff for college. Like, literally every penny, I think. I spent it on, like, a word processor, a mattress pad. I never thought I'd need a mattress pad, but I had to get one of those. And I had to get a raincoat for college. I had to get sheets and stuff like that. I think I spent every last penny on college. Not actual tuition, just the stuff I needed for it." Thus, Kim got an early lesson in funding living expenses herself. Her experience is more typical of the working-class teens I interviewed, who frequently assumed their personal expenses early in high school. More commonly, middle- and upper-middle-class parents make a major event out of sending their child off to college with a trailer full of back-to-school items. Market studies suggest that these families spend upward of $2,000 equipping their new college freshman for school, spawning a trend in "off-to-college gift registries" at several retailers.[23] Many parents make it clear, however, that this back-to-school shopping spree will be their last one. Though parents say it in a variety of ways and show it through a variety of actions, they make their children keenly aware that high school graduation means entering a new stage in their parent-child financial relationship. As Rob Robertson put it, "My parents are making me more and more financially autonomous," and, working ten-hour days in New Jersey's summer humidity, he could literally feel it.

Teens face other financial adjustments during the first year out. These include having to spend money in larger sums and more regularly than at any previous point in their lives. College freshmen must buy textbooks and pay a variety of student fees, and many begin to get their first monthly financial statements (e.g., phone bills, checking statements). College freshmen also witness a rapid acceleration in spending by their new peers and are quick to join in. Teens from less affluent homes discover their new peers spend a lot more money than their high school friends, while teens from affluent homes always find some peer who spends more in a given area than they do. Either way, the effect is the same: increased personal spending. Tammy Biggs went from $20 of spending money a week in high school to $88 of spending money per week in college—a fourfold increase, yet on the low side compared to many freshmen. Electronic equipment, computers, clothes, and entertainment all become arenas of intense competition among freshmen, accelerating the spending of even financially disciplined teens. Recall Carol Thomas, who came home from college with money still in her savings account. Even she admitted that her spending got out of control her first semester and that it took considerable self-discipline ("over the year, I've learned") to limit her spending during her second semester.

Perhaps the most financially significant change made by post-high school teens is the widespread acquisition of major credit cards. Though some high school seniors have store credit cards, none have independent accounts with MasterCard, Visa, Discover, or American Express. This pattern alters profoundly during the first year out. Major card issuers solicit applications from any teen enrolled in a post-high school educational program, and they approve applications readily. In fact, card issuers entice teens with offers of discounted air travel or other desirable goods in exchange for opening accounts. Many of these young credit card holders believe they are managing their accounts well when they pay the minimum balance regularly and show little concern for the growing balances on these cards. Kristi Kramer was quick to join the ranks of the indebted:

> KRISTI: Actually, I have three credit cards *and I use them!* I don't even know what I bought with them, to tell you the truth. Some of the stuff, I don't know why I bought it. I guess because I said, "Oh, I have plastic now; I can get it for myself."
> INTERVIEWER: OK, so you have credit cards and you've run up some charges on them, all three?
> KRISTI: Oh yeah.
> INTERVIEWER: All the way?
> KRISTI: All the way.

Though credit card issuers may treat teens as adults, it is not clear that teen cardholders treat their credit cards with a fully adult perspective. Of course, to read *The Overspent American*, by Juliet Schor, is to learn that many adults treat their credit cards immaturely, too. Though financial responsibilities may enlarge during the first year out, they are not always accompanied by enlarged financial wisdom.

ON THE ROLE OF FAMILY, FAITH, AND COMMUNITY

That most American teens view leisure as a purchased commodity, work as a necessary nuisance, and money as a lifestyle essential strongly suggests that they have learned these views from their families, their faith, and their local communities. Not that most families, faiths, or communities send these messages explicitly, but they do so implicitly as they pattern leisure, work, and money behaviors along these lines. Though children and teens will sometimes listen to what adults tell them, they closely observe what adults actually do. Our actions often betray our most deeply held values (see chapter 2).

Families, then, become the first place wherein children observe and absorb basic practices with respect to work, money, and leisure. Some families want their teens to focus on schoolwork and school activities, reserving paid employment for summertime or future years. Some families live within their means, save money for long-term needs, and give cheerfully. Some families prefer less consumptive leisure activities, such as sports, volunteer work, reading, or watching television. Most families, however, just tolerate the workplace, because it is the source of the income they seek, which in turn allows them to purchase the goods and services they need and desire. Transference of family practices to children is never guaranteed, but behavioral practices inculcated from an early age set the trajectory for teen's behavior.

Faith communities are semi-important to most teens and strongly important to many teens. Among semireligious teens, faith plays no discernible role in their work, money, or leisure practices, save the occasional deposit into the donation basket and the occasional youth group activity. Among strongly religious teens, it is also difficult to identify a sustained role of faith in work, money, or leisure practices. One does finds elements of a traditional moralism among these teens—work diligently because one should, give because it is one's obligation, and avoid objectionable leisure activities. Beyond this, however, there is no general evidence that religious teens either resist or succumb to the American teen lifestyle any more than nonreligious teens. Faith's impact was clearer at the margins: all of the strivers demonstrated an ongoing commitment to religious faith, while none of the pleasure seekers described faith as a significant part of their lives. As theologian Vincent Miller argues compellingly, American forms of faith are themselves too affected by consumerism to effectively challenge the consumerism of the population at large.[24]

Local communities and volunteer organizations often have keen interests in the work, money, and leisure activities of teens. This chapter demonstrates that most teens are willing to accept the work that is available and fulfill work obligations reasonably well. But my study does not offer evidence for a widespread spirit of volunteerism among teens; most teens are not active in organized activities or programs, while those who are active choose activities from their immediate institutional offerings. In other words, most teens do not have "radar screens" that are even tuned to volunteer possibilities, and those that do have small screens. As short-staffed and poorly funded as most volunteer organizations may be, they will need to vastly expand their efforts to even make it into the everyday consciousness of just a portion of American youth.

As for the communities of gender, race, and social class, this chapter highlights a number of important ways all three shape the leisure, work, and money practices of teens during the first year out. But rarely do these differences—so obvious from an outside perspective—percolate up into teen consciousness. Neither male nor female teens question the often gendered patterns they follow with respect to leisure activities, work settings, or spending. The same holds true for race: majority and minority race teens notice few systematic differences beyond preferences for fashion, music, and dance.

Only a few working-class teens indicated awareness of social class differences. Tammy Biggs, for example, secretly resented her best friend's greater spending freedom. And Christine Darden described quitting her job at Big Box Electronics Store for Discount Fashion Clearinghouse, because the "rich" customers at the former were too demanding, while the customers at the latter "were a different kind of people" who expected little attention from store employees. While working-class teens often work at jobs that require them to serve middle- and upper-middle-class Americans, the inverse rarely holds true. This gives working-class teens firsthand knowledge of affluent consumers, while reinforcing the insularity of middle- and upper-middle-class teen experiences. Unfortunately, this knowledge did not lead working-class teens like Tammy or Christine to question the inequities of the American class system. It led instead to feelings of envy, a passion for upward mobility, or a preference for more class-homogeneous social interaction. Hence, affluent Americans need not worry that the system of class privileges they enjoy will be significantly or even modestly challenged by this rising generation of young Americans.

Throughout this chapter, I have examined the moral culture of American teens with respect to leisure, work, and money, describing dominant and variant patterns of teen behavior in each of these areas. Though the first year out might seem like a prime moment for teens to evaluate their behavior, I found that the leisure, work, and money practices of contemporary American teens do not pause, but rather combine to gain momentum as American teens pursue full admittance to the work-and-spend cycle of American adults. Unless a significant downshifting phenomenon exists during the second, third, or fourth years out—and I have seen no evidence that it does—it is doubtful that these new American adults are planning to question this cycle, much less slow their entry into it anytime soon. There is also little hope, given the way American teens approach their post-high school educational experiences, that education will give teens pause about these matters either, as is evident in chapter 5.

FIVE

Cognitively Sharper, Intellectually Immune

Bigger and taller than 95 percent of NJ High's girls and 75 percent of its boys, Cookie Munroe was not a young woman to be overlooked. One of the Girlfriends Seven, Cookie was a well-known varsity athlete and a student government officer. But Cookie was not an honor student like other student government officers; in fact, she was almost the opposite. "I always used to say, 'Oh, I hate school,'" and during Cookie's early high school years, she admitted, she "was kinda a bad student, I . . . didn't care." But Cookie's mother, one of few who could intimidate Cookie, "put me back in my place on that one." So while Cookie found high school to be "really hard," she realized as a senior that it "taught me a lot." Her feelings had thus become more mixed: "I like school, but I don't like school—it's like that."

What made school enjoyable for Cookie were her friends, playing sports, and planning special events. What wore on Cookie's patience were classes, especially math. In fact, with respect to Cookie's poor performance in math, "My mom would [say], . . . 'They're gonna keep you back and you ain't never gonna graduate.'" Yet somehow, after struggling through several years of remedial math, Cookie managed to pass the math portion of NJ High's basic proficiency exam. This made Cookie "very, very happy," because, finally, she knew she would be cleared to graduate.

But the joy of graduating from high school presented Cookie with a new hurdle: earning a vocational certificate in broadcasting. At the time of our first interview, Cookie had not yet been accepted by a broadcasting program. One school rejected Cookie because of low grades, while another put her on a wait list until she received her senior grades. This left Cookie "scared," and she feared she would not do well if admitted. "I say I'm going to be famous," Cookie confided, "but you know how things don't work out for some people." More than anything, Cookie wanted to make her mom proud.

So when an established broadcasting program admitted Cookie, she and her mom were elated. Adding icing to Cookie's cake was the program's location some three hundred miles away in Industrial City, which would give her a chance to live away from home. "I just didn't want to stay in [Suburban Township]—there wasn't really nothin' here." Cookie had considered a four-year college, but "I knew I probably wouldn't have done anything. I know me. . . . I wouldn't have done what I was supposed to do. I probably would have been partying and everything. And I told my mom the main reason I really wanted to go to a four-year school was just to join a sorority." By attending broadcasting school, Cookie would be "done" in a little over a year, and she could then start to earn money. Her plan was to use the school's placement office to enter a good broadcasting company, move up the ranks, and become a television show host:

> COOKIE: I'm going to have a [women in sports] show.
> INTERVIEWER: Your own show?
> COOKIE: Yeah. I just want to have something to have fun with on TV.

Lacking nothing in ambition, Cookie had a clear plan for the future to motivate her to make the most of her training.

So how did Cookie do? I caught up with Cookie during the final weeks of her broadcasting program. She told me, like other teens, how she learned to navigate relationships, manage gratifications, find leisure activities, secure employment, and apportion her spending. These were the things that consumed Cookie's time and attention. Cookie also told me about her schooling. She described how she adjusted to her new school's patterns, successfully maneuvered through school bureaucracy, and learned how to work with her various instructors. One of the skills American teens like Cookie must acquire is learning how to adapt to new formal organizations, and colleges or vocational schools represent a major test of these skills. American adults must possess these skills if they are to maintain employment, obtain health care, make major purchases, or accomplish many other goals. Cookie did so with aplomb.

Cookie learned how to live in a residence hall, where to shop, how to use public transportation, where to register for classes, how to conduct herself in classes and studios, where to submit paperwork, and especially, how to "read" her instructors. A couple of Cookie's instructors were "tough," and they required students to "do it their way," but Cookie used humor and charm to win over even her most difficult instructor. "He'd embarrass you in front of the whole class if you did something wrong. . . . I mean, he liked me. . . . He would pick on me, but he was alright." Still, Cookie seemed to enjoy her classes and expressed satisfaction with her choice of broadcasting.

Still, I have a strong suspicion that, had I not asked Cookie about her classes or instructors directly, she would not have even mentioned them. Though Cookie's broadcasting program was the official reason for her move to Industrial City, her classes were quite secondary to her life. "I do what I gotta do," was how Cookie described her educational experience. Cookie gave no indication of intellectual engagement with any particular topic in broadcasting (such as sensationalism), nor did she show signs of any creative appetite for broadcasting-related matters (such as set design). School was a necessary nuisance, as was her job in the equipment center of a local broadcasting company. Cookie did not care to consider, for example, the place of broadcasting in American culture, the significance of media ownership by a few major corporations, the ethics of interviewing, or even the creative possibilities that broadcasting and the Internet might hold. Even the horrors of September 11, 2001, occurring just a few weeks into Cookie's program, did not spark an intellectual or ethical curiosity within her. To my question of any lasting effect of September 11 on her life, Cookie replied: "I mean, I was upset, you know, sad for everybody and the family members and stuff like that, but no, not really." Cookie simply wanted to earn her broadcasting certificate, begin her career, and become a famous and well-paid television host. Nothing beyond classroom essentials and daily life management gained a foothold in Cookie's consciousness. It was as if Cookie had an immunity to intellectual curiosity or creative engagement.

Some might suggest that Cookie's intellectual immunity was a function of her weak high school preparation and the technical primacy of her vocational broadcasting program. Perhaps, *if* Cookie had been better prepared as a high school student, and *if* she had attended a college where she enrolled in a wide array of courses in the traditional arts and sciences, then she *might* have been stimulated intellectually and engaged creatively. But I seriously doubt it, because neither factor—better high school preparation or classic liberal arts curricula—made much impact on the other teens I observed and interviewed. Except for a handful of teens who become the future intelligentsia, such as Rob Robertson (introduced in chapter 1), the overwhelming majority of teens I studied appeared culturally inoculated against intellectual curiosity and creative engagement. No idea or creative possibility seems capable of penetrating college-going teens' immune systems.

Still, I believe Cookie made important educational gains during her vocational program that go beyond her acquisition of technical broadcasting knowledge. I could not help but observe that Cookie, during our second interview, used longer and more elaborate sentences, described her points more clearly, provided apt examples to illustrate her points, and spoke far more comfortably adult-to-adult. Indeed, the number of unique words Cookie employed during the second interview increased by 9.7 percent over the first interview. Some of this can be attributed to simple maturation, but more of it, I suggest, fits with the cognitive and communication skills required in any classroom. That is, for Cookie to gain and demonstrate a technical understanding of broadcasting, she had to use cognitive and communicative skills. Her instructors sought to teach broadcasting, but Cookie's need to regularly demonstrate that knowledge served to sharpen her cognitive and communication skills. Though Cookie may have been inoculated against intellectual curiosity or creative engagement, her improved cognitive and communicative skills were an important—if latent— educational accomplishment.

In the long run, Cookie's improved cognitive and communication skills may be more valuable than her acquisition of technical broadcasting skills and knowledge. The former are useful in any context (including interviews), while the latter are context-specific and subject to change. Or, to use different example, much of the factual knowledge of sociology I sought to teach in my classes a decade ago is now dated and under revision, but the cognitive skills, data skills, and communication skills that my former students developed in the process of understanding and applying that knowledge remain useful. The pace of technical innovation in broadcasting has surely made Cookie's formal training obsolete, but Cookie's sharpened cognitive and communicative skills, when combined with her drive and diligence, should ensure that she keeps pace with technical innovations during her broadcasting career.

I propose that culturally mainstream American teens are, by the end of the first year out, more similar to Cookie than dissimilar. That is, they have become cognitively sharper and more skilled in adapting to new organizations, but are largely immune to intellectual curiosity and creative engagement. Educationally, then, the glass is neither empty nor full. It is half-empty for those who want the first year out to be about intellectual curiosity and creative engagement,[1] and it is half-full for those who want the first year out to be about becoming smarter and successfully adapting to new formal organizations. In this chapter, then, I describe the educational preparation of high school seniors, the educational experiences of first-year students, and the cultural mismatch between educator hopes, student experiences, and public perceptions.

Doing so requires me to approach this chapter like a cabbie working the New York City rush hour, taking readers through the congested streets of American educational research as I follow teens through various educational systems. In the process, I will guide readers through a couple of debates and past gargantuan research edifices and will hopefully deliver readers to a fuller understanding of the educational lives of American teens during the first year out. Some of what we will pass by is encouraging, and some is disturbing. Readers will see that the education of American teens is not simply about the accumulation of human capital, it is not simply about widespread exploration and identity-formation, and it is not simply about reproducing U.S. social classes—as various theorists allege.[2] While teens make observable cognitive gains, obtain useful credentials, and adapt to new formal organizations, the overwhelming majority of teens remain *under*whelmed by their education and view education as little more than a hurdle on the path to adulthood. Though such findings are hardly new, they have not been sufficiently absorbed by educators, nor have they been interpreted through the cultural lens I employ here.

Many readers, moreover, may be surprised by the sorts of teens who appear among that teen minority which does approach education as an opportunity to thoughtfully explore, create, analyze, or reinterpret. There are not only teens who aspire to become the next generation of professors and allied professionals, but also many teens with strong commitments to religion. I argue that the more removed teens are from popular American moral culture, the less they use the identity lockbox and the more they avail themselves of educational opportunities. Let me start this journey, then, at the beginning of the first year out, the educational preparation of teens in American high schools.

HIGH SCHOOL PREPARATION

All I wanted to do was sit in the back of class and observe, but it just never happened. Every time I observed a class at NJ High, whether English, social studies, science, or wood shop, the teacher would spend more time talking to me than to the students. So the students would talk to each other, make halfhearted attempts to complete the busywork du jour, ask tangential questions to delay and distract the teacher, and do whatever else they could to ensure the least possible time was spent on the course subject matter and the most possible time was spent goofing around. The teachers would explain how they use projects or worksheets because the students liked "active learning" or "group work," then quickly move to venting about the students, the administration, the school, or Suburban Township. Teachers would complain about "kids with ADHD [attention deficit hyperactivity disorder]" placed into their classroom under the rubric of "inclusion" whom they had to manage with no training and no support. They would complain about parents who did not respond to teacher efforts to reach them or, worse, parents who complained to the principal about how the teacher handled a poorly behaved student. Teachers would grumble about the principal who "should have been a cop," and who ran the school "like a [juvenile] detention center." They would complain about the declining academic skills of kids enrolling at NJ High and attribute that to the declining quality (i.e., social class) of Suburban Township. All of this was offered as a foundation for each teacher's main points: you cannot require much from these students, and teachers do the best they can "with what we have."

Perhaps, I thought, this was unique to NJ High. Surely "better" school districts or private schools would have students spending more time on task and teachers requiring more work from their students. And to a degree, this is true. At "better" school districts, which simply mean school districts that contain more homogeneously affluent families, I found students to be relatively more willing to remain on task and teachers relatively more willing to challenge students. But it is a *relative* difference; the primary pattern of teachers content to keep students busy, and students content with less than challenging classes, remains evident. In fact, a 2005 national survey of 10,387 teenagers ages 16–18 by the National Governor's Association found two out of five students characterized high school as "somewhat easy" or "very easy," and just one out of ten characterized high school as "very hard." This survey also found two out of three students agreed with the statement,

"I would work harder if high school offered more demanding and interesting courses."[3] Though NJ High may be unique in some ways, the low expectations many of its teachers held for students and the low expectations many of its students held for classes were not among its distinctions.[4]

"I think senior year is kinda pointless." That was the verdict of Moesha Anderson, a student who earned A's in her honors and advanced placement (AP) courses at NJ High, and whose efforts garnered her a sizable merit scholarship to college. By the end of her senior year, Moesha just went through the motions of being a good student, because she was "tired of" school and had "stopped caring" about her classes. Kristi Kramer (introduced in chapter 1) similarly complained that she was "completely bored with school," because it was "just too much busywork." Kristi described her classes with characteristic bluntness: "They suck." Eric Strauss, though a generally optimistic white, middle-class senior, became uncharacteristically cynical: "It's kind of busywork—give us something to do so that the teachers can grade it and say that they did work." Stuart Jones, another white, middle-class senior, believed the problem was with the "whole system" of high school, because its teachers and administrators just do not understand "how to teach kids." Dennis Jackson, a black, working-class senior at NJ High, took a different approach to the busywork: "You just have to learn to enjoy yourself. The teacher's going to give you work, regardless. It's just how you take the work, you know. It's the classes; you have to make the classes fun, by [adding] a little more excitement." So Dennis, an athlete, got through his classes just like he got though his coach's drills: comply with the demands but make the time pass quickly by joking around with other students and the teacher/coach. Although a few seniors enrolled at private preparatory schools spoke of their classes as challenging and generally interesting, and those taking AP courses described courses that were difficult, the majority of culturally mainstream teens in my sample found American high school to be educationally underwhelming.[5]

TEACHER-COWBOYS

Colleges and universities often refer to their faculty as "teacher-scholars"— that is, as highly educated professionals who combine a commitment to teaching with a commitment to ongoing scholarship. It is a good phrase and represents a goal that many professors endorse, though hearing it less often out of administrators' mouths would do much to preserve faculty endorsement of it. High school teachers are not scholars, however. They are individuals whose primary orientation is to teaching a particular field of study. The term *teacher* does not, however, adequately describe the daily responsibilities and obligations of the dozens of high school teachers I observed. So much of a high school teacher's time is devoted to matters not related to the curriculum that the term *teacher* needs to be augmented.

A high school teacher must establish control, keep order, and maintain school policies. This is not a one-time project, but an ongoing activity, during each class, day, week, and term. This aspect of their work struck me as highly similar to cowboys herding cattle; the cattle must be safely contained in a designated space and kept from becoming rambunctious. Similarly, teacher-cowboys must ensure that students enter their classrooms, stay in their classrooms, and remain in their places. Teacher-cowboys must identify missing students, authorize student excursions to the nurse or bathroom, receive latecomers, and handle sundry but always urgent requests from the "main office." Teacher-cowboys must also prevent their students from doing anything harmful to themselves or each other. And finally, teacher-cowboys must keep students busy (or at least looking busy), with books open or projects in progress, lest the class spin out of control. It is as if the teacher-cowboy's mantra were, "Keep 'em corralled and keep 'em busy." Only after these basic requirements are met, can real teaching—by which I mean introduction of new topics and engagement with course materials—begin. For classes of unmotivated students, there is rarely time for real teaching. For classes of motivated students, real teaching can occur regularly. Intrinsically motivated students are rare, however, and teacher-cowboys compete for assignments to classes with such students. Marginally motivated and unmotivated students are legion, and their abundance leaves many teacher-cowboys resigned to their duties and half-heartedly hoping, as many teachers told me, "that something is getting through."

LIKING HIGH SCHOOL

Surprisingly, most teens will say that they "like" high school, and that they look forward to returning to high school by the end of their summer break. To adult listeners, it is tempting to conclude that this means teens enjoy learning and attending their classes, and teens seem pleased to leave their statements ambiguous. But enjoying classes and learning is not what teens mean at all—such activities are tolerated at best, even among the future intelligentsia (see below). What teens mean by liking school is that they enjoy spending time with peers in a relatively undemanding and comfortable environment for seven hours each day, and they appreciate the opportunities that school provides to participate in sports, performing arts, or special events like the prom.

Ken Drake, a white, middle-class senior, answered my question about liking school this way: "Yeah, I like it—it's a good time to be with friends." Eliza Cheroff, another white, middle-class senior, answered similarly: "This year I kind of like it, because I don't really do anything in my classes. It's more just about the social aspects this year." Both Ken and Eliza were college-bound seniors with promising futures, and neither was destined to be filling orders at a drive-up window. Ken and Eliza simply recognized that, given the minimal effort necessary to complete a high school degree sufficiently well to gain admittance to a four-year college, there is much to like about high school. It certainly beats working, or even staying home being bored. "I'd say I like it, because I am the type of person that needs to always be doing something, and if it wasn't for school I'd be sitting around doing nothing all day." Those are the words of Dwight Stevens, a white, working-class senior, but his sentiments are common. On the one hand, I applaud Dwight's honesty and self-awareness, both signs of emotional intelligence, a valuable characteristic.[6] On the other hand, I believe his answer reveals a stunning absence of creativity and initiative, fostered perhaps by a dozen years of passively receiving a bland public education. Could not Dwight imagine *any* productive or engaging activity that he could pursue if he was not compelled to attend school? Does he possess no interest, hobby, or concern about which he is passionate, about which he would love to learn more and get involved in more? For all the educational rhetoric (mission statements and what not) about schools developing "a love of learning" in their students,[7] American schools have an abysmal record in actually accomplishing this. Even exceptional students who do possess a love of learning do not attribute that love to their schooling.

THE FUTURE INTELLIGENTSIA

Precious few teens possess a love of learning or a breadth of perspective on the world and their place in it. Rob Robertson was the best example of such a teen that I met. I found two others who also qualified. One was Moesha Anderson (introduced in chapter 2), who planned to become a public interest lawyer, and the other was Amy Lawson, a white, middle-class senior, who planned to become a social worker and, eventually, a professor of social work or public policy. Note that Rob, Moesha, and Amy planned careers in fields that value progressive education and intellectual engagement. They represent the future intelligentsia, not American teens at large. Perhaps their breadth of perspective was fostered by their broad involvement in school sports, academic clubs, student government, and church youth groups. Perhaps their love of learning was also nurtured by having parents with graduate degrees, professionally educated aunts and uncles, and college-educated grandparents. Whatever its source, all three had well-informed political views and thoughtful answers about justice, poverty, and racism. All three also seemed particularly comfortable talking to me as high school seniors—speaking with the confidence and maturity that does not come, for other teens, until the end of the first year out.

Rob, Moesha, and Amy's schooling was, to be sure, an important place wherein they expressed their breadth of perspective and found support from teachers for their love of learning. But school was neither the source of their breadth of perspective nor their love of learning. I suggest the source of their breadth and intellectual curiosity lay in the dynamic interplay of their family's nurturance and their individual personalities (as their siblings did not possess the same love of learning). Three cases are insufficient, of course, for conclusions about sources of intellectual breadth or curiosity. But one possible source of intellectual breadth or curiosity that can clearly be ruled out is high school itself. Teachers may be able to lead students to intellectual waters, but they cannot make them drink. Rob, Moesha, and Amy came to school thirsty; their peers did not. School provides drinking water—but it does not create thirst.

A CULTURE OF NONCHALANCE, A CULTURE OF "COOL"?

Some high school seniors take their future plans seriously; they learn about occupational fields, take career interest inventories, talk with parents, teachers, and other adults about their plans, and enroll in high school courses or programs that will best prepare them for their futures. Some of these teens choose vo-tech fields, that is, skilled trades, and they enroll in specialized programs at vocational and technical high schools. Others plan careers that require graduate or professional degrees; these include future engineers, lawyers, scientists, and physicians. At NJ High, however, most high school seniors demonstrated little concern about career planning. Beyond engaging in the status competition of college applications and admissions, they gave only cursory attention to fields of study and long-range plans and projected an attitude of nonchalance—an air of "coolness"—about all such matters. Sounding like breezy teen celebrities being interviewed about their success—"Oh, I just focused on having fun with my music, and everything just fell into place"—NJ High teens adopted a discourse that was similarly nonchalant and wholly likely to take them nowhere.

Steve Moeller, a pleasure seeker at NJ High, exemplified this teen nonchalance. Steve's plan for the future was "the winning-the-lottery plan." If that were to happen, Steve reported, "it would be great." As for "other plans," the ones "where I plan to work and, you know, make money like that—I don't know. I've been really lazy. I'm just hoping I can live up to my goals or whatever." Steve's "goals" were not particularly high, and he should have little trouble meeting his goal "to work as little as possible." Teen nonchalance was not restricted to pleasure seekers, however. Joann McBride, a white, upper-middle-class senior, described her future as if she was watching a television miniseries. She was "curious to see" where she would "end up" in the future: "I'm ready to go to college, but I don't know what I'm going to do once I get there. And I don't know what I'm going to do, like, from that point. So I'm kind of curious to see where I'm going to end up." Okapi Ahmed, a black, working-class, high school senior, knew he needed a plan for the future, but had not identified it: "I don't have a mission, like, an objective yet. I'm just moving, just like leaves in the wind." Okapi seemed to think his "objective" would become apparent to him at some point in college. But given the educational disappointment of most freshmen (see below), his objective was not any clearer at the end of his first year out. Paul Stephens, a white, upper-middle-class senior, had "no clue" about his future plans, but hoped it included a "nice" suburban home and family: "As far as my future goes—I have *no clue*! You know, everybody has those dreams, white picket fence, that kind of thing. That would be nice, I guess." Paul, Steve, Joann, and Okapi all wanted their futures to include a comfortable standard of living, marriage, and parenthood. But because these teens had adopted a discourse of nonchalance, they resisted developing plans that would guide them toward achieving such goals. It is not that teachers or parents fail to guide teens sufficiently, as sociologists Schneider and Stevenson suggest, but rather that teens construct and maintain a screen of nonchalance that deflects messages they do not wish to hear. So long as this screen is in place, it makes little difference what efforts parents or teachers put forth to nurture and guide teens.

ATTAINABLE HIGH SCHOOL GOALS

Though some might use the foregoing report of educationally under-whelmed and nonchalant high school seniors to conclude that American high schools are a complete failure, I do not take that route. High schools need to have goals to give direction to their curricula, programs, and plans, even if they do not fully achieve them. The question is, rather, *which* goals foster the best education for the *largest proportion* of students. Should schools have as their chief goal the inculcation of a love of learning when schools have not, and likely cannot, accomplish this? Might it not be more effective to orient schools toward identifying and developing the preexisting inter-ests of students, helping students apply cognitive and communicative skills to those interests, and assisting students in connecting those interests to established and emerging fields of inquiry? The National Governors Asso-ciation's Rate Your Future survey (cited above) reports that seven out of ten high school seniors believe "taking courses related to the kinds of jobs they want is the best way to make their senior year more meaningful." I believe the process of schooling inevitably hones cognitive skills and communica-tion ability (as it did with Cookie), because teachers require students to use these skills to demonstrate learning of various bodies of knowledge (even though knowledge retention is short-term). But I believe a far more benefi-cial starting point is student interests, not progressive educators' ideals.

EDUCATION AND THE FIRST YEAR OUT

Teens express specific hopes about their education following high school graduation. The baseline expectation, as Jabari Campbell, a black, working-class senior put it, is "to gain a good education and stuff that I can use after college." Eric Strauss was more specific. He hoped for an end to "busywork," so that any course-related "work that I do will have some kind of meaning and bring some kind of understanding to what it is that I'm studying." At-tending college, however, is connected to American folklore. "'The greatest four years of your life,'—I just hope that's true," said Tammy Biggs, a white, working-class senior from NJ High. Or as another white, upper-middle-class teen, Keith LeCourtier, put it: "I want it to be memorable; everybody always talks about 'Oh, back in college . . . ,' and that's what I want to be able to do." Many of these expectations refer to college life in general rather than to col-lege's educational component. But gaining an education and identifying a field of interest are wrapped up in teen expectations. Megan Morici (introduced in chapter 2) combined social, educational, and career expectations into her hopes for college: "I hope I meet a lot of people, have good classes, and I hope I decide on something I want to do, that I *really* like and can get into and am interested in. Something that I'll want to spend the rest of my life doing." Megan, like virtually every other college-bound teen, had practical, career-related hopes about her college education. She hoped that college would offer interesting and relevant classes and present a refreshing change from the uninteresting and irrelevant classes of high school. This hope is, unfortunately, the opposite of what Megan and her peers most likely experienced in their college courses. Megan's and her peers' practical and careerist expectations could not be more mismatched with most colleges' expectations for their freshmen.

EXPECTATIONS AND REALITY

First, the good news: teens are happy to discover that college classes have much less busywork than their high school classes. In fact, many freshmen have no assignments or examinations until halfway through their courses, giving them additional time to navigate relationships, manage gratifications, and adapt their leisure, work, and money patterns. Teens also report that they are impressed by the intelligence and knowledge of their professors: these teacher-scholars represent a striking contrast from the teacher-cowboys they knew in high school. And teens are pleased with fewer class hours and with their new freedom to decide whether even to attend class, arrive late or leave early, eat or drink in class, or simply go to the bathroom without asking permission. All of this adds up to "being treated like an adult," and teens appreciate it.

Now for the bad news: many freshmen find themselves seated in large lecture halls, taught by graduate students and adjunct faculty as often as full-time faculty, and anonymous to the instructor. Compounding matters, instructors typically subscribe to a set of educational goals that are wholly out of step with student interests. These goals often include developing intellectual breadth and curiosity, critiquing various elements of traditional (read: middle-class, familial, and religious) socialization, challenging popular assumptions and norms, and approaching coursework with the same seriousness and perspective as the instructor. Eric Strauss, for example, complained that one professor was:

Not at all understanding about student problems and concerns. . . . If you missed class, he didn't like you 'cause you were "giving up." If you "didn't care about his class," then you "didn't care about academics." He . . . came at it with the attitude that "my class and your academics are the most important things in the world right now." And even if you have family members dying, even if you're sick, it doesn't matter. . . . It made me feel like, you know, he didn't care about the students. All he cared about were the numbers, which bothered me a lot.

Andre Kendall, a black, working-class teen from NJ High, went to talk to one difficult professor. Andre asked his history professor to focus more on the course content and tell fewer stories about his own college and life experiences. "He was talking about himself most of the time during the class. He was always telling us how he wrote twenty-two books, and just all his self-accomplishments. But he never got to the point of history. So it was like, we'd leave class knowing more about him than the history book." But talking did not help, because "he thought that he was doing good." What Andre, Eric, and many other teens discovered was that their college instructors and their college courses were even more irrelevant to "real life" than were their high school teachers or high school courses. In fact, a national survey of college freshmen found fewer than 15 percent were "very satisfied" with the "relevance of coursework to their future career plans" and only 7 percent were "very satisfied" with the "relevance of coursework to everyday life."[8] The primary exception to this occurs among teens who pursued vocational or professional fields; they see that their courses are relevant, just not as interesting as they had hoped.

Amazingly, the irrelevancy of, and boredom with, most college courses does not become a source of great disappointment for most teens. I suggest teens are not very disappointed for several reasons. First, attending irrelevant classes is educationally continuous with high school; though teens hope for something different at college, they are not shocked when the familiar pattern carries over. Second, first-year students accept the necessity of completing their college's core or general education requirements and expect upper-level courses in their major to be more relevant. Third, most teens are too caught up in daily life management to care very much; with so many relationships to navigate, gratifications to manage, and economic expectations to fulfill (see chapters 3 and 4), teens are happy to "just get done with" classes they view as irrelevant and impractical.

Some teens did voice disappointment about their educational experiences during the first year out. I heard this from several students attending community college. "It's thirteenth grade!" Steve Moeller, a freshman who barely graduated from NJ High, exclaimed in frustration. By that, Steve meant that he saw the same students from high school, took the same courses in history, math, English, and writing, and even discovered one of his high school teachers moonlighting as a community college instructor. Christine Darden, a white, working-class teen, hoped that college would be "just like high school." Her plan was to become a teacher, starting first at the community college ("to save money"), then transferring to complete her degree. But the presence of high school classmates only made her experience worse, as these were classmates Christine would have "rather forgotten about." Christine thought community college "would be a lot harder than it was" and stopped attending classes, except for exams, halfway through. Except in one course, Christine still finished with all A's (thus confirming that her classes were not challenging). Christine "just didn't like" college and switched to a vocational photography school. Though not all community college students were as dissatisfied as Christine, only Kristi Kramer expressed enthusiasm for her courses. For most community college students, disengaged tolerance is the best summary of their feelings toward class.

Among teens attending four-year colleges, there was a wider spectrum of reactions. Some freshmen described instructors that they really enjoyed. These instructors were funny, caring, "really good at explaining things," and "made the course interesting." Descriptions of good instructors always preceded descriptions, if any, of course subjects or fields of study. The upside of this is that freshmen are open to learning about fields of study when those fields are presented to them in an engaging way. The downside is that freshmen seem easily swayed and may make decisions about fields of study based primarily on the charisma of a good instructor or two, with little thought given to their long-term interests.

Other freshmen grew cynical about the whole system of higher education. Bob Kohl, a white, upper-middle-class, residential college freshman, was unimpressed with his "Public Ivy" college courses:

> It really isn't much different than high school, other than my professors are like doctors instead of just like regular people. . . . It's just like going to a high school class. You sit down, you listen to them lecture, and that's about it. I mean, it's really boring. . . . I hate learning; I hate sitting

in classes and everything. I just do it for grades. . . . I've never had a class where I was really interested and into it. I just . . . did the work so I could get an "A" pretty much.

Barb Miscoski (from chapter 3) entered college ready for "a challenge" and eager to learn. She discovered instead that her classes were not demanding and that she was stuck taking "classes that I'm never going to use." To make matters worse, Barb was accumulating significant debt for the privilege of doing this: "It's incredibly expensive. And I'm like, what am I paying for? At home, I could learn this stuff out of the book!" But self-taught persons do not possess college credentials, and Barb "needs this degree" to become a certified teacher of the deaf, so she resigned herself to accumulating school debt and less-than-stimulating coursework. Perhaps Barb and Bob are exceptions and students elsewhere enjoy the challenge of their classes and dedicate themselves to mastering the course materials. But results from the National Survey of Student Engagement do not bear this possibility out. This survey reports that two out of three college students do not study even one hour weekly for every hour they spend in class. (Once upon a time, college students were told to plan three hours of study time for every hour they spent in class.) The *Your First College Year Survey* similarly reports 68 percent of freshmen studied or did homework less than ten hours per week.[9] Even at the highest ranked research universities, most full-time students attend class *and study* less than thirty-two hours per week.[10] Being a full-time college student, then, is a terrific part-time activity, freeing its privileged holders to focus intensely on daily life management.

ON GRADES AND GAMES

How do college students manage to remain in good academic standing while spending so little time preparing for class? The immediate answer is twofold. First, grade inflation is rampant at virtually every college and university in the United States. At Princeton University, for example, the problem was so severe (with one-half of students receiving "A" grades) that the faculty adopted voluntary standards to keep the percentage of A, A+, and A– grades below 35 percent. Across the nation, students can be confident that as long as they perform on par with their classmates, their "average" performance will garner them a B+.[11] That means grades of B or lower signify "below average" performance, and grades of C, which once signified "average" or "satisfactory," are now routinely awarded for "poor" or even "failing" academic performances. This may explain why fewer than one out of three college graduates obtained a "proficient" score on the 2003 National Assessment of Adult Literacy of the U.S. Department of Education.[12] It may also explain why some question whether college is really worth its high and rising cost.[13]

The second way college students remain in good academic standing while spending little time preparing for classes involves developing skills in playing "the game of college." The game of college, students tell me, involves, first and foremost, choosing the right instructor. To help with this all-important choice, students can consult numerous Web sites featuring anonymous evaluations of instructors, some of which use the Freedom of Information Act to obtain instructor grading distributions, so students can avoid the few tough graders who remain.[14] After choosing the right instructor, students must next find out "what the instructor wants." This involves talking to past students and often obtaining from them copies of past exams and papers. Studies show that as many as 70 percent of college students admit to cheating on exams, papers, and other course projects.[15] College students defend this by pointing out how "professors cheat" too—in that they make no effort to update their classes, give the same exams each year, and require the same assignments, practically inviting students to choose the "easy way out." The remaining rules of this game involve telling instructors exactly what they want to hear (regurgitating the instructors' own views), learning one topic well enough to write or discuss it intelligently, going to office hours for "a little face time," and, in smaller classes or discussion groups, appearing to pay attention and participating once each class.[16] And if the reports of some observers are accurate, teens from upscale suburban districts enter college with several years of experience playing a similar game during high school.[17]

THE PRACTICAL CREDENTIALISTS

To purists, that is, to present and future members of the American intelligentsia, it can be disconcerting to confront the twin realities of professors' grade inflation and students' game of college. It can be so disconcerting, in fact, that purists will leap to defend the status quo. They will argue, for example, that they teach (and thus grade) "to mastery," that intellectual life is alive and well among *their* students, or that "just last week" they witnessed an entire class engaged in a thoughtful, intellectual discussion. Perhaps, in specific and limited cases, such arguments can be sustained. But given the evidence cited above, neither grade inflation nor student strategies to minimize academic effort can be denied on a national scale.

From a macrohistorical perspective, such phenomena are the natural consequences of the overexpansion of American higher education since the 1950s, the flood of college graduates into the marketplace, and the corresponding escalation of degree requirements for more desirable jobs. Jobs that once required only a high school diploma now require a college degree, while those that required a college degree now require a graduate degree. Retention of college course content is, often, of little import for the performance of most jobs; the general cognitive and communicative skills that college graduates acquire, combined with on-the-job training, are sufficient for most jobs that require a college degree. Though some occupations have become more complex, more of the increase in demand for college degrees can be attributed to the declining value of a high school education and the preservation of occupational statuses. Completing a bachelor's degree does provide an economic benefit relative to those with only high school diplomas (about a 55–59 percent median salary margin), but the benefit is both higher and rising among those with graduate degrees (about 107–119 percent median salary margin).[18]

College freshmen understand little of the foregoing, of course. They just know that there are no good jobs for those without college degrees, that good jobs require bachelor's degrees, and that the best jobs require graduate degrees. Thus, they have enrolled in college to better, as founding sociologist Max Weber put it, "their life chances." The overwhelming majority of college freshmen are, then, *practical credentialists*, not future intelligentsia. It is as if college freshmen have taken the famous campaign motto of President Clinton, "It's the economy, stupid," and adapted it to become "It's the degree, stupid." As Lowanda Smith (from chapter 1) put it succinctly: "All I want to do is to graduate with a diploma. I'm not looking for one of those gold strings around my neck. I'm just looking to graduate." Grades matter to freshmen with higher aspirations, however. Not because they signify mastery of a field of study that is intrinsically interesting, but because freshmen believe grades matter to graduate schools and employers. And to highly competitive graduate schools and employers, grades do matter—but to most graduate schools and most employers, they matter far less than undergraduates would ever imagine. Mona Segall, a white, upper-middle-class, residential college freshman, wanted to attend a top-tier graduate school: "I just want to have good grades so that when I go to graduate school I can have the pick of the litter." Mona's graduate degree would then help her obtain a job "in the medical field," where she would be able to "move up . . . , make enough [money] . . . , and be happy."

That we now have a generation of practical credentialists should not surprise anyone who was listening to sociologist Randall Collins in 1979. He concluded, in his widely cited but little absorbed book *The Credential Society*,

> Students electing to remain within the system have adopted the goal of high grades, irrespective of content and by any means whatsoever, producing an inflation in college grades, while at the same time achievement levels have been steadily dropping. . . . The reasons for going to school are extraneous to whatever goes on in the classroom. Reformers expecting that intellectual curiosity can be rearoused by curricular reforms or by changes in the school authority structure were projecting their own intellectual interests onto a mass of students for whom education is merely a means to a nonintellectual end.[19]

My findings, of a predominantly careerist orientation among students, are consistent with a steady stream of research and observation[20] and confirm Collins's projections of three decades ago. I diverge from Collins on one matter only—his contention "that job skills of all sorts are actually acquired in the work situation rather than in a formal training institution." While I concur that this is generally true, I argue that the cognitive and communicative gains I observed among teens (such as Cookie) are a real, if latent, function of their formal, post–high school education. To borrow a saying I often heard from teens describing older, but operable, cars, "It may not be much, but it's *something*." Higher education's obese "emperor" may not be naked, but he blusters an awful lot for someone wearing only underwear.

COGNITIVE SHARPENING

Just one year after high school graduation, the difference in teens is obvious. High school seniors who talked in phrases or clipped sentences, as college students now talk in full sentences, even paragraphs. Seniors who stumbled and skipped over more challenging questions, as college students now answer and explain themselves. Seniors who seemed awkward and embarrassed by more personal questions, as college students now look me in the eye, speak directly, and talk at length. Some of this is maturity, to be sure, and some of this is familiarity with the interviewing process. But these factors are not sufficient explanations for the thoughtful explanations, apt examples, and intellectual confidence that teens demonstrate at the end of the first year out. Successfully transitioning to a new, and often more challenging, educational environment requires students to use cognitive and communicative skills regularly. Two examples will need to suffice.

Julie Gillmore, a white, middle-class teen, was heavily involved at her semirural public high school. A member of the National Honor Society, a student council representative, captain of her varsity lacrosse team, and a summer camp counselor, Julie was a bright young woman with leadership experience. And yet, when I first interviewed Julie and asked her, as part of a series of questions about gender-related issues, "What does it mean to be a woman?" she stammered:

> JULIE: Uh, I don't know. (*Giggles, then pauses.*) Can I skip that?
> INTERVIEWER: OK. Then, how is being a woman different than being a man?
> JULIE: I don't know, I've never been a man, so. . . . (*Giggles.*) You can have children! (*Laughs.*)

A year later, Julie had a lot to say:

> JULIE: I think that you have to be willing to be challenged. I just think that, you know how everyone's always, like, arguing about men and women and salaries and all—like the whole controversy thing?
> INTERVIEWER: Yes.
> JULIE: But now I feel like it's equal. Like women have high positions in companies, and they have high paying jobs, and they do everything men do. And men do everything women do except have kids. (*Laughs.*). . . I think being a woman you should be, I don't know, well-rounded and be different things. Like fix a car and then go out to dinner all dressed up.
> INTERVIEWER: And how is being a man different from being a woman?
> JULIE: (*Pause.*) I think that maybe men have less. . . . Like society has less expectations for men. Like with housework, for instance, women are basically seen as the person who cleans and cooks and stuff like that, so I think that men have less expectations to live up to.

Julie did not turn into a philosopher. She still sounded like many teens who sprinkle their opinions with qualifications. But she also had something she was trying to say, she supported her claims with evidence, and she showed that she had considered this issue previously.[21] Whereas during the first interview Julie passed on the opportunity to answer this question, at the end of her first year out Julie had the intellectual confidence and the interpersonal poise to tackle it.

Reggie Kraft, a black, middle-class teen, played football for a private preparatory high school and focused all his free time on football—from his own team, to attending games at Flagship University, to watching professional football. Perhaps the most difficult question I asked in my interviews was "What would you say is the meaning, or purpose, of life?" Reggie, like many other high school seniors, struggled to give a coherent answer. "The meaning of life comes by different people and different aspects, but my meaning of life? Probably be, like, to take time and education and wisely . . . pursue what I have to. But other people could have different thoughts on it." A year later, Reggie offered a more direct answer to the question and spoke with more conviction and confidence. "The meaning of life? [Pauses.] The meaning of life . . . is trying to get the most out of it. Like doing what is necessary and learning as much as you can and trying to just be happy. I think that's what life should be about. I mean, getting the most out of it. . . . Being happy and not losing self while doing it." This second answer is not particularly novel, but it is a popular answer and one that Reggie offered without the qualifications that bracketed his first answer. While his first answer has little coherence, his second answer is coherent, it is consistent with American individualism, and it is linked to other ideals he expressed during the second interview.[22]

Reggie, Julie, and Cookie will retain little of the knowledge they processed during their first year out.[23] And intellectual curiosity is not a value that they or most American teens esteem. Yet I would argue that Reggie, Julie, and Cookie did benefit educationally during the first year out. Their improved cognitive and communication skills may not have been the primary goal of their instructors, but their improved skill in these areas should benefit them for the remainder of their educational programs and transfer to their careers thereafter. Thus, I do not conclude, as some do,[24] that education simply certifies the existing social class system. College graduates *have* developed their cognitive skills and communicative abilities more than those outside of educational institutions and thus possess more marketable work skills.

The larger issue, then, is why colleges orient entire curricula around the ideal of developing intellectual curiosity and breadth of perspective, when incoming freshmen are distracted by daily life management and quite immune to intellectual engagement. Why do colleges not pursue ideals that are more likely to garner the endorsement of broader constituencies and more likely to be achieved by most students? At my own institution, faculty were eager to create and teach a newly required seminar designed to intellectually challenge incoming freshmen with scholarly matters and diverse perspectives, only to discover this seminar produced little academic engagement, frequent intellectual regurgitation, and pockets of outright student hostility. We would have done far better had we delivered the kinds of practical but challenging courses that incoming freshmen seek and sought simply to whet freshmen appetites for deeper and broader matters.

Faculty at elite universities and colleges may believe, because a larger proportion of the future intelligentsia attends their schools, that they should preserve elite, progressive ideals. But I contend that even elite universities contain far more practical credentialists than future intelligentsia and that the former learn to become adept at appearing intellectually curious in order to accomplish their practical ends. I recall an intense, intellectually engaged debate in an undergraduate seminar I observed at Princeton University. After class, as the sparring parties descended the staircase, they high-fived each other and said, "Nice bullshitting!" These Ivy League undergraduates had become conversant in intellectual matters and macrohistorical paradigms. But it was technical, Machiavellian knowledge, not deep knowledge that comes from the mind *and* heart. Had these undergraduates gained an education that was oriented less toward intellectual elitism and more toward humility and humanity, perhaps they might have genuinely valued the larger good their university so esteems, rather than bandied about such language to serve their selfish ambitions. In fact, I found it was not Ivy League students but strongly religious teens enrolled at residential, religious colleges who were most likely to express humility and the desire to serve humanity, and who were most likely to be intellectually engaged and receptive to broader perspectives on the world and their place in it (see discussion below).

COLLEGE'S NET EFFECTS?

Perhaps college students become interested in intellectual life and broader perspectives after the first year out, after they master daily life management. Because intellectual engagement requires openness to identity work, college juniors and seniors should possess the confidence and may possess the will to open and evaluate the contents of their identity lockboxes. A few professors have told me that some college seniors who enrolled in broad, introductory courses "got a lot more out of the course" than the freshmen did. If this is true, and not a function of seniors simply being more skilled players of the game of college, then it suggests that upper-level college students may actually be more open to broader and forward-looking intellectual engagement than incoming freshmen. I note, however, that everyday patterns and social behaviors are deeply habitual and that few students appear to make significant individual changes once they settle into their educational environment. Perhaps a future investigation will uncover when and to what extent upper-level college students are open to intellectual engagement or broader perspectives on the past, present, and future. But my evidence offers little basis for such hope.

There is also scant evidence for such a hope in the voluminous publications of UCLA's Higher Education Research Institute (HERI) and its prolific director, Alexander W. Astin. That is not the first impression these publications present, however. In the reports *Four Critical Years*; *What Matters in College? Four Critical Years Revisited*; and "How the Liberal Arts College Affects Students," readers will find an array of interesting analyses, all interpreted to "accentuate the positive." For example, Astin writes, "Undergraduates demonstrate a number of substantial changes in beliefs and attitudes during the college years. The largest positive changes are in feminism, commitment to participating in programs to clean up the environment, promoting racial understanding, developing a meaningful philosophy of life, and support for legal abortion."[25] Elsewhere, Astin presents a college student typology that labels 37 percent of college freshmen as "scholars," which then expands to 40 percent by the time these students become seniors.[26] But readers may be unaware that Astin and HERI are funded to a substantial degree by conducting educational analyses for hundreds of colleges and universities and by selling their own analyses to a higher education readership—so they know exactly how to frame their analyses. A closer reading of Astin's tables reveals the top life goal of college seniors is "raising a family" (72 percent) and the second is "being very well off financially" (62 percent); far fewer students, for example, wish to "promote racial understanding" (39 percent) or become "involved in programs to clean up the environment" (35 percent).[27] A closer reading also reveals that Astin's "scholars" are just students who rated themselves "above average" or "top 10 percent" in "academic ability," "intellectual self-confidence," and "mathematical ability" and who hope to earn a graduate degree. In other words, Astin's "scholars" are simply *studious* practical credentialists who plan to attend graduate school. Applying the term "scholars" to students for whom Astin can give no evidence of intellectual curiosity or breadth of perspective is quite misleading. In fact, despite receiving four years of a college education that proclaims the value of intellectual curiosity and breadth of perspective,[28] one out of two college seniors in Astin's survey still agree that "the chief benefit of a college education is that it increases one's earning power."[29]

Sociologists Mary Jackman and Michael Muha demonstrate, in their study of college-educated survey-takers, that receiving a college education does little to broaden college graduates—it simply cues graduates to the "right" answers about race, poverty, inequality, education, and the like.[30] There is a small but deeply committed minority of college students, to be sure, who view matters of racial, economic, and environmental inequality with utmost seriousness. But most college students do not view these matters as actual priorities, including a large portion of students who say they are important.[31] If even half of the 35–39 percent of college graduates who regularly pledge in Astin's surveys to become involved in promoting "racial understanding" or working with "programs to clean up the environment" actually did so, the United States would have measurably better race relations and cleaner air, water, and soil than it does presently.

Rather than liberalizing college students, or even engaging them intellectually, the primary effect of college on students involves cognitive gains and basic knowledge acquisition. As educational psychologists Pascarella and Terenzini report in their landmark review of research on the impact of college, *How College Affects Students* and *How College Affects Students: A Third Decade of Research*, "There is more extensive and consistent evidence to support the net impact of college on learning and cognition . . . than in the areas of attitudes, values, and psychosocial characteristics."[32] My evidence, though observational, confirms Pascarella and Terenzini's conclusions about primarily cognitive gains being made by college students.

Pascarella and Terenzini further note that the limited evidence they did find of college's effects on attitudes or values showed signs of decline toward the end of the 1980s, which they suggest might be "the precursor of an important generational effect."[33] Their suggestion is based in part on the implicit assumption that the college student generation of the late 1960s was significantly affected by their college experience, while more recent generations have been less affected. Recent research reveals, however, that just one out of four college students in the 1960s participated in protests on college campuses and that most college campuses were politically inactive.[34]

Thus, contrary to popular assumptions and media portrayals, even during the heyday of the 1960s U.S. counterculture, most college students wanted nothing more from their colleges than a diploma. That a disproportionate number of current professors and college administrators were active and involved in the 1960s student counterculture (or wished they were),[35] then, suggests that what lies behind many colleges' impossibly idealistic mission statements may be nostalgia for, and overgeneralizations about, these individuals' unrepresentative college experiences.[36]

In actuality, the nonintellectual interests of college students have been documented for more than a half-century. Political scientist Philip E. Jacob's analysis of college students in the 1940s and 1950s remains hauntingly apropos: "A dominant characteristic of students in the current generation is that they are *gloriously contented* both in regard to their present day-to-day activity and their outlook for the future. . . . Only a minority seem to value their college education primarily in terms of its intellectual contribution, or its nurturing of personal character and the capacity for responsible human relationships" (emphasis in original).[37] Perhaps with the rising significance of assessment in higher education, the reality of colleges' and universities' erudite and unattainable goals will become apparent, and more realistic, widely shared, and broadly achievable goals such as cognitive development, subject retention if not mastery, and appreciation for scholarly contributions to public life will become prominent.

ON THE ROLE OF FAMILY, FAITH, AND COMMUNITY

In my two previous chapters, I closed with a discussion of the important but often limited and indirect ways that family, faith, and community affect teens during the first year out. In this chapter, however, I will describe important but also large and direct impacts of family, faith, and community on teens' educational lives during the first year out, as this corresponds to the critical role of family, faith, and community on teens' educational lives.

THE ROLE OF FAMILY

First and foremost, virtually every teen I spoke with who enrolled at a competitive, four-year residential college described parents who early on established basic ground rules about pursuing a bachelor's degree at a well-respected college or university and who had been active in that teen's post–high school planning. Often, these parents had college degrees themselves, but not always. Some were successful managers who had been promoted without a college degree, but who recognized the critical importance of a college degree in a corporate or organizational setting. Next, I learned of other parents, "too poor" to bankroll their children's college education but "too rich" to qualify for any financial assistance beyond loans, who made it clear that college costs were paramount, more important than school type or reputation. Back in the era of "need-blind" financial aid, college-going children would not have been so affected by their parents' financial status. But colleges increasingly compete against each other, which means that financial aid offices manipulate their assistance packages to recruit applicants with above average scores (and often less financial need), while applicants with average or below average scores (and often greater financial need) receive the least support.[38] As a result, teens whose parents emphasized costs typically chose fairly ordinary local colleges, with little consideration of the college's educational or extracurricular offerings.

Finally, some teens' parents left them to make their own decisions. On the one hand, this could be good in that parents did not micromanage teen decisions about fields of study or school characteristics. On the other hand, this left many of these high school seniors, who were too nonchalant to demand assistance from busy guidance counselors, relying upon the ill-informed opinions of classmates. This was most common among teens whose parents did not complete bachelor's degrees, but it also included a few teens whose parents did not pursue careers relevant to their college degrees and who therefore seemed ambivalent about the value of their college education. These teens applied to colleges for odd reasons (one told me he "just really liked" the college's mascot and logo), failed to be admitted or decided against attending (it was not always clear which happened—students are intentionally vague about such matters), and wound up "taking classes" at their local community colleges. The combination of no parental guidance with teen nonchalance left these youths unengaged with their college experience and quite distracted by the daily management of their relationships, gratifications, and economic life.

THE ROLE OF FAITH

Most teens, as I report in chapter 2, are either semi- or strongly religious. For semireligious teens, education and faith are treated as separate realms. One semireligious teen told me, "Sometimes it feels like God dropped me off at college and said, 'I'll be back to pick you up in four years.'" These teens place their religious identities into a lockbox at the start of their first year out and leave that lockbox undisturbed for the entire year. Because their religious identities are kept preserved, they report few if any cognitive shifts in these identities at the end of the first year out. There is behavioral change, however. Semireligious teens attend worship services much less often during the first year out. This is not a disavowal of their faiths; these teens just "don't have the time right now" or "couldn't find a church" they liked "out at school." The decline in attendance is also true of semireligious commuting students, but to a lesser degree. Ultimately, as adherents of popular American moral culture, these semireligious teens understand that their post–high school years are not a time for religious involvement or engagement; they are a time for navigating relationships, managing gratifications, and earning diplomas (see chapter 2).

For strongly religious teens, however, the occasional faith of semireligious teens is unacceptable. Some strongly religious teens, such as Emily Fisher, a white, upper-middle-class teen, chose to attend a religious college because "Christianity has just been a big part of my life, and so I decided to apply to a Christian college. . . . I like the fact that it was a Christian community, which was not what my environment is like at home, and I really liked the off-campus programs the college offered." Among Emily's hopes for college was "to develop my spiritual side," which would be less likely at "a secular school." Journalist Naomi Schaeffer Riley, who studied a dozen such religious colleges and universities, reports that Protestant, Catholic, Jewish, and Buddhist institutions are growing at a "breakneck pace." Riley argues that these religious colleges, which are capable of attracting "some of America's brightest and most dedicated teenagers," are producing a missionary "generation of smart, worldly, and ethical young professionals whose influence in business, medicine, law, journalism, academia, and government is only beginning to be felt."[39] Though my data are limited to the first year out, I can confirm Riley's claims that strongly religious teens enrolled at religious colleges articulate a strong desire to positively and religiously influence the world.

Strongly religious teens choose religious colleges in part because they *want* to work on their identity, including its religious dimensions. Therefore, students at these religious colleges *allow* their schools to make a deeper impact on their lives than students at nonreligious colleges. For example, Dave Olsen, a white, middle-class, residential student at an evangelical Protestant college, entered college with the goal of becoming a minister. But by the end of his first year of college, Dave reported:

DAVE: I have changed a lot of my ideas as to what I think I will be doing in the future. I have become almost more confused, kind of, as I see more options laid out in front of me. . . . Like, I have been interested in the social sciences field, such as sociology and psychology. I can see myself as more of a researcher than I could before.

INTERVIEWER: Are there other ways you've changed?

DAVE: I think I have become more secure in who I am, like understanding how I deal with people. Like, I think I have a better grasp on some of the things I do wrong. So my coarser tendencies—I am kinda learning how to deal with them.

Similar sentiments were voiced by other religious teens after a year of attending religious colleges. My findings, though among a limited pool, match results from more extensive investigations by sociologist James Hunter in the 1980s and political scientists James Penning and Corwin Smidt in the late 1990s.[40] Both studies, despite the two-decade difference in dates of data collection and some important differences in interpretation, find that evangelical colleges are quite successful at engaging their students intellectually and broadening their students' perspectives on the world and their own lives. It is striking how the very sorts of colleges assumed by many intelligentsia to be anti-intellectual and narrow, in fact produce more intellectual curiosity and breadth of perspective among their religious students than do their nonreligious counterparts.

This being said, the majority of strongly religious teens do not attend religious colleges, for various reasons. One reason is simply the sheer numbers of strongly religious, college-bound American teens compared to the limited seats at religious colleges; religious colleges can accommodate only a fraction of America's college-going, strongly religious teens.[41] Thus, most religious teens never seek an education at a religious college, because of financial or geographic restrictions, because of interest in a field of study that exists on limited campuses, or, I propose, because of no sense of contradiction between their religious activities and their educational pursuits. Fawn Sweitzer, for example, was a deeply religious Jew from a suburban New Jersey enclave of orthodox Jews. Fawn planned to attend the local community college to become a physical therapy assistant and was committed to graduating from her two-year program before she marries. "In this [Orthodox] community, the girls are not so involved in going to college. Like, we're not so independent, y'know? The girls get married very young in this community. . . . I'm sure I'll graduate from [Local] Community College. . . .

I just don't want to sit around all day and do nothing. . . . I want to at least keep myself busy with something." Attending college locally allows Fawn to remain connected to her religious community, and her course of study will fill her time until she marries. More status driven, Paul Stephens, an evangelical Protestant, was consumed by "big name" universities, and he had dreams of suburban affluence after graduation. Paul did not apply to any religious colleges, nor did he seem aware of them. What Paul did was find out which of his schools had sizable religious organizations on campus and added that factor into his college decision. Paul's top choice was Big Southern University, because it "had a beautiful campus" and a "huge Christian fellowship." Both Fawn and Paul chose a middle path between attending religious colleges and locking away their religious identities. Like those attending religious colleges, they wanted to remain religiously active during their college years, and like those using the identity lockbox, they approached college as practical credentialists. Fawn, Paul, and strongly religious teens like them seemed content to open and close their identity lockbox many times each week—keeping it closed, for example, while attending class and opening it up when within their religious circles.

Quite distinct from Emily, Dave, Fawn, and Paul are nonreligious teens. Such teens divide into two subgroups: a smaller number of *antireligious* teens and a larger number of *a*religious, semihedonist teens (see chapter 2). There are few teens who are adamantly antireligious, because such a position requires a level of intellectual engagement that few of them possess. Most common are *a*religious teens. Such teens report "no interest" in religion and sometimes explain that "no one should tell anyone" what they "should do." Such teens, such as Poppy Lopez (from chapter 1), reject religion as part of a larger resistance to social institutions in general, including education, government, and even the family. Areligious teens are practical credentialists in the extreme. They are apolitical or libertarian, often show minimal interest in their own family relationships, and are sometimes dubious about marriage and family life in general. These teens do not articulate the developed, philosophically informed arguments that antireligious teens do, because such arguments require educational engagement. Rather, they seem to rally around the Gadsden flag of the American Revolution (i.e., "Don't Tread On Me"); the key difference is that the Revolutionary soldiers who rallied around that flag were willing to sacrifice for their country, while these teens just want to keep the party going.

Religious faith, strong, semi-, or nonexistent, significantly affects the educational experiences of American teens during the first year out. It does so in two important ways. First, most teens do not wish to examine their faith, nor do they wish to abandon it. Therefore, they deposit their religious identities along with other critical identities into the identity lockbox at the start of their first year out. That seems to preserve their faith, but it also boosts teen immunity to intellectual engagement or thoughtful reflection. Second, and in sharp contrast, I found that strongly religious teens who attend religious colleges and *anti*religious teens who attend nonreligious colleges are more likely to engage themselves intellectually or creatively with their educational experiences. That is because they resist using the identity lockbox and seek to reflect on their own lives and on their wider environment. Strong views on religion, be they positive or negative, appear to be connected with greater openness to intellectual or creative engagement. Such views seem to sensitize their holders to matters of worldview and make them more open to intellectual or creative life, which is not evident among teens who choose mainstream orientations toward religion.[42] If my findings are true generally, and have been true for some time, then they suggest that the American intelligentsia may contain many who are antireligious, many others who are strongly religious (of various sorts), and few who endorse the semireligiosity to which the popular majority of Americans subscribes. This would be, of course, an important question for future inquiry.

THE ROLE OF COMMUNITY

There were two notable but distinct ways that community norms and experiences affected the educational lives of the teens I observed and interviewed. First, there was the bizarre combination of status competition among teens over college admissions alongside nonchalance about career plans and fields of study. Teens particularly concerned with maintaining their present social class position or entering the middle classes gave close attention to the college's "name recognition" and general reputation, though they often conveyed nonchalance about fields of study or long-term career plans. Most of these teens were no more certain about their plans at the end of their first year out than they were at the beginning. These teens, then, pursued various diplomas because it is expected of mainstream American teens and not because they formed plans that oriented their studies and gave direction to their activities. Some might argue this is because teens are too immature when they begin college and that they should take a year off between high school and college to gain life experience and identify their skills and interests more clearly. While this argument has merit, and I return to it in the next chapter, I note that maturity is a cultural construct. Teens in other places and at other times have demonstrated greater maturity about their short- and long-term plans than contemporary American teens. Our present cultural expectations do not seem to challenge teens but rather distract them from thinking about and planning for their futures.

A second impact of community norms and experiences on the educational lives of teens involves NJ High's lower academic expectations for its minority students and the subsequent difficulties these minorities had in adjusting to the academic workload of college. NJ High had three distinct tracks: the top track had "honors" and "AP" classes, the middle track had "general studies" courses, and the bottom track had "principles" courses. Though minorities were enrolled in all three tracks, they were overrepresented in the middle and lower tracks. Many teachers of the middle track assumed few of their students were college bound and thus held significantly lower academic standards for these students than for those in the top track. Teacher assumptions and expectations were even lower for students in the bottom track. Yet most students from the middle track and many students from the lower track *did* go on to college or vocational training—and arrived there quite unaccustomed to their program's (relatively) higher academic standards. The good news is that minority teens from these middle and lower tracks rose to the challenge and began to develop the study patterns and skills necessary to improve their grades. But the bad news is that it took most of these teens the entire first year to accomplish this, many were disheartened by their academic performance the first year, and none were aware that their performances had been systematically affected by not receiving a sufficiently challenging education while in high school. The consensus among NJ High's teachers that middle- and lower-track students were less able to achieve academically not only hindered these students' transition to college, but made the teachers' own jobs less enjoyable as well. The gain of reduced daily teacher-student aggravation is a short-sighted trade for underprepared graduates and diminished job satisfaction.

EDUCATIONAL REALISM

In sum, during their first year out, American teens become cognitively sharper but remain intellectually immune. The overwhelming majority of American teens are practical credentialists. They understand that diplomas are necessary for better jobs and that for the highest status jobs, grades are important, too. Thus, they become adept at playing the game of college, putting in minimal effort to obtain the desired grade. Educators knowingly and unknowingly play this game, too. They do so by steadily inflating their grades, to minimize student complaints and maximize time for individual pursuits. And they do so by maintaining elite educational goals of intellectual curiosity, breadth of perspective, and liberal idealism—which are not only out-of-step with the majority of students they teach, but which limit them from learning who their students truly are and how to communicate effectively with them.

Ironically, colleges of the very type presumed to be intellectually narrow—religious colleges—are in fact more successful at developing intellectual curiosity and breadth of perspective among their freshmen than nonreligious colleges are at developing these qualities among their freshmen. Perhaps the shared faith of religious colleges facilitates greater understanding between instructors and students, and thus increases the effectiveness of instructor-student communication. In any event, America needs a healthy dose of realism about (1) who college students are and what students' goals are and (2) what colleges represent and what they can realistically offer. Scholars often lament how little the public takes notice of their scholarship or areas of expertise; if they truly want to change this, they might start by learning how to honestly communicate with that portion of the public seated directly in front of them: their students. Perhaps if they did, the number of teens comfortable with the narrowed perspectives described in the next chapter might decrease.

SIX

Narrowed Perspectives, Broader Implications

Dennis Jackson and Tammy Biggs were intelligent, well-mannered, and hard-working teens. Besides the obvious differences of gender and race—Dennis was black and Tammy white—both teens had a lot in common. They were both born the same year, they were both reared in working-class families, they have both lived their entire lives in Suburban Township, New Jersey, and they both graduated from NJ High in 2001. Even though Dennis and Tammy were only casual acquaintances, just growing up at the same time in the same suburb gave them countless commonalities. They bowled, for example, at the same alley, shopped at the same stores, played in the same parks, and knew dozens of the same people. So if they run into each other in years to come, whether at a high school reunion or a local 7-11, Dennis and Tammy should be able to find plenty of things to talk about.

What Dennis and Tammy are *not* likely to talk about when they meet, however, is the larger, shared culture that makes their very conversation possible. That includes their socialization as native U.S. citizens, which imparted fluency in American English as well as knowledge of the norms for holding conversations. But it also includes the wider U.S. culture that they shared by coming of age—that is, by being teenagers—between 1995 and 2001.[1] That wider cultural environment includes the widespread use of the World Wide Web and the popularization of cell phones. It also includes a criminal and a civil trial of O. J. Simpson and the host of salacious details surrounding the impeachment trial of President Clinton. It includes the truck bomb explosion at the Murray Building in Oklahoma City in 1995 and the murderous rampage at Columbine High School in 1999. It includes the highly polarized 2000 presidential race between Governor George W. Bush and Vice President Albert M. Gore and its final resolution a full month after election day by a divided U.S. Supreme Court. It includes the terrorist attacks of September 11, 2001, and the subsequent anthrax letter attacks—which every New Jersey resident knows passed through its own state's post offices. While these events affected all Americans, scholars have long documented how major cultural events have a particularly powerful impact on that generation that comes of age during them (such as the "[Great] Depression Generation" and the "World War II Generation").[2] These events become critical components in the unspoken, taken-for-granted conversational foundation of teens like Dennis and Tammy, so that when Dennis remarks, "Y'know what I mean?" or Tammy says, "You know how *that* goes," they *both* understand each other.

I expected September 11, 2001, to be the signal event that affected how teens like Dennis and Tammy viewed the world and chose to live in it. To me, it deeply underscored my perception that the United States had become just one player (albeit a major one) in a political and economic order of global proportions and that it had to take its global interdependency and international perception much more seriously. But that is not how teens interpreted September 11. Teens viewed September 11 as an awful and historically important day, but it was not the *signal* event of their youth. The signal "event" for teens coming of age in the late 1990s, I contend, was the series of school-based, deadly rampages that culminated on April 20, 1999, with the murders of twelve Columbine High School students and one teacher, the wounding of another twenty-four, and the suicides of the two gunmen.[3] These events, which received extensive media coverage, were followed by a wave of anonymous threats, preemptive school closings, and "zero tolerance" policies that affected students across the country.[4] The effect was powerful: because *every* American high school has student outsiders, then *every* high school and *every* high school student were at risk.

Even though my interviews with Dennis and Tammy occurred two full years after the Columbine rampage (a term I use as shorthand for the series of violent school shootings), that tragedy still weighed heavily on their minds. Dennis, a broad-shouldered and athletic senior, who in an earlier era would have intimidated others with his physical size and speed, talked at length about school violence: "Just to know that someone younger than me can *anytime* just come up to me and just, you know, either stab me or shoot me or whatever—that's *crazy*! And it makes you worried." Dennis was worried about his own safety, the safety of his friends, and the long-term safety of the country. "Violence can cause chain reactions. . . . It can cause other things to happen," he said. Dennis wanted to see violent teens treated as adults:

> With some of the killings that's going on today, that the young kids are doing, they're treating them like children and not like adults. You know they're not giving them the same sentence as an adult would have. . . . I just believe that they should be treated as adults. If they just have that type of mentality, just to go kill another student or another child, then I just feel that they should be treated the way that they treated others; just have no heart for them. I don't care *what* age they are.

Given Dennis's impassioned view, I asked if he had taken action to address this problem. Other than voice his concerns with a few friends and family, however, he had not.

Tammy likewise voiced concern about violence in schools. But she went a step further than Dennis, connecting her vote in the 2000 presidential election to her views: "Gun control—that is a *major* thing. I am scared to death of guns." So Tammy voted for Vice President Al Gore, because Gore had proposed several policies to restrict the type and sale of guns following the Columbine rampage. Gore's loss left her disgusted with politics in general. Six months after the election, Tammy explained that she had "no political views at all," stated that there was "no one" in politics that she admired, and concluded that politicians are "all in it for the money."

Another NJ High senior expressed her feelings with particular vividness during one of my lunchtime visits. Attending high school since Columbine made her "feel like I'm playing Russian roulette just coming in here." I asked how she dealt with that feeling, since sixteen months had passed since that violent event. With a seriousness that words cannot convey, she answered: "I just keep my head down, mind my own business, and don't bother nobody." She was not alone in that response. After April 20, 1999, I contend, the majority of culturally mainstream American teens, as an act of self-perseveration, put their heads down, minded their own business, and avoided bothering others. The rampage at Columbine taught a generation of teenagers to mind their own business and avoid making others angry. Disengagement became the path of preservation, and most teens opted for it.

Thus, September 11 did not become the signal event that shaped Dennis's and Tammy's generation, because the rampage at Columbine already had. Rather, September 11 became tragic repetition of a lesson American teens had already absorbed: if you make others angry, you may pay dearly for it. After the initial shock faded, Dennis and Tammy continued in the well-established pattern of their high school years: disengagement from virtually everything except their immediate goals of completing school and pursuing individual happiness. Tammy Biggs recalled that she had been on the Observation Deck of the World Trade Center on Tuesday, September 4, 2001, and her recent visit made it particularly hard for the horrific reality of Tuesday, September 11, 2001, to sink in. Tammy considered herself "lucky," not only for choosing to visit the week that she did, but also because she did "not know anyone [who died] 'cause, you know, I'm really close to there." As for any lasting impact, Tammy reported, "At first it was really hard, but, I don't know. I don't let it really affect me that much. Because, like, I'm going to France in November [of 2002]; . . . you know, can't lose your life in a nutshell." Mixed metaphors notwithstanding, Tammy had become immersed in managing her daily life and did not care to pay attention to national or international news. "I'd rather be doing something else than worrying about politics," she said, even though Tammy's second interview occurred less than a year after September 11, the anthrax letter attacks, and the war in Afghanistan and during stirrings of a future war in Iraq. Thinking about "everything" too much, Tammy believed, just "drives us nuts."

Dennis was similarly disengaged from wider issues, though somewhat less cavalier about matters than Tammy. When I asked Dennis whether his first year out had been a good or a bad year for him, he answered that it had been "all right." By way of explanation, he listed "the September 11 thing" along with "getting hurt" during his varsity sport season as the "downs" for the year. Like Tammy, Dennis was "glad that, like, none of my family was there [i.e., in the World Trade Center]." I asked Dennis whether September 11 had any long-term effect on his life. He replied, "Impact? I'm, I'm glad to wake up each day. That's about it. Like, I realized how, how life can be taken away just like that." And that was all Dennis had to say on the matter. Inexplicable and deadly violence had become a fact of life for Dennis, and his response was gratitude that it had not touched his life yet. Beyond this, though, he saw no value in thinking further about such matters or their broader implications.

Teens like Dennis and Tammy react to larger political and historical events, I suggest, like rush-hour commuters react to tragic accidents on an interstate highway: they are *inconvenient*, because they slow progress to some personal destination; they become moments of *voyeurism*, as drivers rubberneck when they pass by the horrific scene; they can be briefly *sobering*, as drivers consider the tragedy they see; but ultimately they are *professional matters*, too dangerous and too complicated for ordinary citizens to handle. Highway accidents do *not* become occasions when rush-hour commuters pause to question, for example, the ever-accelerating pace of their lives, their dependence on environmentally unfriendly combustion engines, or the reasonableness of suburban dream houses built farther and farther from places of employment. In the same way, larger political and historical events do not become occasions when Dennis, Tammy, or most of their American peers pause to question the larger direction of the United States, its role in the international community, or their role as citizens at this particular moment.

In the remainder of this chapter, I will describe the narrowed perspectives on larger political, economic, and social matters as a general and possibly generational phenomenon among teens, then shift to the broader implications not only of teens' disengagement but also of the project's findings as a whole. The disengagement and narrowed perspectives evident in Dennis's and Tammy's lives are predominant among the teens I observed and interviewed and deserve careful examination. Of course, many researchers and educators have made youth's disengagement from political and civic life a prominent concern for over a decade.[5] Their work identifies growing cynicism about American political life as a root cause, which is exacerbated by mass media framing of political news.[6] My argument about the impact of popular American moral culture on youth disengagement, then, is hardly novel. What is novel is that I specify the identity lockbox as the mechanism of narrowed perspectives, I propose that school rampages affected teens' perspectives on the world more than September 11, and I claim that distinct forms of teen religiosity sustain or challenge youth disengagement. To my knowledge, no one else has made these arguments.

But more than make a novel contribution to scholarship, I hope to make a public one. So I conclude this chapter by suggesting ways that scholars, educators, clergy, parents, and teens might use this book to alter their thinking and revise lines of action. We need to change a number of things we do with teens (or as teens), if we wish to produce youth known as much for their purposeful direction and thoughtful engagement as they are for their generally efficient management of their daily lives. Hopefully this chapter, and this book, will be useful to that important cultural project.

NARROWED PERSPECTIVES

Larger issues, of virtually any sort, barely register on the radar screens, or daily consciousness, of the vast majority of American teens I observed and interviewed. That includes political issues of local, regional, state, national, or global significance; economic issues such as the growth or stagnation of the U.S. economy, our economic interdependence, or the disparities of wealth and poverty; social issues such as gender roles and gendered inequalities, the vexing difficulties of American race and ethnic relations, or the shifting definitions of family and their implications. Asking teens about such matters always produced answers that were liberally sprinkled with "maybe" and "I don't know" and typically supplemented with one of two explanations. Most teens would explain that they do not pay attention to larger issues because they disdain politics and have no hope that any improvement could be made with respect to larger political, economic, or social issues.[7] These teens position themselves somewhere between apolitical and antipolitical. A smaller but sizable minority of teens would explain that they will pay attention to larger issues *in the future*, because they consider such issues to be important, just not important *right now*. Such teens position themselves as temporarily apolitical, with good intentions to become knowledgeable about broader issues in the future. Both sets of teens choose to store their (barely formed) political identities in the identity lockbox and keep them there during their entire first year out.

When I specifically asked teens to describe their political views, most answered that they had no political views, and the rest indicated that they were "kinda" conservative or liberal politically. Ken Drake, an intelligent, white, middle-class senior, was among the majority with no political views. He said simply, "I don't deal with politics, unless I have to." Ken continued: "I really couldn't tell you the difference between Republicans and Democrats. I don't even know what party our president is right now. I mean, I know it's Bush, [but] I don't know what party he is." Not all teens are as politically oblivious as Ken, but most are not too far away. Susie Dane, a white, upper-middle-class senior, wanted to appear informed about political matters, but she quickly backpedaled: "My *political* views? [Sounding bewildered:] I'm not really involved politically. I mean, I know sort of what's going on in the political world, but not so much. I don't really have an interest in it. I think it's very complicated and I can't ever seem to understand everything that's going on. So I'm not really interested in political views." The "no interest, no knowledge" answer was common among teens regardless of their social class and common among teens across races. Cookie Munroe (from chapter 5) confessed that she had absolutely no interest in politics, "but I'll vote, you know." While Cookie, like other minority teens, was slightly more likely to align herself with a political party (usually Democratic), the majority of both minority and white teens indicated no interest in, if not disdain for, political matters.

Some high school seniors said that they would pay attention to political matters "in the future." That future did not arrive during their first year out, however. White, middle-class, NJ High senior Kato Stuart explained that politics "doesn't interest me too much now, but I think as I get older it will interest me more." Kato must have meant more than a year after his first interview, as he gave the same answer at the end of his first year out. Similarly, black, middle-class senior Reggie Kraft explained that "I just never really got into all that [i.e., politics] yet—but I will eventually." Reggie did not get to his "eventually" by the end of his first year out, either. He explained, yet again, that he did not have any political views: "When I'm older I might, when I need to be concerned about it. I mean, I'm actually kind of happy with the way everything is going right now, so I don't have to be concerned about it yet." Cookie, Susie, and Ken were similarly unconcerned. "I don't even care," was Cookie's answer at the end of her first year out—even though Cookie's first year included, along with Kato's, September 11 and its globe-shaking aftermath. For reasons I have already presented in this book, the vast majority of American teens refuse to look up from their management of daily life during the first year out. Just as most American teens view religion as an adult matter reserved for a later time in life (see chapter 2),[8] I find most teens view politics as something they intend to do later in life as well. A question for future researchers, then, is whether and to what extent these teens' good intentions become actual behaviors. Because previous research suggests few changes occur in one's political perspectives on the world following late adolescence,[9] it may be that the road to adult political disengagement has been paved with teens' good intentions.

Perhaps, some might argue, it is the word *politics* itself that is problematic. Because the American public is dubious about political matters, some might contend, the very word *politics* triggers immediate distancing and expressions of indifference.[10] To counteract this possible effect, I asked questions about the teens' political views and level of interest last. After a series of questions that began with a broad query about how teens wished they could change the world, I moved to more specific questions about justice, injustice, wealth and poverty, and race. Teen answers to my broad query, as well as to specific questions about macro issues, however, confirmed that no matter how I asked teens about larger issues, such issues do not appear on their radar screens.

Some teens laughed and called it my "Miss America" question: "If there were three things you could change about the world, what would they be?" In fact, a popular teen movie released during my field research at NJ High, *Miss Congeniality*, poked fun at the ubiquity of "world peace" as the proper answer to that question. Still, it was noteworthy how many teens struggled to answer the question. Thinking from a global perspective, even a Pollyannaish one, stymied nearly half of my interviewees. Of course, ending war or bringing about world peace was one answer given, sometimes embarrassedly, by many teens. But three other answers surpassed that one in frequency: ending violence/crime, ending world hunger/poverty, or ending hatred/discrimination; and three other answers ran close behind: everyone should be nice/kind/loving, everyone should share [my] religious faith, and everyone should be free of all disease/suffering. What I find striking about teen responses to this question, besides the difficulty teens had with it, was how many teens offered answers that projected individual-level changes on a global scale. That is, *individuals* should not commit crime and not be violent, *individuals* should not hate, *individuals* should love each other more, "be nicer," or have more religious faith. Few teens described truly macro-level changes (such as laws to "cut pollution"). Rather, when the vast majority of teens talk about the macro-level, if they talk about it at all, they describe it as the sum of the individuals it comprises. The solution to world poverty and hunger, for example, is simply getting "everyone" to be "less greedy" and "share more." The language of individualism is not only these teens' first moral language, as sociologist Robert Bellah and his coauthors wrote in 1985, it is their *only* moral language.[11]

That point becomes obvious when teens answered my questions about justice, injustice, wealth, and poverty. For *justice*, the most frequent teen definition was "getting what you deserve," the second most frequent definition was being treated "equally," "fairly," or "impartially" before the law, and the third was "I don't know." For *injustice*, the definitions were the inverse: "not getting what you deserve," not being treated equally or fairly before the law, or "I *still* don't know." When I asked teens to tell me what they considered the greatest injustices today, the most frequent answer was "I don't know," followed by a description of the sensationalist crime du jour. And while teens often explained the gap between rich and poor with answers that described larger economic and historical forces alongside individual choices and abilities, nearly every teen said "nothing" can be done to alter poverty or economic inequality, and thus the matter merited little further thought and no action on their part. While there were a few teens who gave atypical answers to these questions, most teens understood justice to be about the legal process and criminal consequences in America—and not about ensuring, for example, that political, economic, and social opportunities are readily available to individuals, families, and communities around the globe.

Perhaps some readers might think I am expecting too much of these teens. They are "just teenagers," after all, and they still have "a lot of growing up" to do. But that would be a tragic misinterpretation of my argument. My argument is not about the individual choices these teens make to track or not track political issues (though the ins and outs of celebrity activities and pairings that dominate many teen conversations are surely as complicated as contemporary politics). Rather, my argument is about how Americans understand "growing up" in the late twentieth and early twenty-first century and how that understanding has powerfully signaled that larger political or social issues are not worthy of attention or action during the teen years. The political and social disengagement of these teens is a *cultural* phenomenon. It is a product, I argue, of popular American moral culture that

1. Views "youth" as extending into one's early 20s,[12] with youth granted full access to adult rights but not assigned the full complement of adult responsibilities;
2. Accepts a wider range of familial and interpersonal relationships, which have made youth microworlds more complex;[13]
3. Distrusts larger institutions and political processes;
4. Believes social and political changes cannot be made through the actions of ordinary citizens;
5. Consumes information about social and political issues from for-profit media outlets that either ignore or oversimplify such issues in seeking to attract the widest possible consumer audience; and
6. Recognizes, ultimately, that its citizens reside in a global superpower that chooses when and whether it pays attention to issues beyond its own immediate interests.

Elements of this popular moral culture have long characterized the United States, but their intensification and convergence during the past two decades has particularly fostered teen disengagement from larger issues.

Consider the difference a half-century makes. A couple of generations ago, Americans age 18–21 accepted that politics had consequences and that actions and events around the globe could affect both their nation and their individual lives profoundly (as World War II demonstrated).[14] Perhaps that contributed to their "growing up" sooner and their early establishment of separate households and work careers. Or consider the difference that a continent makes. In various countries across Europe, Asia, and Latin America, and in Australia, youth possess a wider and deeper understanding of national and international matters than American youth do.[15] Youth in all of these countries have concerns, to be sure, about managing relationships, gratifications, educational requirements, and personal finances. But such matters do not consume their attention as fully, and the wider world is not as ignored among them as it is among American youth.

Two education scholars have argued that a reason for youth's broader disengagement with the world is their preoccupation with gender and race differences. "Today's undergraduates think of themselves in terms of their differences rather than their commonalities," Arthur Levine and Jeannette Cureton conclude in their widely cited study of college students in the early 1990s.[16] Stating that "tension regarding diversity and difference runs high all across college life," they explain that college "students were more willing to tell us intimate details of their sex lives than to discuss race."[17] By the time I began my interviews in the mid-1990s, however, I did not find anything resembling this. Most teens were remarkably oblivious about the significance of diversity, and not just the male, white, and relatively affluent teens that you would expect to be oblivious, but also those teens on the historically subordinate side of these categories—female, minority, and working-class teens. Most teens will acknowledge that gender, race, or class "used to be really important," as most teens have been thoroughly trained by their teachers to accept the historical significance of gender, race, and class. Most teens, including female, minority, and working-class teens, do not, however, consider gender, race, or class to be all that relevant to understanding contemporary, everyday life. Thus, I often found myself listening poker-faced as female, minority, and working-class high school seniors told me that their gender, race, or class status did not affect their lives, while feeling internally incredulous that these teens did not recognize the profound ways their everyday lives and larger structures of opportunity had been shaped by these ascribed realities (see my discussion of the latter below). And despite my hope that this would change by the end of the first year out, it did not.

In contrast to Levine and Cureton, I found that teens were willing to talk about race or gender, but rather frustrated about the topic's ubiquity. With rolling eyes and heavy sighs whenever the subject was broached, they described annoyance with "constant" discussion of race or gender (and to a lesser degree, social class). Teachers, schools, professors, and colleges had "beat this topic to death," and my teen respondents had had enough of it. "They, like, beat it into you during welcome week here [at college]—'Be nice to everyone. Be nice to everyone,'" said one first-year, white male. Another white male concurred, "Yeah, it's always 'Have respect—don't be racist, don't be sexist, don't be homophobic'; and you have to talk about it in, like, *every* class." And it was not just white, male teens who had grown weary of the emphasis on gender and race matters, so had female and minority teens. Kasim Douglass, a black, working-class NJ High graduate, stated that racism, except among a handful of extremists, was not a widespread, contemporary force: "I can't blame the people today for what happened years ago. I can blame the people today who are still doing, like, stupid stuff, like, skinheads, Nazi's." And Julie Gillmore, a white, middle-class teen, described a similar view about the declining social significance of gender:

> JULIE: I think it's, like, equal now. I don't think that women are looked down on anymore. Like, sometimes, women have advantages over men.
> INTERVIEWER: Such as?
> JULIE: Like, because of the whole discrimination thing, that [employers] don't want to discriminate—so sometimes women have better opportunities.

Far from being preoccupied with their differences and resistant to talking about gender and race, most teen interviewees rejected the view that gender and race had contemporary relevance, and once they realized I was not going to disagree or correct them, they had plenty to say about how these "past" differences no longer mattered. Rejecting race and gender identities as salient to interpreting the world, however, leaves teens with only individualistic views of social behavior that reinforce their disengagement with larger issues of all sorts.

It took me quite a while to discover why September 11, 2001, did not affect teens more. I could not understand why that powerful event did not drive home the limited value of individualistic interpretations of social behavior or the critical importance of being aware of and engaged with the larger world. It was only after much trolling through interview transcripts and field notes that I finally saw what was so readily apparent: the violent rampages at Columbine and other schools had already affected how teens viewed the wider world and profoundly underscored their disengagement from it. My initial oblivion to the potential impact of the Columbine rampage is particularly embarrassing, as I had myself been anxious about the very same violent possibility during my first day of field research at NJ High. Thankfully, qualitative social research is an iterative process, and researchers can correct early oversights during later stages in the process.

Readers not enrolled in junior or senior high school on April 20, 1999, need to imagine what it felt like to be a junior or senior high student after that awful day. Imagine being an early or middle adolescent without the experience or perspective of adulthood. Imagine what it felt like to look at every school "outcast" with suspicion, to evacuate one's school multiple times because of a bomb scare or phoned-in death threat, to regularly practice "intruder" or "lockdown" drills during the school day (announced by an ominous "Code Red" over the PA system and requiring one to crouch along the walls of a darkened classroom with the most obscured line of sight from the door), to be required to wear visible student ID cards at all times, to experience random book bag and locker searches, and to have various security measures added—from security cameras, to added security staff, to a regular police presence in the school.[18] These actions ritually reenacted violent school rampages and powerfully reinforced their possible repetition. Even getting a "hall pass" to use the restroom or the library, many teens reported, became far more difficult and involved a process that underscored the possibility of every teen being a violent risk. And teens who preferred a "Goth" clothing style or wore trench coats found themselves carefully scrutinized by peers and school officials. Such teens were questioned regularly and at length by school officials, and one even reported that his parents were called in to the principal's office and told that their son was a "potential Columbine."

In the wake of the Columbine rampage, teens reported that parents who had previously resisted purchasing cell phones for their children now supplied them readily, talked to them about safety in their schools, and even considered enrolling them in private schools. Many teens also described "intense" new school policies about "no bullying," strict "zero tolerance" policies toward any sign of hostility or misbehavior, and school assemblies that stressed "being kind" to others and "reaching out" to peers who "may be struggling." And, teens being teens, this became a source of macabre humor: "My friends would joke and say, 'Better not make him mad or else

he'll shoot you,'" or "During a 'Code Red,' we'd have to go sit in the football stadium, where we would become even easier shooting targets." The
most common teen responses, however, were anxious ones: "[I was] scared
regarding future situations like this"; "I realized it could have been my
school"; "I started to question if I was on everyone's good side"; and "I used
to think violence was something that was found more in the urban areas,
but seeing this happen I realized that *everyone* was susceptible to violence."
In short, this cohort of American teens shifted into survival mode: keep a
low profile, focus on individual goals (e.g., finish school), and otherwise
"mind your own business."

What September 11, 2001, did, then, was underscore the reality of random, inexplicable violence that teens had already come to expect. Lowanda
Smith (introduced in chapter 1) recalled: "There was so many people that
were affected by 9/11. This girl—we were in a church service—and her cell
phone went off. She was keepin' her cell phone on, and she wanted to know
about her parents, and both of them had died. And she found out like right
then! . . . I was just so scared." As poignant and powerful as that event was,
however, Lowanda did not interpret it as a reason to try to understand September 11's precursors more fully or to track its global aftermath. While
Lowanda did state that the television "news has become more interesting to
me as I get older," she also said that she did not have "any" political views—
"I should have some, but I don't." I suggest, however, that September 11 did
affect Lowanda, in a way that emerged in her answer about what she would
change about the world: "The violence, I just can't stand it. I don't like [that]
people have to get to the point where they have to make sure every door
in their house is, you know . . . I mean, just livin' in fear or something. . . .
I don't like the fact that I have fear in my heart. I would just change that
so that wouldn't be there." "Violence" was the number one thing Lowanda
wished to change about the world—not terrorism, not war, but violence
and people's fear of it. The Columbine rampage, September 11, perhaps even
the violent stories on the local news—Lowanda classified them all as examples of (random) "violence." Once classified in this way, there's nothing
Lowanda feels she can do about them except make sure her doors are locked
and live in fear.

I am not suggesting that most teens live in a state of constant fear of
violence, however. Not even Lowanda. Rather, I argue that because teens
preoccupy themselves with daily life management, they returned to their
daily lives after September 11 as a way of distracting themselves. That is
what Chuck Barker, a white, middle-class, NJ High graduate did even

though he attended a funeral for his best friend's uncle, a New York City firefighter who perished on September 11. I asked whether September 11 had any long-term effect on him: "I don't think so," Chuck answered. Chuck had no interest in larger issues of any sort at the end of his first year out, though he "guess[ed] that'll change when I'm older." Chuck, like his classmates Lowanda, Dennis, and Tammy, and the vast majority of his American peers, had long learned to disengage and "mind his own business" after Columbine's rampage. He had also absorbed throughout his entire life the frequent American pattern that paying attention to and being engaged with larger issues is something that teachers, select adults, and highly trained experts do. Not even the collapse of the World Trade Center buildings could rattle Chuck or his peers from their deeply habituated, narrowed perspectives on the world.[19]

ON THE ROLE OF FAMILY, FAITH, AND COMMUNITY

As much as I critique organized schooling in America for expecting too little of American youth in chapter 5, I will not do so here. Teachers and schools work hard to get students to understand and engage in larger political, social, and economic issues. Part of the problem may be, in fact, the strong association between knowledge of larger issues and schooling itself, as popular American moral culture is suspicious of both political processes and large institutions, especially education. But I do not suggest that teachers or schools curtail their efforts in an attempt to use a cultural "reverse psychology." Schools should continue their efforts to inculcate knowledge of and engagement in larger issues of political and social significance. Their teaching staffs, however, should recognize that they are engaged in an uphill cultural battle, because American youth absorb a far louder message about the irrelevance of larger issues to their daily lives and long-term goals. Youth absorb that louder message, I contend, from their families, their faiths, and their communities, and then reinforce it among themselves through the popular and peer cultures they inhabit. Put differently, American teens are not alone in their possession of narrowed perspectives on the larger world; they are much like the American adults who have shaped them.[20] The apple never falls far from the tree.

That minority of teen respondents who described "some" political views, who guessed they leaned more toward the Democratic or Republican party, almost always described having parents (usually fathers, as political interest remains notably gendered in culturally mainstream U.S.

families) who paid attention to political matters and talked about politics with their children. When I asked these semipolitical teens where they got their information about politics, the primary response was through their parents, with teachers and "the news" (i.e., the television news) tied for a distant second. Understand that these teens do not sit around the dinner table engaging in thoughtful political discussions with their parents; rather, the dominant pattern is that teens occasionally hear their fathers offer a partisan interpretation of some current news event, and the teens decide (privately) that they agree or disagree with it. That is the extent of the political socialization occurring in most of these teens' families. And recall that these teens are atypical; most teens did not report any conversations with others about political (or economic or social) issues of any sort and had no political views or interests. If such matters are not important to most American parents, then we surely should not expect them to be important to most American teens.[21]

As for religious faith and narrowed perspectives of American teens, I observed three patterns. First, most teens are semireligious and politically uninterested, and thus they assign both faith and political issues to their identity lockbox, in seemingly separate compartments. Or, to use a different analogy, if religion represents vegetables in the grand buffet of teen lives, then larger social and political issues represent Geritol, the vitamin supplement marketed to senior adults. While most teens recognize the value of religious vegetables and continue to include some on their plates during the first year out, albeit in reduced quantities, they see no need to begin taking a vitamin supplement that they "know" is for senior adults. Jabari Campbell, for example, is a black, middle-class, residential college freshman who grew up attending his local United Methodist Church. Like most teens, Jabari's religious participation dropped during the first year out, but not his deeper identification as a Christian. And like most teens, Jabari expressed little interest in and no knowledge of politics, but he knew that someday he would identify his political views and obtain political knowledge. Jabari stated, "I wish I knew more [about politics]," but the problem was that "I usually change the channel when that [i.e., political news] comes on." Jabari explained, "Whatever they [politicians/news reporters] are talking about is not going to affect me," and thus Jabari confidently assigned his future political identification to his identity lockbox, keeping it in a compartment separate from his religious identification. Jabari could barely articulate his religious beliefs; it is no surprise that he had not considered their possible implications for social and political matters.

A second pattern exists among those teens who are strongly religious and who believe that their faith has a connection to certain larger issues, but they can offer as evidence only sensationalized issues such as abortion and cannot describe even a rudimentary framework for connecting faith and larger issues. Indeed, for many strongly religious teens, faith *is* the larger political and social issue, and the expansion of faith worldwide is cited as the solution to all political and social issues, great or small. Christine Darden, a white, working-class evangelical teen, believed, "If everybody had a faith in God, not like any god, but like one God, *God*-God [i.e., my God] ..., then I think that people would be more honest ..., look out for their beloved ..., [be] willing to help everybody, and not be selfish." Christine asserted that if the whole world shared her evangelical faith in God, then all other worldly problems would cease. Other faith traditions, and even other evangelicals, believe resolving social and political problems will require more than just a common faith. Many religious bodies have, in fact, issued eloquent statements about human rights, economic opportunity, the pursuit of peace, or the need for social justice.[22] Strongly religious teens do not demonstrate any knowledge of these statements, however, and give only cursory thought to the implications of their faith for the wider world. Although it is youth who have historically been the vanguard of social change in societies around the globe, American religious groups have failed to mobilize legions of their youth on behalf of the social changes they seek.[23]

A third pattern is evident among those teens who are nonreligious. Most common within the nonreligious, semihedonist camp is rejection of the wider world. Just as religious faith is rejected primarily for the claims it attempts to make on these teens' lives, so are larger political and social issues rejected for the same. Poppy Lopez (from chapter 1) said he would like to see the federal government eliminated and replaced with a "localized government," where "whatever they [i.e., the locals] say, they can do that; whatever they choose, they can do that." Such a political structure could then "legalize marijuana," "make abortion legal," "lower taxes," and generally "not bother" its citizens. The less common response, found among the antireligionists, is to value knowledge of and engagement in larger social and political issues and to combat the impact of religion on such issues. Nick Lawrence, a white, middle-class, commuting college student, "got fed up with the Christian thing, [where] people were more interested in themselves rather than the actual religion." Though reared in his mother's Episcopal church, Nick viewed religion as hypocrisy and heaped scorn on its self-righteous practitioners—in particular, President George W. Bush: "I feel like of all the people we could possibly have running this country at this time [June 2002], I think George W. Bush is the last guy I would ever pick. I mean, the man can't even finish a basic thought! I just feel like he's just kinda screwing things up all over the place; he's doing more harm than he is good. The whole war on Afghanistan didn't work at all. He's just kinda sticking his nose where he shouldn't be." Thus Nick, who followed politics closely and read a variety of news magazines and newspapers, was registered to vote and could hardly wait until 2004, so he could vote against Bush and elect a more "liberal" and less religious President. Antireligious teens like Nick can be adamant about reducing the impact of religion on political and social matters—which is striking, given that most American religious organizations can barely interest, much less mobilize, their own teens about such matters.

Perhaps part of the reason why many teens are so comfortably disengaged from the wider world may be because political leaders successfully present themselves as custodians of popular American moral culture and, in particular, its theistic components. Several teens explained that they were generally happy with how things were going and did not see larger political or social issues affecting their own lives anyhow. Perhaps teens relinquish concern for the wider world to others because they believe that these political custodians, and the various teachers and other adults who watch them, will hew closely enough to popular American moral culture that teens need not burden themselves with political or social matters. Moreover, because most teens believe that God is somehow watching over all of this, they are comfortable assigning concern for the wider world to grown-ups and devoting their attention to the pressing matters of their own microworlds. That the overwhelming majority of their peers do the same further undergirds this practice.

As for the role of teens' communities of origin, I can describe but a hodgepodge of ways communities sometimes affect how teens understand and engage larger social and political issues. Some community groups, for example, will plan "awareness-raising" activities for national holidays: a high school social studies class might plant trees with a park ranger on Arbor Day, or the public library might sponsor a lecture and pull together a display for Black History Month. Other community groups will mount larger-scale events such as fundraising walks or sport contests that may involve a number of teen volunteers. Teen volunteers enjoy these larger events, because they provide ways to demonstrate visible concern for issues that many people support, such as disease research or the Special Olympics, and because these events often have a celebratory character to them. Yet only a fraction of teens get involved in these events or activities, and, even for the teens who are involved, the long-term impact seems negligible. Among teens, it may be that "awareness" activities and events function more as cultural vaccinations *against* further action than as stimuli *for* further action.

As for the "communities" of race, class, and gender, I found that only race seems to be connected with broader perspectives on social and political issues among a minority of minorities only. That is, most of the culturally mainstream minority teens I interviewed did not demonstrate any racial consciousness. They described having never experienced a discriminatory action or prejudicial attitude personally, they did not believe that their future plans or opportunities would be affected by their race, and they generally identified racism with extremist groups and "places we drove through in the South." Just a handful of minority teens possessed an identifiable racial consciousness. They recognized that race is always in the background, and often in the foreground, of all social interaction. One such teen, Moesha Anderson (introduced in chapter 2), explained that this had made her "pretty radical a lot of the time; I'm very pro-black." Moesha's recognition of race imparted to her a sense of belonging to a racial "community" wider and deeper than herself and increased her attention to matters that might affect her "community." Moesha therefore described paying close attention to news of racial profiling, racial "mistreatment," and discussions about affirmative action, a policy she supported "right now, because I think we need it." That Moesha used "we" to refer to the black American "community" itself speaks volumes about Moesha's racial consciousness. Most minority teens, however, did not use a "we" discourse—because most minority teen interviewees did not articulate consciousness of race. Perhaps these suburban, minority teens will develop a racial consciousness later in life, as they move out of more egalitarian educational settings and into less egalitarian settings;[24] that is a possibility deserving future research.

I could discern no connection between gender and broader perspectives, nor between class and broader perspectives, however. Despite the significant accomplishments of the women's movement and the labor movement in U.S. history, I found no evidence of a wider gender consciousness or class consciousness among female or working-class teens. The "communities" that the women's movement and the labor movement painstakingly created are moribund, at least among these American teens.

BROADER IMPLICATIONS

During the first year after high school graduation, the teens I observed and interviewed accepted and largely followed the prevailing American cultural patterns: they prioritized the management of relationships, gratifications, educational requirements, and money matters; they stored their religious, political, and other critical identities in a lockbox; and they gave little heed to anything else beyond their microworlds. The upside to American teens' focus on this cluster of cultural practices is that mainstream teens do become competent in daily life management and relatively successful in the pursuit of their private and largely conventional goals. The downside is that most culturally mainstream teens do not set goals with much care or thought, because they have not learned to balance individual desires, interpersonal worlds, or efficiency preferences with wider interdependencies, global realities, or larger purposes. While this may have been a common pattern among previous generations of American teens, this pattern has become particularly well-established among culturally mainstream teens who came of age during the rampage at Columbine. Having learned early in their teen years to avoid unnecessary engagement with others for fear of deadly repercussions, contemporary youth refuse wider engagement despite historic and horrific events that cry out for understanding and thoughtful response.

These youth, then, will accomplish their private and conventional goals of finding work, creating families, and consuming leisure, *so long as* the United States's cultural stability and its relatively predictable economy persist. Should one or both of these foundational supports weaken substantially, by some action gradual or cataclysmic, these American young people will lack the cultural resources with which they can construct lives of purpose that are meaningfully connected to the global context that envelops them. To return to the analogy I made in my introduction, contemporary teens are quite capable at pitching the tents of their lives and attending to their daily business in the campground they have chosen. The problem is that the campground containing most teens lies in a flood plain, and, despite its damage following September 11's flood, its residents continue to attend to their daily lives ignoring the mud and deaf to the cracking noises they hear from the faltering dam just a mile upstream.

Some might think that I am being dramatic or alarmist. I am sure some residents of New Orleans thought the same about those who, prior to Hurricane Katrina, claimed that the city's levees would fail if a hurricane hit their city directly. But the global conditions that create terrorists have not lessened in the years since September 11, despite two wars and America's varying attention to matters of public safety. It is only a matter of time before the next attack on the United States occurs—on our food or water supply, our power supply, our transportation systems, or our cities—to say nothing of the "normal" sorts of natural disasters such as hurricanes.[25] My concern is that we are not ready as "a people" for another devastating attack and that this generation of American teens, in particular, is not ready. Hurricane Katrina dramatically illustrated how unprepared the United States is to evacuate large numbers of its citizens and attend to their basic needs following a (forewarned) devastation, much less to address longer-term issues such as housing and employment for affected citizens or to plan the reconstruction of an entire region. I do not say this to denigrate the generosity or the individual resourcefulness of U.S. citizens following Hurricane Katrina. But private or local actions, as important as they are, are like first-aid: they provide affected families with a bag of clothes, a basket of food, a place to sleep, and a school for the children. What affected citizens need for long-term recovery requires physical *and* cultural resources. Better-built cities, stronger levees, and more efficient evacuation plans are a first step; but as a people, Americans must recognize that it is essential to understand, be engaged with, and hold politicians accountable for the critical issues that undergird our shared lives, so that future devastation might be less likely, or at least less deadly.

The vast majority of teen Americans in this book have responded to devastating events in the exact opposite manner, however. They have narrowed their perspectives to the private worlds that they can capably and efficiently manage and left the wider world to its own devices. This is not only a problem for our public life, it is also a problem for these teens' private worlds. Lacking a broader perspective that meaningfully links their private worlds to local communities, national issues, and global realities leaves these teens charting the course of their lives with dated and erroneous cultural maps. Some will therefore run aground, others will be lost at sea, still others will land in an undesirable place, and some will arrive at the desired location quite by accident. Few will understand how any of these outcomes happened, however, and fewer still will realize that the cultural map they inherited was flawed. America cannot correct these cultural maps overnight, of course, but we do possess the resources to begin the correction process and the capacity to alert teens to flaws in their maps. It is a question of how many adults have the will to start and how many teens have the desire to listen.

In this final section of the book, I will suggest implications of my study for several audiences. First, I will convey the significance of my analysis to scholarly types like me—to those who conduct or track research on youth, family, education, religion, community, and American culture. Scholars, I contend, need to more clearly understand the moral culture and everyday lives of American teens, so they might better communicate with teen publics who could benefit from their knowledge. Second, I will offer implications for educators at the secondary and collegiate levels, for clergy and other religious professionals, and for concerned parents of current or future teens. All of these audiences seek to produce young people known as much for their purposeful direction and thoughtful engagement as they are for the effective management of their daily lives. Finally, I will offer implications for American youth themselves—to those who came of age in the late 1990s and early 2000s, who seek to understand some of the cultural factors that have shaped their own lives and wish to deepen their sense of purpose and direction as new adults and as a rising cohort of American citizens. I admit that sociologists are better at cultural diagnoses than they are at cultural cures; so please view this as but one starting point in a conversation about how we might better equip American teens for adult life and not as the final word. There is far too much at stake for mine to be the only voice heard.

IMPLICATIONS FOR SCHOLARS

With apologies to F. Scott Fitzgerald, I propose that scholars post in a prominent place this adaptation of his famous quote: *Let me tell you about teens— they are different from you and me.* Scholars need to let go of their expectations that American teens will (or should) demonstrate the kind of intellectual and worldly curiosity that we (allegedly) demonstrated during our first year out. We were the teen intelligentsia, not like most teens, and we ought not expect most teens to think or behave as we did. Though we may lament a popular American culture that is suspicious of intellectual life and prefers oversimplified interpretations of national and global matters, we do our cause a disservice if we expect teens to abandon these perspectives during the first year out, and we frustrate ourselves when our educational institutions do not reverse these powerful cultural trends. Rather, we should lower our lofty ideals to ones that are more widely attainable and that, over time, will lay the groundwork for a public that is more open to the contributions that scholars wish to make.

Our status as scholars has not, in the United States, conferred to us the cultural authority that it does in other societies. So if we wish to reach contemporary American teens, to say nothing of American citizens in general, scholars need to become public intellectuals, or more precisely, scholarly apologists. Just because we as scholars give academic disciplines the authority to make claims about our fields of study does not mean the American public does the same. Witness, for example, the continuing difficulty of biologists to convince local school boards about the empirical basis of an evolutionary paradigm for biological life. Testimonies by leading biologists are not assigned widespread cultural authority in the United States. As much as we might bristle at the suggestion, scholars must *earn* the right to be heard, and that requires speaking plainly, marshaling evidence, evaluating dispassionately, and leading our audience to logical conclusions. It is not enough to prove our case with our scholarly peers, we must also do so with the general population, and thus our challenge lies in effectively communicating evidence and argument to a general audience.

Can it work? I think there is a good possibility that it can, because I have observed two phenomena with respect to teens and American education. The first is that, despite minimal subject retention, teens do make cognitive gains as a result of their educational experience, and these gains should help them understand and appreciate more complex lines of argument. The second is that teens will consider new subjects and fields of inquiry *when presented to them in an engaging manner*. While the latter may trouble purists and certainly has its downsides (see chapter 5), it does convey that intellectual curiosity is not dead among teens, just dormant. As scholars, we can curse the cards that our culture has dealt us or we can work with the hand we have. Thankfully, there is increased attention to the importance of public intellectualism in many fields, and that is a trend I hope both continues and expands. But it will require scholars in every field to recognize and reward such public intellectual activity as crucial to that discipline, and not merely pay it lip service while continuing to prioritize internal, disciplinary activities such as journal publications.

IMPLICATIONS FOR EDUCATORS

Expectations are powerful. I often intentionally set my expectations low regarding a new experience, so that I will be more readily pleased when that experience exceeds my expectations. While that may be individually helpful, especially for someone with perfectionist tendencies, it is not helpful when educators do so with respect to teens' capacities to learn. Teens have surely mastered the art of divining minimal expectations and meeting them, and they have also mastered the art of pressuring aberrant educators to lower their expectations. Rather than buck the system, most educators identify a balance point that meets local expectations of students, conforms to that of other local educators, and falls within the demands of administrators. The result is a tolerable, but not very fulfilling, educational process for everyone. There are certainly exceptions to this pattern, but far more schooling fits this pattern than does not. Clearly, educator expectations need to change—but an effort to simply raise them will surely backfire, as lowered expectations are deeply embedded in the institutional patterns of schooling.

I suggest that educators, instead of raising existing expectations, create new expectations about what students can learn and do. These new expectations should not begin with what *educators* want students to learn, but rather should begin with helping *students* identify their interests and then move to (1) engaging those interests to develop cognitive and communicative skills, (2) connecting those interests to existing bodies of knowledge, and (3) applying knowledge in practical and creative ways. There is, to be sure, a common core of knowledge that every culture must transmit to persist. But that body of knowledge is far smaller than curriculum experts suppose,[26] and its retention will be higher if students find their education to be generally interesting, useful, and engaging. Instead of focusing on what educators ought to cover, I suggest that we focus on what knowledge our graduates retain and what skills they actually use, and work backward to develop a student-centered curriculum that imparts knowledge worth retaining and skills worth developing. In this era of overwhelming information and endless data, American adults need skills in how to thoughtfully navigate the sea of information and chart a course through the data that surrounds them.[27] The whole of the arts and sciences are well suited for teaching these things; the critical factor is whether they are taught with the student's interests as primary or the teacher's interests as primary.

What I am advocating to educators, then, is not that different from what I am advocating to scholars. Both groups need to look past their immediate professional circles to make a priority of the needs of their audiences. Just as scholars need to become public intellectuals, so do educators need to become learning facilitators. Both groups will be more effective if they approach their work from an end-user's perspective.

To gain an end-user's perspective will require educators to understand more than just their current students. Educators will need to understand past and future students, too. I have spent time with a number of alumni, and I can attest to the impact that getting to know alumni offers: it convinced me to raise my standards for writing, speaking, and analysis even higher, as these are critical skills for the workplace and graduate school; it convinced me that developing quantitative and problem-solving skills deserve more pedagogical attention than covering some set of valued disciplinary "facts"; and it gave me a reservoir of real-world examples to use in teaching my classes. Though some might believe an end-user perspective will involve a reduction in the educator's work, I can attest to the opposite. Shifting to a user orientation has demanded a lot more work from me, as developing student skills requires more intensive teaching labor than simply presenting a unit of knowledge and then testing for its (short-term) retention.

I can also attest to the value of spending time with future students. Because this project put me into contact with a range of high school seniors, it aided my teaching of college students significantly: it convinced me to upgrade my expectations in freshmen-level courses, because freshmen expect substantially more difficult courses in college than they had in high school; it convinced me that starting with sociological studies of interpersonal relationships engages incoming students far more than macrohistorical theories of social order; and it gave me a host of examples from teen culture to use in illustrating sociological concepts. An end-user perspective has resulted in more meaningful work for me and my students and in more lasting effects on students.

Gaining an end-user perspective does not mean that educators do not challenge students. But it does mean that some challenges may be more appropriate at certain times in a teen's life than others. I am quite concerned about the consequences of narrowed perspectives for American teens and for American culture, but I am convinced that educators waste their breath if they attempt to challenge these during the first year out. During this year, the vast majority of teens are too involved in daily life management to manage anything else. I believe this also holds true for seniors in high school, when teens prepare to exit high school. The prime years, I suggest, for challenging American youth to broaden their perspectives—with respect to both their long-term goals and their wider engagement with the world—are the sophomore and junior years of high school and sophomore and junior years of college. During these years, youth are not transitioning into or out of their primary roles and have settled sufficiently into their roles that they may be more open to looking beyond their local contexts. This may make sophomores and juniors more amenable to broadening challenges. Such challenges will require an uphill battle, as these remain *American* youth, and the forces of individualism, pragmatism, and nationalism are strong. But efforts during the sophomore and junior year may have better odds of success than efforts during either the senior year of high school or the first year afterward, and educators would be wise to focus on broadening perspectives during these two periods.

IMPLICATIONS FOR CLERGY

Some clergy may find comfort in learning that most American teens do not, by and large, abandon their identification with religious faith during the first year out. Religious involvement drops, to be sure, but not teens' self-identification as a religious person and not their hopes to become reinvolved in religious faith sometime "in the future." But most clergy will not find this of much comfort, because teens who deposit their religious identities in a lockbox during the first year out do so because they see everyday life and religious identification as separate and distinct entities. Teens view religious faith and practice as largely irrelevant to this stage in their life cycle. Religion is something they did as "kids" and something they will probably do again as "adults." But, for now, teens tune out religion—at the very moment when they make decisions that can affect the rest of their lives and during the very time when they individually establish patterns of everyday living. One of the largest and longest-established cultural sources of direction and purpose, then, is frequently muted, leaving teens fewer resources with which they can evaluate goals or prioritize daily tasks.

The religious story of most teens, then, is the story of a thousand missed opportunities. Given the seeming importance of retaining youth for most religious groups in the United States, it is striking how haphazardly most congregations go about it. Teens report attending religious services or participating in various religious activities more often than I expected, yet they gain only sketchy and frequently mistaken understandings of what their religion believes and practices (see chapter 2). Many teens get confirmed or bar/bat mitzvahed by their local congregations but report that the rigid way that process occurred left them with unanswered questions and little regard for their religious teachers. Parents are rarely a religious resource, either. Few teens talk on a deeper level with their parents, and some teens relayed stories of parents becoming frustrated by teens' religious questions, of parents disagreeing with each other about religious matters, or of parents simply issuing edicts to teens about religious activities. When all is said and done, what most teens gain from this haphazard religious socialization is reinforcement of the theistic and moral dimensions of popular American culture: "There is a God; God wants me to be a *nice person*; and he'll help me out if I am" (see chapter 2). It is a simple faith, but a surprisingly enduring one, as it can withstand long stays in an identity lockbox.

In striking contrast to semireligious teens are the American teens who have stronger feelings, pro or con, about religion. Fifteen percent of American teens are nonreligious, and some adamantly so, while 30 percent view religious faith positively and assign great importance to it. The former group should remind clergy to consider carefully that for which they want their congregations to be known, as most of these teens know religion for what it opposes and few know for what it stands. This is not to say that congregations ought not oppose objectionable matters; but they should carefully consider the message they communicate from an outsider's perspective, as some choices may do more harm to their larger cause than good. The latter group, by contrast, includes many youth already quite familiar to clergy, particularly campus-based clergy. These youth value their religious life deeply, and they do not wish to keep their faith in an identity lockbox like semireligious peers do.

That 30 percent of American teens strongly value faith does not imply, however, that these teens possess a wide or deep understanding of their faith. Religiously committed teens often described religious socialization processes that were as haphazard as those that produce semireligious teens. Intensity of faith, depth of religious knowledge, and consistency of religious practice do not walk hand-in-hand. Religiously committed teens often need basic instruction in religious life and seek guidance about how to meaningfully connect their faith to the rest of their lives and how to integrate their faith with future plans and with the world at large. The need for support from clergy and other religious leaders runs high among these teens during the first year after high school, and it is costly support. Programmatic approaches are of little interest; one-on-one conversations with trusted and religiously respected adults are most desired.

Finally, it was almost exclusively among these strongly religious teens that I heard indications of interest in spirituality. Though many American adults separate religion and spirituality,[28] I found little evidence for such a separation among teens. Given that established and institutionalized religious traditions are often haphazard about their efforts to socialize teens, it comes as no surprise that amorphous spirituality would not register an observable effect. The few teens who express interest in spirituality largely do so within traditional religious frameworks. In other words, were a university to arrange lectures on "cultivating Jewish spirituality," "understanding Catholic devotions," "practicing biblical spirituality," and "spirituality and well-being," the first three would attract a sizable and rather serious teen audience, while the latter would attract a handful of graduate students from the counseling program. At some point after the first year out, Americans begin to distinguish between religion and spirituality, but it certainly is not during the first year out.

IMPLICATIONS FOR PARENTS

Parents provide the critical infrastructure that makes teens' everyday lives possible. They provide various forms of financial support, from basic provision of housing, laundry privileges, and meals that some working-class, commuting students receive, to deluxe provision of tuition, on-campus housing, meal plans, spending money, and transportation that some upper-middle-class, residential college students receive. Parents also provide emotional support and serve as a safety net should their offspring stumble, fall, or develop significant health-related issues. Yet only when I drew teens' attention to their relationships with their parents did most teens consider the infrastructure their parents provided. Just like the technical marvel of modern air travel does not register with frequent fliers, so the economic marvel of the first year out did not register with my teen respondents. Unless there is some emergency, frequent fliers and first-year-out teens do not question the infrastructure that makes their very existence possible.

But beyond providing infrastructure, a safety net, and general emotional support, most parents' roles are relatively limited. Parents and culturally mainstream teens seem to have an unspoken agreement that parents are to watch from the sidelines while teens manage the first year out. The last major influence that most parents have in their teens' lives (except when the teens' first year out goes seriously awry), involves teens' post–high school plans. This means, for the majority of my teen respondents: (a) what form of post–high school education teens choose—vocational, two-year college, or four-year college; and (b) whether teens will reside on campus or remain at home. Financial factors are, of course, critical in this decision, but so is parents' willingness to allow their children to live away from home and parents' involvement in post–high school educational planning. From this project, and from more than a decade as a professor, I believe there are several important ways parents can make this last major influence on their teens a helpful one.

First, I would strongly encourage all parents to be partners in their children's post–high school planning process, even if they do not feel particularly competent or knowledgeable about the various possibilities. This is an important decision, and parents need to help teens with the decision *process*: Ask teens whether they have sought help from their high school's guidance office. Ask whether they have identified teachers or coaches who will write letters of recommendation. And ask teens to describe and think through their preferences for the post–high school period.

Second, I would remind parents that while post–high school planning is an important process, a far more important process is teens' life and career planning. Too many teens and parents become consumed by the college admissions process and give short shrift to considering longer-range plans (or possibilities) for which the teen is pursuing a college degree. This leads to a large number of teens enrolling in college ten weeks after high school graduation because "it's what everyone else does," unenthusiastically attending "required classes," and never finding the drive to make the most of their college education. Because of this, I offer a daring recommendation to teens and parents: let high school graduates take a year off to work (in settings that are related to their interests), volunteer, travel, and gain some independent life experience. Teens who do this subsequently enter college with a clearer purpose and firmer conviction about making the most of their college experience.[29] Gaining a college education requires a major investment of time and money; teens should enter it prepared to make the most of that investment, not just to obtain a diploma.

Third, while I certainly encourage parents to make sure teens' decision-making process is a thoughtful and careful one, I strongly encourage parents to let (even require that) their teens make the final decision. A number of teens, because of their own indecisiveness or their parents' pressure, end up making decisions that are ill-suited to their own interests or preferences, with unhappy results for all parties. Teens gain much when their parents offer guidance in their decision process, but lose much when parents make decisions for them.

The post–high school planning process is one of the last moments when parents have a direct role in their teens' lives. The primary years when parents influence children come well before the first year out. During those earlier years, parents play a significant role in all of the areas addressed in this book: teens' religious life, community awareness, interpersonal skills, gratification patterns, leisure preferences, money management, work practices, schooling interests, and general knowledge of world issues and their significance. For example, teens who managed their money well reported parents who did the same; teens who wisely moderated their gratifications reported the same by their parents; teens who were immersed in work-and-spend cycles reported parents who were similarly consumed; and teens who prioritized education, athletics, and community involvement reported parents who did the same. Parents influence their children profoundly through their own behavioral patterns—which is good and bad news for parents, because it reminds us that our words matter little if not matched by our actions. I found teens were highly skilled in identifying gaps between what their parents said and what their parents actually did. Our children know our flaws intimately. Thankfully, wise parents refuse to give up, because their children's future as well as our shared future depends on nurturing youth as effectively as we can.

IMPLICATIONS FOR TEENS

Those who passed through their teen years during the period of my research (1995–2004) and current teens may find this book resonates with some of their own experience. They deserve respect for the accomplishments their generation has made. Their generation was born and reared in an increasingly diverse set of family environments, grew up in a time when real incomes where flat but consumption expectations were rising, resided in changing communities where older modes of interaction were declining while newer modes were forming, and participated in a culture still adapting to its role in an increasingly interdependent world. That they have succeeded in managing the complex microworlds they live in is no small accomplishment. Only young and energetic Americans could adapt so readily to such a nonstop, complex, and shifting cultural environment; many in my cohort, myself included, would find it physically and emotionally overwhelming if we had to travel back in time and come of age in this environment.

With all strengths, individual or collective, come corresponding weaknesses, however. A gregarious person may not be particularly analytical, for example, just as an analytical person may not be particularly gregarious. Similarly, a generation may capably manage a shifting and complex microworld but do so at the expense of considering the wider world and developing longer-term perspectives. Some might argue that this is a temporary developmental phenomenon that will change with further maturation, but I am dubious. Many researchers have documented how everyday patterns and perspectives on the wider world remain relatively unchanged after the college years and that the daily patterns and social networks formed early in the college experience undergo few subsequent changes.[30] Others might argue that short-term, disengaged, and quasi-nationalist perspectives are typical of Americans of all ages and not unique to this particular generation. Although there is truth in such a claim, I suggest that the very factors that have made this generation's success in managing microworlds a particular achievement have also made this generation's disengagement with the wider world and shorter-term perspectives a particular weakness. The critical questions, then, are how might this particular weakness be hindering individual and generational effectiveness, and how to minimize its effect.

The answers to those questions will vary from reader to reader. Members of this generation who voluntarily read this book are probably among the current or future intelligentsia and thus are not disengaged from wider issues or longer-term perspectives. Reading this may have helped them better understand the context behind what they have witnessed among peers, and I hope this book will be useful to their own efforts to convey the importance of a wider and longer perspective to others. Members of this generation who are reading this book as an educational requirement will hopefully realize that disengagement from wider issues and resistance to longer-term perspectives will negatively affect both their individual lives and the lives of their peers. Thankfully, we do live in a democracy. Thus, we can readily obtain a variety of information about our local, regional, national, and international contexts; we can seek or create cultural resources that will support a desire to widen and deepen perspectives; and we can individually and collectively make our voices heard. I am not so idealistic as to believe that the well-habituated practices of an entire generation can be altered. Indeed, the macroeconomic and larger cultural forces that have shaped this generation's distinctive traits are only marginally more manipulable than the slowly shifting plates that give the American continent its geological foundation. However, if sufficient teens step forward and speak up, the narrowed perspectives of others will be challenged, and the small fraction of teens who understand the importance of broader perspectives might enlarge. Hope, even if only modest, is better than despair.

CONCLUSION

We are all, in the end, deeply cultural beings. Mainstream American teens have largely become what popular American moral culture has shaped them to become. They form more-or-less successful patterns of navigating relationships and managing gratifications, they prefer consumptive leisure and willingly insert themselves into the work-and-spend cycle, they pursue the practical educational credentials necessary to sustain these patterns and preferences, and they give little attention to that which lies beyond their microworlds. Most teens, moreover, ignore (if not resist) all opportunities to critically evaluate these patterns or to understand the wider world. To do so, they use an identity lockbox. Procuring the private happiness that popular American moral culture holds dear requires keeping religious, political, civic, socioeconomic, ethnic, and gender identities in a lockbox, as tampering with any of these identities could diminish the odds of attaining this happiness. This is further underscored by the changing global economic realities of the United States. In other words, the vast majority of teens do not seek to understand why the first year out table (to return to my opening metaphor) is wobbling or to consider whether its wobble might mean that the identity lockbox might not be so secure after all. They simply want to learn how to play, and win, the daily life management game (see chapter 3) —that is more than enough.

Some teens, however, resist using the identity lockbox. They learn how to play the daily life management game, as it represents an important set of skills to learn. But they also want to understand why the table is wobbling, and they question placing important identities into a lockbox that could very well slide off the table and burst apart. These teens have been reared to see the gaps and understand the weaknesses in popular American moral culture and to recognize the global economic realities that shape contemporary life. They come from diverse cultural streams: some represent the future intelligentsia, others are antireligious, and still others possess a strongly religious heritage. Their impact on their peers is limited, however, in part because the roughly one out of five teens[31] who fall into this category see *different* gaps and identify *different* weaknesses. Thus, most culturally mainstream teens, the remaining four out of five, ignore the noise about gaps and weaknesses, make quick use of the identity lockbox, concentrate on daily life, and remain oblivious to the flood plains on which they have pitched their life tents. I only hope that the next flood is not cataclysmic, that enough reside beyond the flood plain to rescue those within it, and that those who are rescued subsequently identify firmer cultural grounds on which to pitch their tents.

Methodological Appendix

This project is based on two primary data sources and two supplemental data sources. The primary data sources are 125 in-depth interviews with seventy-five different teens and a year of field research at a public high school (NJ High) in Suburban Township, New Jersey. The supplemental data sources are a focus group with twelve college teens about interpersonal relationships and substance use, and an open-ended group survey of twenty-four college teen volunteers that explored teens' recollection of the violent rampage at Columbine and its impact on their schools and their own lives. Though no project possesses perfect data, these data provided me with a diverse, nuanced, and in-depth portrait of American teens who graduated from high school between 1995 and 2003, of the paths they traveled during the year that followed their graduation, and of the moral culture they inhabit. In this appendix, I will describe my research methods in greater detail, but I will also narrate the microhistory of this research project so that readers can see why I structured my research project the way I did and how to avoid some of the setbacks I experienced.

I can remember watching, as a kid, a 1970s ABC television sitcom called "Operation Petticoat," based on the 1959 Blake Edwards film of the same name, starring Tony Curtis and Cary Grant. The show explored the comic adventures of an all-male WWII submarine crew that had to unexpectedly transport a dozen Army nurses. The submarine crew ran into a variety of mishaps, of course, but the nurses always proved their value, particularly the nurse whose donated girdle held damaged but critical engine gears in place, and thus saved the entire submarine and crew. I sometimes thought of that girdle holding those gears in place when I was collecting data for this project, as I had no major research grant or graduate research assistants, but instead kept puttering forward with a changing crew of eager undergraduate assistants, a half-dozen tiny (but precious!) grants for transcription and other miscellaneous expenses, and even an assortment of donated gift certificates from chain restaurants to use as initial interviewee honorariums. It is amazing what one can accomplish on a shoestring budget with diligent undergraduates and sheer determination!

Because I am not the first person to study American teens and will not be the last, I hope future researchers will benefit from this description of my project's methods and data. This all began in the summer of 1995 with a seven-page list of interview questions, a few (false) hunches, and eight in-depth interviews. I learned a lot that summer, and I am particularly indebted to the cohort of 1995 for bearing with me. Following is a list of some things I learned in the course of my project.

1. In-depth interviews are far superior to survey methods for understanding teen lives in teens' own terms and following teens' own logic.

2. Teens were quick to trust an interviewer whom they had some knowledge of, but suspicious of cold contacts.

3. By listening actively and by asking for examples, I could draw out amazing stories from teen interviewees.

4. Interpersonal relationships, sex, and substance use were more important to teens than I had expected, and I needed to probe these areas more than I initially planned.

5. Trained undergraduate interviewers can do a good job conducting interviews, and they had an immediate rapport advantage over me with high school seniors.

6. Although my rapport was less immediate, I could also help interviewees feel relaxed, I probed responses better than my undergraduate interviewers did, and my presence lent an air of importance to the interview (and increased sample retention).

7. I learned to schedule appointments with teens a week in advance, follow-up with an official letter, and call to remind students the day before the interview—as teens can be less reliable than adults.

8. It was better to shift my first interviews to the weeks preceding high school graduation—to both ask students about their high school experience while it was still current and take advantage of the greater predictability of teens' schedules during the school term.

9. Few studies of American teens had focused on the first year out, and none had used the two-wave panel interview method I intended to follow.

In short, I learned firsthand the advantages of field research methods, of making creative use of the resources that I had available, and of letting the evidence give birth to hypotheses (and not vice versa).

By the end of the project, my assistants and I completed 125 in-depth interviews with seventy-five different teens who graduated from high school between 1995 and 2003. Of these in-depth interviewees, 45 percent were male and 55 percent were female, 23 percent were black, 3 percent were Latino, 3 percent were mixed race, and 71 percent were white. Almost a third (31 percent) were from working-class families, almost a fourth (23 percent) were from upper-middle-class families, and the rest (47 percent) were middle class. Seventeen percent identified as black Protestant, 20 percent as conservative Protestant, 16 percent as mainline Protestant, 15 percent as Roman Catholic, 9 percent as adherents of other religions, 5 percent as adherents of two religions, and 16 percent did not identify with any religion. Teen interviewees came from high schools in New Jersey (both in and beyond NJ High), Pennsylvania, Connecticut, Massachusetts, New Hampshire, Maine, and Oregon, and they spent their first year out in colleges, vocational programs, and workplaces across the nation (though most stayed within a few hours' drive of their homes). I conducted one-time interviews with seven of my seventy-five interviewees; three were residents of Oregon and four were residents of an orthodox Jewish enclave. All seven were interviewed because I took advantage of a one-time opportunity to explore possible regional and cultural/religious differences (I did not find any that undermined my interpretations).

This left sixty-eight first-wave interviewees, of which we retained fifty for the second wave (giving a sample retention rate of 74 percent). These fifty teens are my primary focus in this book. Of the eighteen who were not retained, four indicated that they did not wish to participate in a second interview; another three scheduled follow-up interviews, but various factors and delays prevented those interviews from occurring; three could not be found; and eight never answered our inquiries. Chief commonalities among panel dropouts were that they belonged to early cohorts, that they were not given cash honorariums, and that they were first interviewed by one particular assistant. Later cohorts received cash honorariums ($10 to $20), and among the final two cohorts we obtained a sample retention rate of 88 percent. Future researchers are advised to use cash honorariums, to increase the honorarium for second-wave interviews, and to monitor the work of their assistants closely—no matter how dedicated they appear.

The in-depth interviews lasted 90 to 120 minutes on average, though a couple concluded after just 70 minutes (shy high school boys), and one went more than 180 minutes. The interviews covered many topics. During the first interview, teens evaluated their senior year of high school, their secondary and primary schooling as a whole, their academic likes and dislikes, their school involvements, and their post–high school plans. They described family backgrounds and relationships, neighborhoods and communities, friendships and romantic partners, religious origins and involvements, work experiences, leisure pursuits, volunteering activities, and monetary practices. They shared their future aspirations, including educational goals, careers, marriage, and children. They explained their views on love, sex, gender roles, religion, politics, work, leisure, justice, equality, and even life's meaning. Follow-up interviews repeated most of the interview questions, but started with general questions about teens' first year out, so teens could describe their experience using their own words.

I had initially hoped to interview some high school graduates who planned to attend four-year colleges, some who planned to attend community colleges, some who planned to enter vocational programs, some who planned to enlist in the military, and some who planned to enter the workforce directly. This would have allowed me to compare teens across institutional contexts and separate institutional factors from more general maturational effects. Several things altered those plans. First, to make the project manageable, I needed to limit my focus to teens from the American cultural mainstream—that is, high school graduates from working-, middle-, and upper-middle-class households—and not teens from poor or elite households. The life circumstances of poor or wealthy teens vary too greatly from mainstream teens to include them here. Elijah Anderson, *Code of the Streets: Decency, Violence, and the Moral Life of the Inner City* (New York: Norton, 1999); Frank F. Furstenberg et al., *Managing to Make It: Urban Families and Adolescent Success* (Chicago: University of Chicago Press, 1999); Jay MacLeod, *Ain't No Makin' It* (Boulder: Westview, 1995); and Peter Cookson and Caroline Persell, *Preparing for Power: America's Elite Boarding Schools* (New York: Basic Books, 1985), provide good introductions to the circumstances of poor and rich teens in America. Second, teens revise their post–high school plans often, particularly those considering direct entry to the workforce or enlistment in the military. (Several teens shared an interest in entering military service with me, but none did so, while one teen who planned to attend college ended up enlisting in the Armed Forces—and was soon assigned to several post–September 11 military actions and could not be reached for a formal follow-up interview. Even if every teen who indicated possible military service chose to enlist, I would not have had sufficient teen participants for more than anecdotal observations.) Third, teens do not believe attending community college or vocational programs excludes them from significant workforce participation; in fact, the dominant pattern for teens who attend community college or vocational programs full-time is to also work twenty-five or more hours weekly. Fourth, as pressure to apply to college is widespread among teens in the American cultural mainstream, I found it nearly impossible to identify and interview high school seniors in that mainstream who did not articulate plans to attend some form of postsecondary education.

Though I made a significant effort to reach high school seniors directly entering the workforce at two high schools, there were fewer than thirty such students in total, and none had any interest in talking to a college professor, even if paid for their time. One guidance counselor described these as "troubled kids"—teens from dysfunctional homes, who had behavior problems, substance abuse problems, cognitive deficits, and so on. Schneider and Stevenson report a similar phenomenon: fewer than "5 percent of high school seniors expected to complete their formal education with high school" (*Ambitious Generation*, 74), and "those who go directly to work after high school today are more likely to have had behavioral problems in school, such as skipping classes, getting suspended, and troublemaking" (70). Such teens are worthy of attention, but reaching them was beyond my resources and their stories beyond my project's focus.

After several years of conducting panel interviews, I began to realize a number of things about the project. First, I wanted to know more about my interviewees. I wanted to talk to their friends, meet their teachers and coaches, get to know their families, and see something of their world. Second, I wanted to diversify the teens I was interviewing. Snowball and purposive sampling kept netting me mostly white and college-bound teens, and I wanted a broader representation of teens. And third, I wanted to contrast what teens were telling me about their world with my own observations of it. Perceptions can be easily swayed by others, and I wanted to perceive for myself the situations I was hearing about from teens. To do these things, I knew I needed to augment the project significantly.

I chose to add a year of field research at a carefully selected high school. I did not want one of those "top school district" high schools; I already had enough teens from those sorts of places. But I also knew I did not want Small City's high school, which was an urban school serving a mostly poverty-level population; such high schools have already been well studied, and I wanted to focus on teens from more stable environments. I wanted a high school that had a good number of working-class teens and a fair degree of ethnic diversity. That is exactly what I found with NJ High. Suburban Township, where NJ High is located, is an "old ring" suburb of Small City; many of its homes were constructed between 1950 and 1965, and it now houses a mix of working-class, middle-class, and a few upper-middle-class residents. Though the township is 75 percent white and 25 percent nonwhite, the high school's ratio was 50 percent white and 50 percent nonwhite, as many white parents pull their children out of the public schools before high school. Thanks to connections that my college's Dean of Education had with school districts throughout the state of New Jersey, I was warmly received by Suburban Township's school superintendent and my project unanimously approved by its board of education.

I met in the summer of 2000 with the principal, two vice principals, and their staff to work out the details of my field research. Because I had no desire to go "undercover" (besides being troubled by deceiving others, I had too many gray hairs and no acting skills), I was issued a "staff" school ID card, which I had to keep visible at all times. That was not unusual, however, as all staff and students had to do the same. This was, after all, just after a tragic series of violent, murderous school rampages in the United States. A pleasant vice principal gave me a tour of the building and introduced me to a few of the staff working there that summer day.

I returned to NJ High the day before the 2000–2001 school year began, to attend a meeting of NJ High department heads. I explained my presence and purpose in being at NJ High, and they mainly wanted to know whether I was going to be observing classes. I explained that I would always get the teacher's permission first, told them I was going to keep names and identifying information confidential, and let them know I would be spending most of my time in the lunchroom and attending events with students. Their eyes widened on hearing the last part, and they wished me a hearty "Good luck!" while the principal glowered. The principal seemed a little nervous about my presence and often talked to me about wanting to get a job teaching at my college when he retired. Still, he made sure that his staff knew of my presence and instructed them to facilitate my research there.

After meeting with the department heads, the social studies and history head enthusiastically invited me to "give a talk" in his sociology elective class. "It has a lot of seniors in it, it would be great for them to meet an actual sociologist, and it meets right before lunch." I thought that sounded like a great way to introduce myself to a dozen seniors at once, so I arranged to visit his class the first Friday of school. Because the class was just beginning to learn about sociology, I kept my presentation at a very basic level. I talked about what sociology is and the kinds of things that sociologists study. I told them about my own interest in sociology as a college student and how I became a sociologist. I introduced quantitative research and passed around one of my journal articles and a copy of my dissertation. (The length of a dissertation really amazed them; I always knew that bound dissertation would be more than a good paperweight.) Then I talked about participant observation, inductive research, and my presence at the school over the next year. I explained that I wanted to understand what it was like to be a high school senior "in the year 2000," that I planned to keep track of what happens to "a small sample" of seniors during the first year after graduation, and that I hoped to write a book about all of this when I was done. The class became quite excited about all of this; several seniors immediately volunteered to be interviewed (including Lowanda Smith and Raquel Johnson) and to introduce me to other seniors. Several juniors volunteered to be interviewed, too. They were all incredulous when I said I was going to hang out in the lunchroom and eat the lunchroom food with them. "You're taking your life in your hands," they teased me. All in all, it made for a great entry into the students' world at NJ High.

I spent the fall term just getting to know the seniors. Though some embraced my presence immediately, like the Girlfriends Seven, others were more wary. Some asked, given my staff identification card, whether I was a teacher or a security aide at the school. A couple heard that I was a "narc," that is, an undercover narcotics officer. That one especially amused me; because I wore a photo ID and made no effort to disguise myself or my intentions, I would surely qualify as the worst undercover investigator in history. One senior wrote an article about me for the student newspaper, which was accurate but very short. No NJ High student admitted to reading the school newspaper, however. "The principal and teachers write that," they told me.

In time, I got to know some seventy NJ High seniors by name, participated in many hours of lunchroom conversation, and observed plenty of teen antics in the lunchroom, hallways, library, and outside.

I also got to know a dozen teachers (several of whom also coached varsity teams) and talked with four teachers on a regular basis. I became acquainted with several security aides, a couple of cafeteria workers, the library staff, a school social worker, the director of the guidance counseling, the main office secretaries, two vice principals, and the principal. My focus, however, was always on the seniors. Besides spending Fridays at the school, I attended pep rallies, spirit week events, games, concerts, rehearsals, and shows. I also visited several students who worked at Suburban Township businesses. Beginning in February 2001, I began to ask seniors to sit for in-depth interviews. I used quota sampling to do this, balancing interviewees by race, gender, involvements, and future plans. To answer student questions and reassure parents, I created a trifold brochure about the in-depth research interviews, including in it answers to frequently asked questions, and adding my contact information at the college. My twenty-one in-depth interviews with NJ High students all occurred after the school day in an empty conference room or classroom, and I gave each interviewee $10 in appreciation for their time. All interviewees received informed consent forms in advance, which their parents signed if they were under eighteen years old, and all retained a copy of the brochure and informed consent form for their records. These interviews took place between March and June of 2001. My field research at NJ High ended in June 2001, when 220 seniors enthusiastically graduated from high school and began their first year out.

During the process of writing this book, I realized I needed to explore a few issues further. I did so in two ways. First, I recruited twelve college teen volunteers to participate in a focus group on interpersonal relationships and substance use. This focus group asked questions about a number of matters about which I had drawn some preliminary conclusions, but for which I wanted to check my conclusions against teens' own experiences. By using a focus group, I could contrast answers, interpretations, and patterns among the participants. We had a wide-ranging and engaging discussion, and many participants stayed afterward to talk with me further about their experiences and observations. I was also happy because I was correct in my preliminary conclusions, but gained more nuanced information and solicited some rich examples from the focus group participants.

The second way I supplemented my data was through recruiting twenty-four college teen volunteers, who sat for a group survey and follow-up discussion. These teens first completed and handed in answers to open-ended questions about the potential impact of the violent rampage at Columbine High School on their schools and their own lives and then discussed their answers as a group. (By turning in their written answers before the discussion, I prevented these responses from being influenced by the subsequent discussion.) This, too, produced a wide-ranging discussion that was also quite emotional (even though the discussion occurred more than six years after the Columbine rampage). Review of survey responses confirmed my preliminary conclusions, but in far more significant ways than I had expected.

A strength of qualitative research is, of course, the opportunity it gives researchers to improve their questions and methods as their investigation proceeds. I shifted the first-wave interview to before high school graduation, developed a process to increase participation in those first interviews, probed issues of interpersonal relationships, sex, and substance use more fully, switched to cash honorariums, increased the proportion of interviews I conducted personally, supplemented in-depth interviews with field research, and then supplemented these with a focus group and open-ended group survey to evaluate a few preliminary conclusions. I hope describing these adjustments will assist future researchers.

An important aspect of qualitative research is determining its "end." Data collection ends when researchers reach the "point of saturation," that is, when researchers no longer discover important new information from their data sources and can largely anticipate what respondents will say. Though the breadth of this inquiry meant that I left a few interesting but more peripheral matters for future investigators, I did reach saturation in both in-depth interviews and field research. I began to hear the same answers again and again and could predict how teens would answer the second half of my questions based on their answers to the first half, or second-wave questions based on their first-wave answers. I also reached saturation at NJ High. Beyond growing weary of the lukewarm, carbohydrate-laden offerings of NJ High's cafeteria, I had learned the organization of the school and the culture of its senior students and shared something of their elation in being "done with high school" on that June graduation night. After spending a *fifth* year of my life in high school, I too was happy to "graduate" back to the colleagues, lectures, coffee shops, and campus quads of my college "home."

Notes

INTRODUCTION

1. A presumption shared by some prominent scholars of adolescence as well. In "Introduction: Late Adolescence and the Transition to Adulthood," Lonnie R. Sherrod, Robert J. Haggerty, and David L. Featherman assert: "College provides a slowed passage to certain adult behaviors and a safe haven to experiment with a variety of adult behaviors, values, and life styles; the developmental opportunities provided by this privilege are not well explored, but that half of the population not attending college may be missing more than continued academic achievement." *Journal of Research on Adolescence* 3, no. 3 (1993): 219.
2. Loren Pope, *Colleges That Change Lives* (New York: Penguin, 1996), 1.
3. G. K. Chesterton, *What's Wrong with the World* (1910), x.

CHAPTER ONE

1. Eliminating households earning less than $25,000 per year in 2002, and subtracting from the denominator those not yet graduated from high school, census figures indicate 75.5 percent of dependent youth aged 18–24 were enrolled, had attended, or had completed college. This figure is biased downward, as it does not include college graduates living independently at ages 22, 23, and 24. Moreover, enrollment in or completion of vocational programs is not included and would add 2–3 percent to this figure. The vast majority of high school graduates (likely 80 percent or more) from households earning over $25,000 per year, then, pursue some form of postsecondary education. (These numbers are

based on my own analyses of October 2002 Current Population Survey summary tables, U.S. Census Bureau, released January 2004.) Schneider and Stevenson, analyzing U.S. Department of Labor data, report even fewer high school seniors (5 percent) plan to end their education with their high school degree. Barbara Schneider and David Stevenson, *The Ambitious Generation: America's Teenagers—Motivated but Directionless* (New Haven, CT: Yale University Press, 1999), 74. Whether its 80 percent or 95 percent of high school seniors, the obvious conclusion is that the new American norm is to continue education in some form beyond high school.

2. As popularized in psychological theories of Anna Freud (Sigmund Freud's daughter), which appeared in "Adolescence," in *Psychoanalytic Study of the Child* (New York: International Universities Press, 1958), 13:255–78; and Erik Erikson, *Identity, Youth, and Crisis* (New York: Norton, 1968). More recent scholarly work in psychology rejects these theories, estimating that just 10–20 percent of adolescents manifest emotional disturbances. See Stuart T. Hauser and Mary K. Bowlds, "Stress, Coping, and Adolescence," in *At the Threshold: The Developing Adolescent*, ed. S. Shirley Feldman and Glen R. Elliott (Cambridge, MA: Harvard University Press, 1990), 388–413. That scholarship has neither slowed the production of pop psychology and journalistic accounts of dramatic and traumatic adolescent rebellion and self-destruction nor filtered into American popular culture generally. (What film or television producer could sell shows about teens who manage their daily lives reasonably well and who like their parents?)

3. See Barbara Ehrenreich, *Fear of Falling: The Inner Life of the Middle Class* (New York: Harper, 1989); and Katherine Newman, *Falling from Grace: The Experience of Downward Mobility in the American Middle Class* (New York: Free Press, 1988).

4. By "increasingly complex," I am referring to the steady rise of complex interpersonal relationships, which arise out of a greater variety of family structures, more diverse means of communication, and shifting cultural forms of dyadic relationships. See Reed W. Larson et al., "Changes in Adolescents' Interpersonal Experiences: Are They Being Prepared for Adult Relationships in the Twenty-First Century?" in *Adolescents' Preparation for the Future: Perils and Promise*, ed. Larson, Brown, and Mortimer (Malden, MA: Blackwell Publishing, 2002), 31–68.

5. Erving Goffman, *The Presentation of Self in Everyday Life* (New York: Anchor, 1959).

6. Kristi has lots of company in this regard. Christian Smith's national study of teen religion reports: "If there is indeed a significant number of American teens who are serious and lucid about their religious faith, there is also a much larger number who are remarkably inarticulate and befuddled about religion." *Soul Searching: The Religious and Spiritual Lives of American Teenagers* (New York: Oxford University Press, 2005), 27.

7. Schneider and Stevenson, *Ambitious Generation*.

8. To borrow a term that anthropologist John Ogbu used to describe the anti-learning attitudes of black teens in several urban high schools he studied. John U. Ogbu, "Minority Status and Schooling in Plural Societies" *Comparative Education Review* 27, no. 2 (1983): 168–90; Ogbu, "Variability in Minority School

Performance: A Problem in Search of an Explanation," *Anthropology and Education Quarterly* 29, no. 2 (1987): 155–88.

9. See the methodological appendix.

10. Thus, the approximately 20 percent of teens from households earning less than $25,000 annually (2002 dollars) who graduated high school and directly entered the ranks of the workforce, the unemployed, or the military are not included here.

11. Based on my own analyses of the 2003 Community College Survey of Student Engagement. Of community college students enrolled full-time, 46 percent worked twenty or more hours weekly (with 25 percent working thirty hours or more weekly). Of community college students enrolled part-time, 68 percent worked twenty or more hours weekly (with 53 percent working thirty or more hours weekly).

12. Internal or organizational reports by American college personnel on the effects of their educational programs on students had been legion since the start of the twentieth century. While some of these reports aspired to social science, most fell short of that goal, and few had gained an audience beyond their institution's boundaries. Thus, Jacob's *Changing Values in College: An Exploratory Study of the Impact of College* (New York: Harper & Row, 1957) represents the first major scholarly effort in this area. This book, undertaken with the support of the Hazen Foundation, assembled, evaluated, and summarized the whole of these miscellaneous college and organizational reports. But Jacob, a professor of political science at the University of Pennsylvania, offers some highly unexpected conclusions. He argues that not only was there no discernible, liberalizing effect of college on student values but that student values actually grew more homogeneous and "self-important" over the course of four years in college: "The main overall effect of higher education upon student values is to bring about a general acceptance of a body of standards and attitudes characteristic of college-bred men and women in the American community. . . . To call this process a *liberalization* of student values is a misnomer. The impact of the college experience is rather to *socialize* the individual, to refine, polish, or 'shape up' his values so that he can fit comfortably into the ranks of American college alumni. The values of the college graduate do differ in some respects from the rest of society. He is more concerned with status, achievement, and prestige. . . . The college man or woman thus tends to be more self-important . . . than those who have not been 'higher educated'" (4–5; emphasis in original). Such candid conclusions triggered wide discussion before the book was even published, which the book's foreword suggests was "explained in part by the shock effect of negative findings concerning many long-cherished but little-examined assumptions of rival [college] programs and theories of higher education" (viii). One prominent discussant was David Riesman, who argued, "the lack of specific impact of colleges today on many of their students is a tribute to their *general* effectiveness. The middlebrow culture of America has been decisively influenced by academic values." "The 'Jacob Report,'" *American Sociological Review* 23, no. 6 (1958): 737. But I suppose few faculty members then, and even fewer today, would consider the "middlebrow culture" of 1950s America an accomplishment they would point to with pride.

CHAPTER TWO

1. The worst offender of this sort is Tom Wolfe's *I Am Charlotte Simmons: A Novel* (New York: Farrar, Straus & Giroux, 2004), but there are plenty of "nonfiction" accomplices. See, for example, Neil Howe, William Strauss, and R. J. Matson, *Millennials Rising : The Next Great Generation* (New York: Vintage, 2000); Patricia Hersch, *A Tribe Apart: A Journey into the Heart of American Adolescence* (New York: Ballantine, 1998); Meredith Maran, *Class Dismissed: A Year in the Life of an American High School, a Glimpse into the Heart of a Nation* (New York: St. Martin's/ Griffin, 2000); Elinor Burkett, *Another Planet: A Year in the Life of a Suburban High School* (New York: HarperCollins, 2002); Zack Arrington, *Confessions of a College Freshman: A Survival Guide for Dorm Life, Biology Lab, the Cafeteria, and Other First-Year Adventures* (Tulsa, OK: River Oak, 2001); or Karen Leven Coburn and Madge Lawrence Treeger, *Letting Go: A Parents' Guide to Understanding the College Years*, 4th ed. (New York: Harper, 2003).

2. See Alexander T. Astin, *What Matters in College : Four Critical Years Revisited* (San Francisco: Jossey-Bass, 1997); Ernest T. Pascarella and Patrick T. Terenzini, *How College Affects Students: Findings and Insights from Twenty Years of Research* (San Francisco: Jossey-Bass, 1991); Pascarella and Terenzini, *How College Affects Students: A Third Decade of Research* (San Francisco: Jossey-Bass, 2005); Kenneth A. Feldman and Theodore A. Newcomb, *The Impact of College on Students* (San Francisco: Jossey-Bass, 1969); and Howard R. Bowen, *Investment in Learning: The Individual and Social Value of American Higher Education* (San Francisco: Jossey-Bass, 1977).

3. See Rebekah Nathan, *My Freshman Year: What a Professor Learned by Becoming a Student* (Ithaca, NY: Cornell University Press, 2005); Michael Moffat, *Coming of Age in New Jersey* (New Brunswick, NJ: Rutgers, 1989); Dorothy C. Holland and Margaret A. Eisenhart, *Educated in Romance: Women, Achievement, and College Culture* (Chicago: University of Chicago Press, 1990); Arthur Levine and Jeannette Cureton, *When Hope and Fear Collide: A Portrait of Today's College Student* (San Francisco: Jossey-Bass, 1998); and Helen Lefkowitz Horowitz, *Campus Life: Undergraduate Cultures from the End of the Eighteenth Century to the Present* (New York: Knopf, 1987).

4. See Erik H. Erikson, *Identity, Youth, and Crisis*; and Anna Freud, "Adolescence."

5. For example, on September 7, 2004, Wellesley College's president, Diana Chapman Walsh, welcomed new freshmen with an invitation to "probe" and examine "assumptions," and so gain lifelong protection against "indoctrination": "The ideal of a liberal education rests on the understanding that probing the assumptions behind high-stakes ideological debates, subjecting them to informed examination, speaking one's own truth and hearing the truth of others, practicing the art of honing, defending, and revising a sustained and serious argument is the best lifelong protection against any kind of indoctrination, perhaps the only effective one." "A Year for Integrity," www.wellesley.edu/ PublicAffairs/President/Speeches/2004/2004Convocation.html. At Ripon College that same fall, retired general (and former Democratic candidate for U.S. president) Wesley Clark challenged freshmen to "take a very, very broad view of what is it that's of interest to you in life. . . . I hope you'll be courageous enough to pursue ideas even if they're a little bit disturbing. I hope you won't instantly

reject that which is different or shocking or frightening. . . . Finally, I hope you'll be committed to others . . . setting aside the self and giving to others." "Gen. Wesley Clark Provides Opening Convocation Address," *Ripon Magazine* (Winter 2005): 28–29, www.ripon.edu/news/magazine/Winter2005/Wesley Clark.pdf. And on August 22, 2002, President Nannerl O. Keohane of Duke University cautioned incoming freshmen: "If you emerge from Duke unfamiliar with and suspicious of other kinds of people, you will not be well prepared to be a citizen and leader of the 21st century. So get to know people who come from a different country, speak a different language at home, have skin of another color, worship in a different way. Befriend someone with a lot less money than you have, someone from a part of the world you've never visited, or someone whose moral and political views are much more conservative or much more liberal." "2002 Opening Convocation Address for Undergraduate Students," www.lib.duke.edu/archives/documents/speeches-nok/NOK20020822.pdf.

6. William Foote Whyte, *Street Corner Society: The Social Structure of an Italian Slum* (Chicago: University of Chicago Press, 1943); Robert S. Lynd and Helen Merrell Lynd, *Middletown: A Study in Modern American Culture* (New York: Harcourt, Brace, & World, 1929); David Riesman, with Nathan Glazer and Reuel Denney, *The Lonely Crowd* (New Haven, CT: Yale University Press, 1950); Robert N. Bellah et al., *Habits of the Heart: Individualism and Commitment in American Life* (Berkeley: University of California Press, 1985).

7. Anne Swidler, *Talk of Love: How Culture Matters* (Chicago: University of Chicago Press, 2001), 21, 100, 103.

8. See Christian Smith, *American Evangelicalism: Embattled and Thriving* (Chicago: University of Chicago Press, 1998).

9. I use the term *antireligious* as shorthand for religious skeptics and avowed atheists. Though there are differences between these two types, members of either generally hold that religion does (and has done) more harm than good and that humanity would be better off without it.

10. See Calvin Wayne Gordon, *The Social System of the High School: A Study in the Sociology of Adolescence* (Glencoe, IL: Free Press, 1957); Robert J. Havighurst et al., *Growing Up in River City* (New York: John Wiley, 1962); and James S. Coleman, *The Adolescent Society: The Social Life of the Teenager and Its Impact on Education* (Glencoe, IL: Free Press, 1961). See also Joseph E. Illick, *At Liberty: The Story of a Community and a Generation: The Bethlehem, Pennsylvania, High School Class of 1952* (Knoxville: University of Tennessee Press, 1989).

11. There is, of course, a sizable literature in journal articles that qualifies as sociology of adolescents and their life transitions. Because I am targeting a wide and more general readership for this book, I cite only the key macrosociological books most likely to be known or read by this audience. Alas, I do not have the space to review the valuable journal literature in this area. Interested readers can consult excellent reviews by Frank Furstenberg, "The Sociology of Adolescence and Youth in the 1990s: A Critical Commentary," *Journal of Marriage and the Family* 62 (November 2000): 896–910; and Sanford Dornbusch, "The Sociology of Adolescence," *Annual Review of Sociology* 15 (1989): 233–59. There is also good work emerging from the Research Network on Transitions to Adulthood at the University of Pennsylvania (accessible at www.transad.pop.upenn.edu). For a

thorough review of the literature on the transition to adulthood that appeared in the late 1980s and 1990s, see Michael J. Shanahan, "Pathways to Adulthood in Changing Societies: Variability and Mechanisms in Life Course Perspective," *Annual Review of Sociology* 26 (2000): 667–92.

12. For an early review, see Peter L. Bensen, Michael J. Donahue, and Joseph A. Erickson, "Adolescence and Religion: A Review of the Literature from 1970 to 1996," *Research in the Social Scientific Study of Religion* 1 (1989): 153–81. One of the only manuscript-length works during these years is Raymond H. Potvin, Dean R. Hoge, and Hart M. Nelson, *Religion and American Youth: With Emphasis on Catholic Adolescents and Young Adults* (Washington, DC: U.S. Catholic Conference, 1976).

13. The first disestablishment occurred, of course, with the ratification of the Bill of Rights. The second disestablishment was a dissolution of Protestantism's cultural hegemony, caused by the immigration of millions of non-Protestants to the United States between 1870 and 1920. See Phillip E. Hammond, *Religion and Personal Autonomy: The Third Disestablishment in America* (Columbia: University of South Carolina Press, 1992).

14. See Ross M. Stolzenberg, Mary Blair-Loy, and Linda J. Waite, "Religious Participation in Early Adulthood: Age and Family Life Cycle Effects on Church Membership," *American Sociological Review* 60, no. 1 (February 1995): 84–103.

15. Pascarella and Terenzini, for example, note that the limited evidence they did find of college's effects on attitudes or values showed signs of decline toward the end of the 1980s, which they suggest might be "the precursor of an important generational effect." *Findings and Insights*, 569. And several books about baby-boomer religion suggest that cohort may possess unique characteristics; see Wade Clark Roof, *A Generation of Seekers* (New York: HarperCollins, 1993); and Dean R. Hoge, Benton Johnson, and Donald A. Luidens, *Vanishing Boundaries: The Religion of Mainline Protestant Baby Boomers* (Louisville, KY: Westminster/John Knox Press, 1994).

16. Smith did receive funding to make his "Youth and Religion" survey and interview project longitudinal, and the data for that project was collected in 2005. His book summarizing his longitudinal research is forthcoming.

17. See the Higher Education Research Institute's Web-published survey report, "The Spiritual Life of College Students: A National Study of College Students' Search for Meaning and Purpose" (Los Angeles: Higher Education Research Institute, University of California, Los Angeles, 2004), www.spirituality.ucla.edu.

18. As evidence, see "A Forked River Runs through Law School: Toward Understanding Age, Gender, Race, and Related Gaps in Law School Performance and Bar Passage," *Law and Social Inquiry* 29, no. 4 (2004): 711–70; "Toward Understanding the Role of Bible Beliefs and Higher Education in American Attitudes toward Eradicating Poverty, 1964–1996," *Journal for the Scientific Study of Religion* 38, no. 1 (1999): 103–18; "Family Behaviors among Early U.S. Baby Boomers: Exploring the Effects of Religion and Income Change, 1965–1982," *Social Forces* 76, no. 2 (1997): 605–35.

19. See Robert D. Putnam, *Bowling Alone: The Collapse and Revival of American Community* (New York: Simon & Schuster, 2000).

20. I acknowledge that there are no monolithic communities of gender, race, or class. There is, for example, no single black community in the United States, but a variety of proto and actual black communities spread throughout the United States. But because ascribed characteristics often form a basis for sustained social interaction, and because sustained social interaction in turn forms the frequent basis for community, and because it makes exposition a bit simpler, I place my discussion of gender, race, and social class under the banner of "community."

21. For example, Patricia Pasick, *Almost Grown: Launching Your Child from High School to College*, 2nd ed. (New York: Norton, 1998); and Laura Kastner and Jennifer Wyatt, *The Launching Years: Strategies for Parenting from Senior Year to College Life* (New York: Three Rivers Press, 2002).

22. Hogan and Astone distinguish the term *trajectories* from the term *pathways*, arguing that the former term "implies a greater amount of individual initiative than actually occurs" while the latter term signals "a course laid out for people, strongly encouraging them to take a particular route to get from one place to another." Because I use *trajectory* within the context of "launching" (as in a rocket), I find that word does a better job conveying what Hogan and Astone mean by *pathways*. Thus, I differ in nomenclature only, not argument. See Dennis P. Hogan and Nan Marie Astone, "The Transition to Adulthood," *Annual Review of Sociology* 12 (1986): 109–30.

23. See, for example, Deborah Carr, "The Psychological Consequences of Work-Family Trade-Offs for Three Cohorts of Men and Women," *Social Psychology Quarterly* 65, no. 2 (2002): 103–24; or Judith Stacey, *Brave New Families: Stories of Domestic Upheaval in Late-Twentieth-Century America* (New York: Basic Books, 1990).

24. The General Social Survey (GSS) is a nationally representative in-person survey, conducted biannually by the National Opinion Research Corporation, located at the University of Chicago. The GSS is the largest sociology research grant of the National Science Foundation. Further information on the GSS can be found at www.norc.uchicago.edu/projects/gensoc.asp. With regard to *theism and belief in an afterlife*, the 2004 GSS reveals that 89 percent of the U.S. population agree or strongly agree that "I believe in a God who watches over me," and 82 percent believe "there is life after death"; and the 1998 GSS reveals that 67 percent of Americans believe in "Heaven." With regard to *patriotism*, the 2004 GSS reveals that 90 percent of Americans "agree" or "strongly agree" that "I'd rather be a citizen of America than any other country in the world"; and the 1994 GSS reveals that 86 percent of Americans are "extremely" or "very" proud to be Americans. With regard to *hard work* and *individual achievement*, the 1993 GSS reveals 94 percent of Americans affirm that "willpower" and "hard work" are "important" or "very important" reasons "why a person's life turns out well or poorly"; and the 1988 GSS reports that 65 percent of Americans agree that "in America people get rewarded for their effort." With regard to *friends and family*, the 2002 GSS reveals that 68 percent of Americans stay in contact with their closest friend at least weekly; the 1988 GSS reveals that 77 percent of Americans wish they could spend "a little" or "a lot more" time with their families, and 64 percent wish they could spend more time with their friends; and the 1982 GSS reveals that 90 percent of

Americans rank "one's own family and children" as "very important . . . aspects of life," and 83 percent rank "friends and acquaintances" as important "aspects of life." With regard to *coworkers*, the 2002 GSS reveals that 86 percent of Americans affirm that "the people I work with take a personal interest in me," and that 91 percent of Americans affirm that "the people I work with can be relied on when I need help"; and the 1991 GSS reveals that 83 percent of Americans describe relationships with their coworkers as "very" or "quite" good. With regard to *personal moral freedom*, the 2000 GSS reveals that 78 percent of Americans believe "being left alone" is "very" or "extremely" important for their "freedom." With regard to suspicion of large organizations and political processes, the GSS in 2004 reveals that 43 percent of Americans have "a great deal" of confidence in the scientific community, 38 percent have the same level of confidence in medicine, 32 percent in the U.S. Supreme Court, 29 percent in banks and financial institutions, 28 percent in education, 22 percent in the federal government, 22 percent in the executive branch of the federal government, 15 percent in the U.S. Congress, 13 percent in organized labor, 11 percent in television, and 9 percent in the press. That the remaining answer options for this list of institutions are "only some" confidence and "hardly any" confidence demonstrates the suspicion that most Americans have toward these large organizations and political branches of government. With regard to the *importance of personal relationships and financial satisfaction to happiness*, the GSS in all years reveals a high and statistically significant correlation between general happiness and marital happiness, and between general happiness and financial situation; in other words, Americans who are happily married almost always report being very happy in general, and Americans who are satisfied with their financial situations are also very likely to report that they are very happy in general.

25. Smith, *Soul Searching*, 124, 171.

26. See Smith, *Soul Searching*; Higher Education Research Institute, "Spiritual Life of College Students"; and Christian Smith, Robert Faris, and Mark Regnerus, "Mapping American Adolescent Religious Participation," *Journal for the Scientific Study of Religion* 41, no. 4 (December 2002): 597–612.

27. Will Herberg, *Protestant—Catholic—Jew: An Essay in American Religious Sociology* (Chicago: University of Chicago Press, 1955), 3.

28. Smith, *Soul Searching*, 116.

29. National survey evidence supports this decline. The *Your First College Year* survey reports 57.2 percent of college freshmen attended religious services "frequently" or "occasionally" at the end of their first year of college, compared to 82.7 percent at the start. This is a significant decline; but the significant religiosity of American teens is also affirmed by the 57 percent who attend at least occasionally. Jennifer R. Keup and Ellen Bara Stolzenberg, *The 2003 Your First College Year Survey: Exploring the Academic and Personal Experiences of First-Year Students*. Monograph no. 40 (Columbia: University of South Carolina, National Resource Center for the First-Year Experience and Students in Transition, 2004), 33.

30. Using the Your First College Year survey, Keup and Stolzenberg report that 57.4 percent of college freshmen report "no change" in religious beliefs/convictions, and 34.6 percent report "stronger" religious beliefs. Keup and Stolzenberg, *2003 Your First College Year Survey*, 37. Similarly, a peer-reviewed study by Mark D.

Regnerus and Jeremy E. Uecker that analyzes the National Longitudinal Study of Adolescent Health reveals that just 4–6 percent of adolescents reported "a considerable increase or decrease in" religiosity during a one-year period in the mid-1990s, though the rate may be a couple of points higher among later adolescents. Regnerus and Uecker, "Finding Faith, Losing Faith: The Prevalence and Context of Religious Transformations during Adolescence," *Review of Religious Research* 47, no. 3 (2006): 217–37.

31. What else could I cite here but George Herbert Mead, *Mind, Self, and Society* (Chicago: University of Chicago Press, 1934).

32. By this, I mean the global interconnectedness of the American economy, the disappearance of the "company job" (i.e., one employer who hired, kept, and valued employees for their entire careers), and the critical importance of having proper and extensive educational credentials to obtain more secure employment and satisfying work conditions. For a thorough introduction to the "new economic realities" of U.S. workers today, see Lawrence Mishel, Jared Bernstein, and Sylvia Allegretto, *The State of Working America 2004/2005* (Ithaca, NY: Cornell University Press, 2005).

33. See Ehrenreich, *Fear of Falling*; and Newman, *Falling from Grace*.

34. Smith, *Soul Searching*, 27.

35. Ibid., 162.

36. Which, of course, takes us back to Will Herberg's astute observation. Herberg, *Protestant—Catholic—Jew*.

37. Smith, *Soul Searching*, 261.

38. See James A. Baldwin, "Fifth Avenue, Uptown: A Letter from Harlem," originally published in *Esquire*, July 1960, and reprinted in the author's book, *Nobody Knows My Name* (New York: Dell, 1961), 61–62.

39. See Carol Gilligan, *In a Different Voice: Psychological Theory and Women's Development* (Cambridge, MA: Harvard University Press, 1982).

40. See Sabrina Oesterle, Monica Kirkpatrick Johnson, and Jeylan T. Mortimer, "Volunteerism during the Transition to Adulthood: A Life Course Perspective," *Social Forces* 82, no. 3 (March 2004): 1123–49.

CHAPTER THREE

1. See, for example, Hersch, *Tribe Apart*; Maran, *Class Dismissed*; Burkett, *Another Planet*; Henry Wechsler and Bernice Wuethrich, *Dying to Drink: Confronting Binge Drinking on College Campuses* (New York: Rodale Press, 2002); Judith S. Wallerstein, Julia M. Lewis, and Sandra Blakeslee, *The Unexpected Legacy of Divorce: A 25 Year Landmark Study* (New York: Hyperion, 2000); David Wheaton, *University of Destruction: Your Game Plan for Spiritual Victory on Campus* (Minneapolis: Bethany House, 2005). Also see various reports by the Alan Guttmacher Institute (www.guttmacher.org), including Hillard Weinstock, Stuart Berman, and Willard Cates, Jr., "Sexually Transmitted Diseases among American Youth: Incidence and Prevalence Estimates, 2000," *Perspectives on Sexual and Reproductive Health* 36, no. 1 (2004), www.guttmacher.org/pubs/journals/3600604 .html: "Our estimate of 9.1 million new infections in 2000 among 15–24-year-olds demonstrates the tremendous toll these infections continue to have on

youth in America: representing one-quarter of the ever-sexually active population aged 15–44, young people acquire nearly one-half of all new STDs. This burden is reflected not only in morbidity among the individuals affected but also in economic and psychological costs."

2. Social desirability is also at work; many culturally mainstream teens may believe that they should have "close" relationships with their parents, and thus they have an additional impetus to report the same.

3. See discussion in chapter 4 of teens' preferences for a "good boss," who lets them socialize with coworkers and customers and tolerates a fair amount of "goofing off." See also discussion in chapter 5 of the "game of school" and the "game of college."

4. Nathan's ethnography, *My Freshman Year*, does a particularly good job pointing out the shallowness of American friendship, particularly as evident from interviews with international students.

5. See, for example, Anthony Giddens, *The Consequences of Modernity* (Palo Alto, CA: Stanford University Press, 1990); or *Modernity and Self-Identity: Self and Society in the Late Modern Age* (Palo Alto, CA: Stanford University Press, 1991).

6. Schneider and Stevenson, *Ambitious Generation*, 203.

7. Teens, of course, are not unique in this regard. Americans in general report a sharp decline in the number of nonkin confidants between 1985 and 2004. See Miller McPherson, Lynn Smith-Lovin, and Matthew E. Brashears, "Social Isolation in America: Changes in Core Discussion Networks over Two Decades," *American Sociological Review* 71, no. 3 (2006): 353–75.

8. Hersch, *Tribe Apart*.

9. For my conclusions about adult sexual behavior, I draw upon the landmark study of American sexuality by Edward O. Laumann et al., *The Social Organization of Sexuality: Sexual Practices in the United States* (Chicago: University of Chicago Press, 1994).

10. And made defining contemporary relationships a major source of angst, at least for college women. See Norval Glenn and Elizabeth Marquardt, *Hooking Up, Hanging Out, and Hoping for Mr. Right: College Women on Dating and Mating Today*, Report to the Independent Women's Forum (New York: Institute for American Values, 2001), www.americanvalues.org/Hooking_Up.pdf. I discuss their important report later in the chapter.

11. The 2004 Monitoring the Future survey of American teens reveals 7 percent of eighth graders had used "tranquilizers, barbiturates, or sedatives for nonmedical use" in the last year, 8.1 percent had used other illegal drugs in the last year, and 12.2 percent had smoked marijuana in the last year. Among twelfth graders, the rates were 14 percent, 20 percent, and 34 percent. Kate Zernike, "Drug Survey of Students Finds Picture Very Mixed," *New York Times*, December 20, 2005; for more complete information, visit www.monitoringthefuture.org/.

12. U.S. Centers for Disease Control and Prevention (CDC), "QuickStats: Pregnancy, Birth, and Abortion Rates for Teenagers Aged 15–17 Years—United States, 1976–2003," *MMWR Weekly* 54, no. 4 (February 4, 2005): 100, www.cdc.gov/mmwr/.

13. See Carolyn Halpern et al., "Implications of Racial and Gender Differences in Patterns of Adolescent Risk Behavior for HIV and Other Sexually Transmitted Diseases," *Perspectives on Sexual and Reproductive Health* 36, no.6 (2004): 239–48.

14. W. I. Thomas and Dorothy Swaine Thomas, *The Child in America: Behavior Problems and Programs* (New York: Knopf, 1928), 572.

15. And so do many adults, with help from the public discourse of mass media. See Axel Aubrun and Joseph Grady, "Aliens in the Living Room: How TV Shapes Our Understanding of 'Teens,'" (white paper, FrameWorks Institute, September 18, 2000), www.frameworksinstitute.org/products/youth.shtml.

16. According to the 1991–2003 Youth Risk Behavior Surveillance Surveys of the CDC. Percentages were obtained by the author in March 2006 through online analysis options available at the CDC Web site, www.cdc.gov/healthyyouth/yrbs/index.htm.

17. Hersch, *Tribe Apart*, 366.

18. See Murray Milner, *Freaks, Geeks, and Cool Kids: American Teenagers, Schools, and the Culture of Consumption* (New York: Routledge, 2004), 3. Milner offers a footnote to his question, "Why have alcohol, drug use, and casual sex become widespread?" (which appears on pp. 239–40), but it cites evidence about alcohol and drug use only and does not provide evidence to support his assumption of widespread casual sex among high school students.

19. According to the 2003 Youth Risk Behavior Surveillance Survey of the CDC, 45.3 percent of female high school students and 48 percent of male high school students reported having sexual intercourse. Percentages were obtained by the author in March 2006 through online analysis options available at the CDC Web site, www.cdc.gov/healthyyouth/yrbs/index.htm.

20. See Schneider and Stevenson, *Ambitious Generation*; Havighurst et al., *Growing Up in River City*; and Coleman, *Adolescent Society*, for a fuller discussion of American teen norms in the 1950s.

21. Glenn and Marquardt, *Hooking Up, Hanging Out*.

22. Because asking interviewees about sexual activities at length made a number of teens feel uncomfortable, I would gather basic information and move on to other topics quickly. As it became clearer just how important it was to understand "hookups," I conducted a 90-minute group interview with twelve residential and commuting, male and female, college students to deepen my understanding of this increasingly important teen phenomenon. This was quite helpful, as interviewees felt comfortable talking about what goes on, without revealing their specific activities. It was a lively interview with complete participation, as teens reported they had never had a focused, objective discussion of this phenomenon before and learned a lot from each other about this phenomenon and its prominence in post–high school teen culture.

23. Elizabeth L. Paul, Brian McManus, and Allison Hayes, "'Hookups': Characteristics and Correlates of College Students' Spontaneous and Anonymous Sexual Experiences," *Journal of Sex Research* 37, no. 1 (2000): 76–88.

24. See also Glenn and Marquardt, *Hooking Up, Hanging Out*.

25. See Laumann et al., *Social Organization of Sexuality*.

26. See Paul, McManus, and Hayes, "Hookups." See also, Elizabeth L. Paul and Kristen A. Hayes, "The Casualties of 'Casual' Sex: A Qualitative Exploration of the Phenomenology of College Student Hookups," *Journal of Social and Personal Relationships* 19, no. 5 (2002): 639–61.

27. Glenn and Marquardt, *Hooking Up, Hanging Out*, 6, 23.

28. Glenn and Marquardt make hay of this in their report, pointing out, "While hooking up is portrayed by some students as a bold move made by modern woman, it is interesting to note how often these women end up in a distinctly vulnerable position, waiting by the phone for the guy to call and allowing the guy to define the status of the relationship." They continue, "Although many people would say that women today have more power in relationships than women did in the 1950s—and women indeed do have far more social power today—in reality they may not have nearly as much power in relationships with men as they appear to. . . . Women and men hook up, and men decide whether anything more will happen." Glenn and Marquardt, *Hooking Up, Hanging Out*, 19, 39–40.

29. To wit, a 2005 survey of undergraduates attending six different colleges, three public and three private, found 84 percent of students reported zero or one sexual partner in the previous year, yet these same students estimated that just 22 percent of their peers had a similar behavior pattern. See Kristen Scholly, Alan R. Katz, Jan Gascoigne, and Peter S. Holck, "Using Social Norms Theory to Explain Perceptions and Sexual Health Behaviors of Undergraduate College Students: An Exploratory Study," *Journal of American College Health* 53, no. 4 (2005): 159–66.

30. According to national surveys by the CORE Institute at Southern Illinois University Carbondale, 17.7 percent of college freshmen are "heavy and frequent drinkers." That is, they consume twenty drinks per week on average, on three or more occasions per week. www.siu.edu/departments/coreinst/public_html.

31. My estimates here are based on what my interviewees told me about their own activities and on national survey results, including the following. The CORE Institute 2004 report showed that 17.7 percent to 27.5 percent of college students are "heavy and frequent drinkers," and 18.8 percent of college students used marijuana in the past thirty days, www.siu.edu/departments/coreinst/public _html/. The 2003 Your First College Year survey found that 25.2 percent of freshman nationally spent six or more hours "partying" each week, but that 38–43 percent did *not* drink wine, beer, or liquor "frequently" or "occasionally." Keup and Stolzenberg, *2003 Your First College Year Survey*, 21, 33. The Glenn and Marquardt report, in which 8 percent of its national survey of college women strongly agreed that "going out in a group, drinking a lot, and then having sex is common at my college," 10 percent indicated having six or more "hook-ups," and 39 percent reported that they were virgins. Glenn and Marquardt, *Hooking Up, Hanging Out*, 74, 4, 13. And the 1995 National College Health Risk Behavior Survey of the CDC reported that 25.7 percent of college students ages 18–24 had more than six sexual partners during their lifetime, 37.9 percent did *not* have sexual intercourse in the preceding three months, and 20.5 percent have *never* had sexual intercourse. Table 15 of the NCHRBS summary report, www.cdc.gov /mmwr/preview/mmwrhtml/00049859.htm.

32. Some of this can be attributed to the nebulousness of the term *hooking up* itself; it can mean anything from kissing to intercourse. This allows participants to acknowledge the activity, while leaving its content ambiguous, which, Glenn and Marquardt suggest, may be particularly important for college women's "reputations." Glenn and Marquardt, *Hooking Up, Hanging Out*, 21–22.

33. And an accomplishment that many freshmen achieve. Sixty-three percent of college freshman reported they were "completely successful" in "developing

close friendships with other students," and another 31 percent reported being "somewhat successful." Keup and Stolzenberg, *2003 Your First College Year Survey*, 12.

34. The Glenn and Marquardt report, however, confirms the impact of parental divorce on college women's dating and mating behaviors. Glenn and Marquardt, *Hooking Up, Hanging Out*.

35. See Mark D. Regnerus, "Religion and Positive Adolescent Outcomes: A Review of Research and Theory," *Review of Religious Research* 44, no. 4 (2003): 394–413; and Christian Smith and Robert Faris, "Religion and American Adolescent Delinquency, Risk Behaviors, and Constructive Social Activities," (Chapel Hill: University of North Carolina, National Study of Youth and Religion, 2002), www.youthandreligion.org.

36. According to the 2003 Youth Risk Behavior Surveillance Survey of the CDC, 4 percent of white high school students reported having sexual intercourse before the age of thirteen, compared to 19 percent of black high school students. Similarly, 30.8 percent of white high school students reported having sexual intercourse with one or more persons in the last three months, compared to 49 percent of black high school students. Finally, 10.8 percent of white high school students reported having sexual intercourse with four or more persons during their life, compared to 28.8 percent of black high school students. Percentages were obtained by the author in March 2006 through online analysis options available at the CDC Web site, www.cdc.gov/healthyyouth/yrbs/index.htm.

CHAPTER FOUR

1. In fact, in 2005 two Roman Catholic high school principals canceled their schools' senior proms, citing the *thousands* of dollars many couples were spending as a "show of affluence" and thus "opposed to [the school's] value system." Paul Vitello, "Hold the Limo: The Prom's Canceled as Decadent," *New York Times*, December 10, 2005.

2. See Greenberger and Steinberg, *When Teenagers Work* (New York: Basic Books, 1986), 6–7.

3. See Jerald Bachman, "Premature Affluence: Do High School Students Earn Too Much?" *Economic Outlook USA* 10, no. 3 (Summer 1983): 64–67.

4. See Milner, *Freaks, Geeks, and Cool Kids*, 57.

5. See Jeylan Mortimer, *Working and Growing Up in America* (Cambridge, MA: Harvard University Press, 2003), 25–27.

6. See Schneider and Stevenson, *Ambitious Generation*.

7. With hats off to the many astute observers of this phenomenon, including Juliet Schor, *The Overworked American* (New York: Basic Books, 1991); Schor, *The Overspent American* (New York: Basic Books, 1998); Vance Packard, *The Status Seekers* (New York: D. McKay, 1959); and even Max Horkheimer and Theodor W. Adorno, *Dialectic of Enlightenment* (1944; various translations available).

8. Douglas Kleiber, Reed Larson, and Mihaly Csikszentmihaly used the experience sampling method with seventy-five adolescents in the early 1980s to identify two forms of leisure: "relaxed leisure" and "transitional activities," the latter

of which includes sports, games, art, and hobbies. These two categories overlap considerably with my "quiet" and "active" leisure clusters; however, these authors did not have the data to differentiate consumptive leisure activities, which emerged distinctly in qualitative interviews. A more recent paper by Leslie A. Raymore, Bonnie L. Barber, Jacqueline S. Eccles, and Geoffrey C. Godbey used formal, statistical cluster analyses of the Michigan Study of Adolescent Life Transitions (MSALT) to identify eight leisure behavior clusters: four for boys, and four for girls. Their clusters typology is fairly complex, however, and requires multiple quantitative indicators to create. Because my project is a qualitative project with a small sample, I simply asked teens about the kinds of things they liked to do in their "free time" or "for leisure" and noted that three generally distinct clusters appeared in their answers. See Kleiber, Larson, and Csikszentmihaly, "The Experience of Leisure in Adolescence," *Journal of Leisure Research*, 18, no. 3 (1986): 169–76; and Raymore et al, "Leisure Behavior Pattern Stability during the Transition from Adolescence to Young Adulthood," *Journal of Youth and Adolescence* 28, no. 1 (1999): 79–103.

9. Classic critiques of organized schooling may ring truer now than ever. See Samuel Bowles and Herbert Gintis, *Schooling in Capitalist America* (New York: Basic Books, 1976); John W. Meyer, "The Effects of Education as an Institution," *American Journal of Sociology* 83, no. 56 (1977); Raymond S. Moore, *Better Late Than Early: A New Approach to Your Child's Education* (New York: Dutton, 1975); John Holt, *How Children Fail* (New York: Pitman, 1964), idem, *How Children Learn* (New York: Pitman, 1967), and idem, *The Underachieving School* (New York: Pitman, 1969).

10. For example, Christina Hoff Sommers, *The War against Boys: How Misguided Feminism Is Harming Our Young Men* (New York: Simon & Schuster, 2000).

11. See Neil Gilbert, "Family Life: Sold on Work," *Society* 42, no. 3 (March/April 2005): 12–17.

12. See Mortimer, *Working and Growing Up in America.*

13. Perhaps this is a result of regional differences in our samples. My sample, though from working-class to upper-middle-class homes, comes largely from more affluent, East Coast states. Mortimer's sample comes from St. Paul, Minnesota, a city with a prominent history of German, Swedish, and Norwegian immigrant populations that long valued economic thrift, and a state population that particularly enjoys outdoor activity. Hence, preferences for active versus consumptive leisure may vary considerably between these two regions, making Mortimer's St. Paul teens distinct from my East Coast teens. Thus, I take a position more aligned with Bachman's "Premature Affluence" and situate my study of adolescents between the adult subjects of Schor's *The Overspent American* and the children and child marketers of Schor's *Born to Buy: The Commercialized Child and the New Consumer Culture* (New York: Scribner, 2004). Teen employment is not inherently harmful to teens' psychological development, and, in fact, their work and spending surely contributes much to the U.S. economy. My critique lies primarily in the consumerism of American teens and the degree to which teen work represents early and uncritical entry into the all too dominant American pattern of work and spend.

14. See Janet B. Bernstel, "Teens: Give 'Em Credit!" *Bank Marketing* 34 (March 2002): 14–19; Deborah J. C. Meyer and Heather C. Anderson, "Preadolescents and

Apparel Purchasing: Conformity to Parents and Peers in the Consumer Socialization Process," *Journal of Social Behavior and Personality* 15 (2000): 243; Stanley C. Hollander and Richard Germain, *Was There a Pepsi Generation before Pepsi Discovered It?* (Lincolnwood, IL: NTC Business Books, 1992); Carol Angrisani, "Cool Rules for Teen Marketing," *Business and Industry* 11 (2000): 32. See also results from the 1999 Youth and Money survey and the Parents, Youth, and Money 2001 survey conducted by Mathew Greenwald and Associates for the TIAA-CREF Institute. (For summaries of both surveys: www.ebri.org/publications/ prel/index.cfm?fa=prelDisp&content_id=3555; for the 1999 survey: www.tiaa-crefinstitute.org/research/speeches/062999.html; for the 2001 survey: www .tiaa-crefinstitute.org/research/surveys/ps_overview.html.)

15. See two books by Viviana Zelizer: *The Social Meaning of Money: Pin Money, Paychecks, Poor Relief, and Other Currencies* Princeton, NJ: Princeton University Press, 1997, and *Pricing the Priceless Child: The Changing Social Value of Children* (Princeton, NJ: Princeton University Press, 1994).

16. Statistics from the Bureau of Economic Analysis at the U.S. Department of Commerce reveal that personal savings rates were almost always above 8 percent prior to 1986, but have plummeted since then to rates of 2 percent and even lower.

17. See Carol B. Stack *All Our Kin: Strategies for Survival in a Black Community* (New York: Harper & Row, 1974).

18. See Dalton Conley, *Being Black, Living in the Red: Race, Wealth, and Social Policy in America* (Berkeley: University of California Press, 1999).

19. See Raymore et al., "Leisure Behavior Pattern Stability"; and Leslie A. Raymore, Bonnie L. Barber, and Jacqueline S. Eccles, "Leaving Home, Attending College, Partnership, and Parenthood: The Role of Life Transition Events in Leisure Pattern Stability from Adolescence to Young Adulthood," *Journal of Youth and Adolescence* 30, no. 2 (2001): 197–223.

20. And even then, reduction is more likely to be symbolic, as second semester freshmen usually improve their grades by better learning how to play the academic "game of college" (see chapter 5).

21. See chapter 1's analyses of the National Survey of Student Engagement (2000–2004) and the Community College Survey of Student Engagement (2003).

22. While the latter's experiences are important, their stories diverge too far from the culturally mainstream American teens whose stories are this book's focus. See discussion in the methodological appendix.

23. See Katherine Zoepf, "Retailers Make Sure Freshmen Live in Style," *New York Times*, September 1, 2003.

24. See Vincent J. Miller, *Consuming Religion: Christian Faith and Practice in a Consumer Culture* (New York: Continuum, 2003). See also Robert Wuthnow, *God and Mammon in America* (New York: Free Press, 1994).

CHAPTER FIVE

1. One need not read through many issues of the *Chronicle of Higher Education* before finding some professor's essay about nonintellectual or academically disengaged college students. Here are three: Stuart Rojstaczer, "When Intellectual

Life Is Optional for Students," *Chronicle of Higher Education*, April 20, 2001; Jonathan Malesic, "The Smell of Indoctrination in the Morning," *Chronicle of Higher Education*, October 17, 2005; and Mark Bauerlein, "A Very Long Disengagement," *Chronicle of Higher Education*, January 6, 2006.

2. For human capital theory, see Gary S. Becker, *Human Capital: A Theoretical and Empirical Analysis, with Special Reference to Education*, 3rd ed. (Chicago: University of Chicago Press, 1993). For identity development theory, see Erik Erikson, *Identity, Youth, and Crisis*. For social reproduction theory, see Bowles and Gintis, *Schooling in Capitalist America*; and MacLeod, *Ain't No Makin' It* (Boulder: Westview, 1995).

3. National Governors Association, Rate Your Future survey. Results were released July 16, 2005, at www.nga.org (summary results at www.nga.org/Files/ppt/ rateyourfuturesurvey.ppt) and described in many major media publications, including Michael Janofsky, "Students Say High Schools Let Them Down," *New York Times*, July 16, 2005.

4. See also Paul R. Gross et al., *The State of Science Standards: 2005* (Washington, DC: Thomas B. Fordham Institute, 2005).

5. A study by Jean Johnson and Steve Farkas of Public Agenda, titled *Getting By: What American Teenagers Really Think about Their Schools* (New York: Public Agenda, 1997), drew this conclusion from their national survey of public and private school teens: "Most view their high school careers as an exercise in the art of 'getting by'—doing as little as possible to get the grades they need. And, while they accept society's judgment that 'getting an education' is essential to their future, they express minimal interest in—and virtually no sense of curiosity about—the subjects they study in school" (11). The same point is made by Denise Clark Pope in *Doing School: How We Are Creating a Generation of Stressed Out, Materialistic, and Miseducated Students* (New Haven, CT: Yale, 2001).

6. See Daniel Goleman, *Emotional Intelligence* (New York: Bantam Books, 1995).

7. A Web search of school district mission statements turned up the following on September 5, 2005: the River Forest (IL) School District seeks to prepare its students by "instilling the love of learning"; the Julian (CA) Union School District wishes to "create an environment that develops a lifelong love of learning"; the Warrensville Heights (OH) School District wants "to foster a love for learning while stimulating students' intellect for creative and productive thinking"; the Martinsville (IL) School District aims "to instill in each student a love of education and a desire to be life-long learners"; the Warren Woods (MI) Public Schools believe "you can teach a love of learning"; and the Richland County (SC) School District pledges "to educate every student to become a productive citizen [and a] life-long learner."

8. Keup and Stolzenberg, *2003 Your First College Year Survey*, 10.

9. Ibid., 14.

10. From the 2005 National Survey of Student Engagement, available at http://nsse .iub.edu/index.cfm. Roughly two-thirds of full-time first-year students enrolled in any of the six Carnegie classifications spent fifteen or fewer hours preparing for class each week.

11. In fact, 77 percent of American college freshman reported earning "at least a B average." Keup and Stolzenberg, *2003 Your First College Year Survey*, 29. See also

Henry Rosovsky and Matthew Hartley, "Evaluation and the Academy: Are We Doing the Right Thing? Grade Inflation and Letters of Recommendation" (occasional paper, American Academy of Arts and Sciences, Cambridge, MA, 2002); and Richard Kamber and Mary Biggs, "Grade Conflation: A Question of Credibility," *Chronicle of Higher Education*, April 12, 2005.

12. Just 31 percent of American college graduates scored, in 2003, at the "proficient" level—meaning "they were able to read lengthy, complex English texts and draw complicated inferences." In 1992, 40 percent of college graduates scored at the "proficient" level. See the U.S. Department of Education, *2003 National Assessment of Adult Literacy Report*, http://nces.ed.gov/naal/; see also Sam Dillon, "Literacy Falls for Graduates from College, Testing Finds," *New York Times*, December 16, 2005.

13. See, for example, William Strauss and Neil Howe, "The High Cost of College: An Increasingly Hard Sell," *Chronicle of Higher Education*, October 21, 2005.

14. As of September 2005, readers can consult www.pick-a-prof.com, www.virtualratings.com, and www.ratemyprofessor.com. The first offers grade distribution summaries for instructors, while the third offers evaluations of the professor's "hotness" (i.e., sexual desirability).

15. Donald McCabe, professor at Rutgers University and founder of the Center for Academic Integrity (www.academicintegrity.org), has consistently found 70 percent of undergraduates at most colleges admit to some cheating. The presence of hundreds of Web sites offering term papers for sale reinforces this finding.

16. Nathan, *My Freshman Year*, suggests that the reason why national surveys reveal that students ask more questions in class and talk more with professors out of class is not because students are growing more interested in the topic, but because they increasingly realize the grade value of "creating and using relationships with professors" (118).

17. See Burkett, *Another Planet*; or Denise Clark Pope, *Doing School*. See also Arthur G. Powell, Eleanor Farrar, David K. Cohen, National Association of Secondary School Principals (U.S.), and National Association of Independent Schools Commission on Educational Issues, *The Shopping Mall High School: Winners and Losers in the Educational Marketplace* (Boston: Houghton Mifflin, 1985).

18. For a broad discussion of U.S. income inequality and changes in real incomes, see Mishel, Bernstein, and Allegretto, *State of Working America 2004/2005*.

19. Randall Collins, *The Credential Society* (New York: Academic Press, 1979), 192.

20. Beginning with Jacob, *Changing Values in College*; Christopher Lasch, *Culture of Narcissism* (New York: Norton, 1979); Pascarella and Terenzini, *Findings and Insights*; Arthur Levine and Jeanette Cureton, "Collegiate Life: An Obituary," *Change* 30, no. 3 (May/June 1998); Ted Marchese, "Disengaged Students," *Change* 30, no. 2 (March/April 1998); idem, "Disengaged Students II," *Change* 30, no. 3 (May/June 1998); and David Brooks, "The Organization Kid," *Atlantic Monthly*, April 2001.

21. In fact, the number of unique words Julie used during her second interview increased by 48.8 percent over her first interview—which a linguist friend tells me is an enormous increase for the "everyday conversation" of an interview.

22. Reggie expanded his unique word use in his second interview by 3.8 percent over his first interview, which is a modest gain. But his logical coherence, for which I do not have a quantitative measure, gained enormously.

23. Consider how little of the reader's own knowledge has been retained from first-year college courses. For scholarly discussion of knowledge retention, see Steven G. Brint, *Schools and Societies* (Thousand Oaks, CA: Pine Forge, 1998); Ulric Neisser, *Memory Observed: Remembering in Natural Contexts* (San Francisco: Freeman, 1982); or Harry Bahrick, "Maintenance of Knowledge: Questions about Memory We Forgot to Ask," *Journal of Experimental Psychology: General* 108 (1979): 296–308.

24. Such as Bowles and Gintis, *Schooling in Capitalist America.*

25. Astin, *What Matters in College*, 159.

26. Ibid., 107.

27. See ibid., 147.

28. A Google Web search of college mission statements on September 15, 2005, uncovered the following. Vassar College seeks to educate "distinguished, diverse students motivated toward intellectual risk." The College of William and Mary "encourages the intellectual development of both student and teacher" and introduces "students to the challenge and excitement of original discovery, and is a source of the knowledge and understanding needed for a better society." Occidental College seeks "to instill a lifelong love of learning." Oberlin College hopes "to cultivate in [students] the aspiration for continued intellectual growth throughout their lives." And Agnes Scott College hopes that its students will "engage the intellectual and social challenges of their times . . . [and] realize their full creative and intellectual potential."

29. Astin, *What Matters in College*, 145.

30. Mary R. Jackman and Michael J. Muha, "Education and Intergroup Attitudes: Moral Enlightenment, Superficial Democratic Commitment, or Ideological Refinement?" *American Sociological Review* 49 (1984): 751–69.

31. Evidence for Jackman and Muha's point can be seen plainly in the Your First College Year survey that Keup and Stolzenberg analyze. Table 22 of their report contains three columns. The first column lists twenty-one different life goals—such as "keeping up to date with political affairs," "writing original works," or "becoming a community leader." The second column lists the percentage of freshmen who, at the *outset* of their first year of college, endorsed these life goals. The third column lists the percentage of freshmen who, by the end of their first year of college, endorsed these life goals. The purpose of the table is to show that freshmen's life goals are changing in ways that progressive educators desire, since *twenty* out of twenty-one life goals show the percentages increased. What Keup and Stolzenberg gloss over, however, is that it matters little how many teens endorse a particular goal or value—endorsing a goal or value is easy. What matters is where these goals or values rank in each teen's *priority system*. Teens will be fortunate if they accomplish two or three of these life goals—and with the top two goals being "raising a family" and becoming "very well off financially," most have little room to prioritize anything else. The goal of financial success is the only life goal that witnessed a decline—and arguably because freshmen are learning to be more circumspect about expressing such

goals to academic researchers. Keup and Stolzenberg, 2003 *Your First College Year Survey*, 23.

32. Pascarella and Terenzini, *Findings and Insights*, 567.

33. Pascarella and Terenzini, *Third Decade*, 569.

34. See Robert A. Rhoads, *Freedom's Web: Student Activism in an Age of Cultural Diversity* (Baltimore: Johns Hopkins, 1998); Richard Peterson, *The Scope of Organized Student Protest in 1964–1965* (Princeton, NJ: Educational Testing Service, 1966); Leonard Baird, "Who Protests: A Study of Student Activists," in *Protest! Student Activism in America*, ed. Julian Foster and Durward Long (New York: William Morrow, 1970), 123–33; Seymour Martin Lipset and Philip Altbach, "Student Politics and Higher Education in the United States," in *Student Politics*, ed. Lipset (New York: Basic Books, 1967); and Lipset, *Rebellion in the University* (Boston: Little, Brown, 1972).

35. Darren E. Sherkat and T. Jean Blocker, "The Political Development of Sixties' Activists: Identifying the Influence of Class, Gender, and Socialization on Protest Participation," *Social Forces* 72, no. 3 (1994): 821–42.

36. For a particularly provocative interpretation of the American university along these lines, see James Piereson, "The Left University: How It Was Born, How It Grew, and How to Overcome It," *Weekly Standard* 11, no. 3 (October 3, 2005).

37. Jacob, *Changing Values in College*, 1, 3.

38. See Matthew Quirk, "The Best Class Money Can Buy," *Atlantic Monthly*, November 2005.

39. Naomi Schaefer Riley, *God on the Quad: How Religious Colleges and the Missionary Generation Are Changing America* (New York: St. Martin's, 2005).

40. See James Penning and Corwin Smidt, *Evangelicalism: The Next Generation* (Grand Rapids, MI: Baker Academic, 2002); James Davison Hunter, *Evangelicalism: The Coming Generation* (Chicago: University of Chicago Press, 1987).

41. Religious colleges are expanding at an astounding speed to accommodate students. For example, the number of students attending the 105 schools in the Council of Christian Colleges and Universities increased 64 percent between 1990 and 2002, compared to a negligible increase in attendance at nonreligious schools (data as of September 26, 2005, at www.cccu.org). Even still, the 220,000 seats that the colleges in this organization offer are but a fraction of the 4.2 million college *freshmen* that the U.S. Census Bureau reports were enrolled in October 2004, of which we can estimate that 1,260,000 (30 percent) are strongly religious (see chapter 2).

42. I would include here semireligious teens as well as strongly religious teens like Fawn and Paul. The latter do not challenge the cultural "wall of separation" between their religious identities and their educational identities. While attending a nonreligious college need not result in compartmentalization for strongly religious teens necessarily, it seems to do so practically.

CHAPTER SIX

1. Dennis and Tammy were both born in 1982; they reached adolescence in 1995 (turning 13 years old) and finished adolescence in 2002 (turning 20 years old).

I begin with 1995 on the assumption that few children 12 years and under give even passing attention to cultural and political events.

2. See, for example, Ole R. Holsti and James N. Rosenau, "Does Where You Stand Depend on When You Were Born? The Impact of Generation on Post-Vietnam Foreign Policy Beliefs," *Public Opinion Quarterly* 44, no. 1 (1980): 1–22; Morton Keller, "Reflections on Politics and Generations in America," *Daedalus* 107, no. 4 (1978): 123–35; David I. Kertzer, "Generation as a Sociological Problem," *Annual Review of Sociology* 9 (1983): 125–49; Wilbur J. Scott and Harold G. Grasmick, "Generations and Group Consciousness: A Quantification of Mannheim's Analogy." *Youth and Society* 11, no. 2 (1979): 191–213; M. E. J. Wadsworth and S. R. Freeman, "Generation Differences in Beliefs: A Cohort Study of Stability and Change in Religious Beliefs," *British Journal of Sociology* 34, no. 3 (1983): 416–37.

3. For a thoughtful and thorough analysis of the entire series of 1990s school shootings, see Katherine S. Newman et al., *Rampage: The Social Roots of School Shootings* (New York: Basic Books, 2004).

4. Local and national newspapers abounded with such stories in days and months that followed Columbine's rampage. A few examples include Peter Grier and Gail Russell Chaddock, "Schools Get Tough as Threats Continue," *Christian Science Monitor*, November 5, 1999; "Five Schools near Littleton Get Letters with Threats," *New York Times*, September 5, 1999; "Monmouth [NJ] Regional High School Closed after Columbine Threat," *Associated Press*, October 29, 1999.

5. For a general introduction to this literature, see William A Galson, "Political Knowledge, Political Engagement, and Civic Education," *Annual Review of Political Science* 4 (2001): 217–34; and Stephen E. Bennett, "Why Young Americans Hate Politics, and What We Should Do about It," *Political Science and Politics* 30, no. 1 (1997): 47–53. For an example of a major educational project, see the American Democracy Project of the American Association of State Colleges and Universities (www.aascu.org). This project, rooted in Ernst Boyer's notion of the "new American college," presented in his book *Scholarship Reconsidered* (San Francisco: Jossey-Bass, 1997), advocates that all campuses recognize the central importance of "community engagement" not just with regard to their service activities, but with respect to core teaching and research activities. The project encompasses programs on 144 state colleges and universities.

6. See, for example, James Fallows, *Breaking the News: How the Media Undermine American Democracy* (New York: Vintage, 1997).

7. Keup and Stolzenberg report that just 17.3 percent of first-year American college women believe it is "very important" or "essential" to "influence the political structure," and 24.5 percent of first-year college men believe the same. Virtually the same proportions (17.7 percent and 24 percent) report "frequently" discussing politics. Keup and Stolzenberg, *2003 Your First College Year Survey*, 54.

8. See also Smith, *Soul Searching*.

9. Duane Alwin and Jon Krosnick offer the most robust study of continuity in political attitudes across the life course. They conclude that their results "provide strong support for the view that attitude stability increases with age. This increase appears to occur immediately following early adulthood, and attitude stability appears to remain at a constant, high level throughout the remainder of the life cycle." "Aging, Cohorts, and the Stability of Sociopolitical Orientations

over the Life Span," *American Journal of Sociology* 97, no. 1 (1991): 169–95. Rebekah Nathan, in her participant observer study at a state university, suggests this may be because traditional-age college students form homogeneous social networks by the end of their first year of college and generally stay within these networks for the remainder of their college years. *My Freshman Year*, 63.

10. See, for example, E. J. Dionne, Jr., *Why Americans Hate Politics* (New York: Simon & Schuster, 1991).

11. See Bellah et al., *Habits of the Heart*.

12. A point now taken for granted by "emerging adulthood" researchers, such as those who contributed to Richard A. Settersten, Jr., Frank F. Furstenberg, Jr., and Ruben G. Rumbaut, eds., *On the Frontier of Adulthood: Theory, Research, and Public Policy* (Chicago: University of Chicago Press, 2005).

13. See Larson et al., "Changes in Adolescents' Interpersonal Experiences."

14. Two valuable period sources are Havighurst et al., *Growing Up in River City*, and Coleman, *Adolescent Society*. Also helpful is Schneider and Stevenson's reanalysis of Havighurst's materials in their 1999 study, *The Ambitious Generation*.

15. Of course, teens in certain countries are keenly aware of political and international matters because of national turmoil and international threats, such as Israeli and Palestinian teens, Serbian teens, and Irish teens. But even in more politically stable countries, teens possess more knowledge of and interest in political and global matters than teens in the United States. See, for example, Judith Torney-Purta et al., "Trust in Government-Related Institutions and Political Engagement among Adolescents in Six Countries," *Acta Politica* 39, no. 4 (2004): 380–406; Marc Hooghe, "Political Socialization and the Future of Politics," *Acta Politica* 39, no. 4 (2004): 331–41; Lawrence J. Saha, "Political Activism and Civic Education among Australian Secondary School Students," *Australian Journal of Education* 44, no. 2 (2000): 155–74; Richard and Margaret Braungart, "Youth Problems and Politics in the 1980s: Some Multinational Comparisons," *International Sociology* 1, no. 4 (1986): 359–80.

16. See Levine and Cureton, *When Hope and Fear Collide*, 75.

17. Ibid., 72.

18. I learned much of this by asking twenty-four East Coast college teens, in late 2005, to voluntarily and anonymously write (1) where they were when they first heard about the rampage at Columbine, and (2) how it affected their schools, their families, and themselves. After having a student collect and shuffle these sheets, I asked students whether they wanted to talk about what they wrote. Many did; it was an impassioned discussion about fears, school and parent reactions, and more. Even though Columbine had occurred more than five years previously, these college students, who were in eighth to tenth grades at the time of the shootings, had no difficulty describing exactly where they were when then heard about the event and writing about the range of effects that event had on them, their families, and their schools. Fear, suspicion, and hopeless fatalism were dominant themes in the oral and written responses—and it confirmed directly and explicitly what was more indirect and implicit in my in-depth interviews and field research. (See also the methodological appendix.)

19. Some political scientists, for example those who wrote Harvard's Institute of Politics report "Redefining Political Attitudes and Activism: A Poll by Harvard's

Institute of Politics," claim that "the generation that has come of voting age in a post–September 11 world reports that political participation is vital to their lives, and they are strongly committed to having their voices heard." April 11 2006, p. 2; see www.iop.harvard.edu. However, 54 percent of the respondents to their national survey of college students did not consider themselves "political engaged or politically active," and only 14 percent used their facebook.com profile to "promote a political candidate, event, or idea" (see p. 3 and p. 15 of their April 11, 2006, "Top Line" data). College teens "know" they are supposed to be interested in politics and know that they are supposed to pay attention to it—many of them told me so. But when asked for specifics about what they know, how they gain political information, or what matters they have acted upon, many quickly explain how little they really know or pay attention to.

20. See, for example, Nina Eliasoph, *Avoiding Politics: How Americans Produce Apathy in Everyday Life* (New York: Cambridge University Press, 1998); Carl Boggs, "The Great Retreat: Decline of the Public Sphere in Late Twentieth-Century America," *Theory and Society* 26, no. 6 (December 1997): 741–80.

21. Again, see Dionne, *Why Americans Hate Politics*; Eliasoph, *Avoiding Politics*; and Boggs, "Great Retreat."

22. Such as the U.S. Catholic Bishops' "Economic Justice for All: Pastoral Letter on Catholic Social Teaching and the U.S. Economy" (1986); the National Council of Church's "Love for the Poor: God's Love for the Poor and the Church's Witness to It" (2005); the National Association of Evangelicals, "For the Health of the Nation: An Evangelical Call to Civic Responsibility" (2004); or the Union for Reform Judaism's "K'hilat Tzedek: Creating a Community of Justice" (2005).

23. This is all the more notable in contrast to the involvement of religious groups in organizing scores of college students for voter registration during the civil rights movement. See Doug McAdam, *Freedom Summer* (New York: Oxford University Press, 1988).

24. See Moffat, *Coming of Age in New Jersey*, for a parallel argument about gender consciousness and female college students.

25. See Philip Shenon, "9/11 Panel Issues Poor Grades for Handling of Terror," *New York Times*, December 6, 2005; see also National Commission on Terrorist Attacks, *The 9/11 Commission Report: Final Report of the National Commission on Terrorist Attacks upon the United States* (New York: Norton, 2004).

26. I doubt, for instance, whether many dedicated and selfless Americans could pass a test based on E. D. Hirsch's *Cultural Literacy: What Every American Needs to Know* (Boston: Houghton Mifflin, 1987), much less Americans at large. More important than formal knowledge, I argue, are sustained practices of concern and action for the public good. A pedagogy that begins with student interests and expands these to broader fields of knowledge and larger concerns is far more likely to produce concern and action for the public good. Consider, for example, a little boy with a keen interest in trains. Imagine if teachers, over that boy's life, connected his interest in trains to engines and the various means by which they generate power, to the impact of trains on American history and culture, to the relatively limited use of passenger trains in the United States, and to advantages and disadvantages of America's primacy in automotive transportation. That little boy would be far more likely to become a citizen who, through technical innovation

or political activism, sought to influence local, regional, and national transportation policy than a whole class of students who were taught various "units" that eventually conveyed most of same knowledge, but were left to make the connections on their own.

27. See Robert Reich, *The Work of Nations: Preparing Ourselves for 21st-Century Capitalism* (New York: Knopf, 1991).

28. See Robert Wuthnow, *After Heaven: Spirituality in America since the 1950s* (Berkeley: University of California Press, 1998).

29. See Richard J. Light, *Making the Most of College: Students Speak Their Minds* (Cambridge, MA: Harvard University Press, 2001). See also student testimonials from the Center for Interim Programs, LLC, with offices in Princeton, New Jersey, and Cambridge, Massachusetts (www.interimprograms.com), as well as this account of this intriguing program: Jodi Wilgoren, "Before College, Year Off Beckons to Well Off," *New York Times*, April 17, 2001.

30. See notes 2 and 5 above.

31. This is my guesstimate, based on 2–3 percent of culturally mainstream teens qualifying as the future intelligentsia, 2 percent of teens qualifying as antireligious, and 15 percent (or about half) of teens as strongly religious—for a total of 19–20 percent.

Selected Bibliography

Alwin, Duane, and Jon Krosnick. 1991. "Aging, Cohorts, and the Stability of Sociopolitical Orientations over the Life Span." *American Journal of Sociology* 97 (1): 169–95.

Astin, Alexander W. 1978. *Four Critical Years: Effects of College on Beliefs, Attitudes, and Knowledge.* San Francisco: Jossey-Bass.

———. 1993. *What Matters in College: Four Critical Years Revisited.* San Francisco: Jossey-Bass.

———. 1998. "How the Liberal Arts College Affects Students." *Daedalus* 128 (1): 77–100.

Bachman, Jerald G. 1983. "Premature Affluence: Do High School Students Earn Too Much?" *Economic Outlook USA* 10 (3): 64–67.

Baird, Leonard. 1970. "Who Protests: A Study of Student Activists." In *Protest! Student Activism in America,* ed. Julian Foster and Durward Long, 123–33. New York: William Morrow.

Bauerlein, Mark. 2006. "A Very Long Disengagement." *Chronicle of Higher Education* 52 (18): B6.

Bellah, Robert N., Richard Madsen, William M. Sullivan, Ann Swidler, and Steven M. Tipton. 1985. *Habits of the Heart: Individualism and Commitment in American Life.* Berkeley: University of California Press.

Bensen, Peter L., Michael J. Donahue, and Joseph A. Erickson. 1989. "Adolescence and Religion: A Review of the Literature from 1970 to 1986." *Research in the Social Scientific Study of Religion* 1:153–81.

Bowen, Howard R. 1977. *Investment in Learning: The Individual and Social Value of American Higher Education.* San Francisco: Jossey-Bass.

Brint, Steven G. 1998. *Schools and Societies.* Thousand Oaks, CA: Pine Forge.

Brooks, David. 2001. "The Organization Kid." *Atlantic Monthly* 287 (4): 40ff.

Burkett, Elinor. 2002. *Another Planet: A Year in the Life of a Suburban High School.* New York: HarperCollins.

Carr, Deborah. 2002. "The Psychological Consequences of Work-Family Trade-Offs for Three Cohorts of Men and Women." *Social Psychology Quarterly* 65 (2): 103–24.

Cherry, Conrad, Betty A. DeBerg, and Amanda Porterfield. 2001. *Religion on Campus: What Religion Really Means to Today's Undergraduates.* Chapel Hill: University of North Carolina Press.

Clark, Lynn Schofield. 2003. *From Angels to Aliens: Teenagers, the Media, and the Supernatural.* New York: Oxford University Press.

Coburn, Karen Leven, and Madge Lawrence Treeger. 2003. *Letting Go: A Parents' Guide to Understanding the College Years.* 4th ed. New York: Harper.

Coleman, James S. 1961. *The Adolescent Society: The Social Life of the Teenager and Its Impact on Education.* Glencoe, IL: Free Press.

Collins, Randall. 1979. *The Credential Society: An Historical Sociology of Education and Stratification.* New York: Academic Press.

Cookson, Peter W., Jr., and Caroline Hodges Persell. 1985. *Preparing for Power: America's Elite Boarding Schools.* New York: Basic Books.

Currie, Elliott. 2005. *The Road to Whatever: Middle-Class Culture and the Crisis of Adolescence.* New York: Metropolitan Books.

Dornbusch, Sanford. 1989. "The Sociology of Adolescence." *Annual Review of Sociology* 15:233–59.

Ehrenreich, Barbara. 1989. *Fear of Falling: The Inner Life of the Middle Class.* New York: Harper.

Eliasoph, Nina. 1998. *Avoiding Politics: How Americans Produce Apathy in Everyday Life.* New York: Cambridge University Press.

Elkind, David. 1997. *All Grown Up and No Place to Go: Teenagers in Crisis.* Rev. ed. New York: Perseus.

Erikson, Erik H. 1968. *Identity, Youth, and Crisis.* New York: Norton.

Feldman, Kenneth A., and Theodore A. Newcomb. 1969. *The Impact of College on Students.* San Francisco: Jossey-Bass.

Flory, Richard W., and Donald E. Miller, eds. 2000. *Gen X Religion.* New York: Routledge.

Freud, Anna. 1958. "Adolescence." In *Psychoanalytic Study of the Child*, 13:255–78. New York: International Universities Press.

Furstenberg, Frank F. 2000. "The Sociology of Adolescence and Youth in the 1990s: A Critical Commentary." *Journal of Marriage and the Family* 62 (November 2000): 896–910.

Furstenberg, Frank F., Thomas D. Cook, Jacqueline Eccles, Glen H. Elder, Jr., and Arnold Sameroff. 1999. *Managing to Make It: Urban Families and Adolescent Success.* Chicago: University of Chicago Press.

Gilbert, Neil. 2005. "Family Life: Sold on Work." *Society* 42, no. 3 (March/April): 12–17.

Glenn, Norval, and Elizabeth Marquardt. 2001. *Hooking Up, Hanging Out, and Hoping for Mr. Right: College Women on Dating and Mating Today.* Report to the Independent Women's Forum. New York: Institute for American Values. www.americanvalues.org/Hooking_Up.pdf.

Gordon, Calvin Wayne. 1957. *The Social System of the High School: A Study in the Sociology of Adolescence.* Glencoe, IL: Free Press.

Greenberger, Ellen, and Laurence D. Steinberg. 1986. *When Teenagers Work: The Psychological and Social Costs of Adolescent Employment.* New York: Basic Books.

Gross, Paul R., Ursula Goodenough, Lawrence S. Lerner, Susan Haack, Martha Schwartz, Richard Schwartz, and Chester E. Finn, Jr. 2005. *The State of Science Standards: 2005.* Washington, DC: Thomas B. Fordham Institute.

Hammond, Phillip E. 1992. *Religion and Personal Autonomy: The Third Disestablishment in America.* Columbia: University of South Carolina Press.

Hauser, Stuart T., and Mary Kay Bowlds. 1990. "Stress, Coping, and Adaptation." In *At the Threshold: The Developing Adolescent,* ed. S. Shirley Feldman and Glen R. Elliott, 388–413. Cambridge, MA: Harvard University Press.

Havighurst, Robert, Gordon P. Liddle, Charles V. Matthews, and James V. Pierce. 1962. *Growing Up in River City.* New York: John Wiley.

Herberg, Will. 1955. *Protestant—Catholic—Jew: An Essay in American Religious Sociology.* Chicago: University of Chicago Press.

Hersch, Patricia. 1998. *A Tribe Apart: A Journey into the Heart of American Adolescence.* New York: Ballantine.

Higher Education Research Institute. 2004. "The Spiritual Life of College Students: A National Study of College Students' Search for Meaning and Purpose." Los Angeles: Higher Education Research Institute at University of California, Los Angeles, www.spirituality.ucla.edu.

Hogan, Dennis P., and Nan Marie Astone. 1986. "The Transition to Adulthood." *Annual Review of Sociology* 12:109–30.

Hoge, Dean R., Benton Johnson, and Donald A. Luidens. 1994. *Vanishing Boundaries: The Religion of Mainline Protestant Baby Boomers.* Louisville, KY: Westminster/John Knox Press.

Holland, Dorothy C., and Margaret A. Eisenhart. 1990. *Educated in Romance: Women, Achievement, and College Culture.* Chicago: University of Chicago Press.

Horowitz, Helen Lefkowitz. 1987. *Campus Life: Undergraduate Cultures from the End of the Eighteenth Century to the Present.* New York: Knopf.

Howe, Neil, William Strauss, and R. J. Matson. 2000. *Millennials Rising : The Next Great Generation.* New York: Vintage.

Hunter, James Davison. 1987. *Evangelicalism: The Coming Generation.* Chicago: University of Chicago Press.

Illick, Joseph E. 1989. *At Liberty: The Story of a Community and a Generation: The Bethlehem, Pennsylvania, High School Class of 1952.* Knoxville: University of Tennessee Press.

Jackman, Mary R., and Michael J. Muha. 1984. "Education and Intergroup Attitudes: Moral Enlightenment, Superficial Democratic Commitment, or Ideological Refinement?" *American Sociological Review* 49:751–69.

Jacob, Philip E. 1957. *Changing Values in College: An Exploratory Study of the Impact of College.* New York: Harper & Row.

Johnson, Jean, and Steve Farkas. 1997. *Getting By: What American Teenagers Really Think about Their Schools.* New York: Public Agenda.

Kamber, Richard, and Mary Biggs. 2005. "Grade Conflation: A Question of Credibility." *Chronicle of Higher Education* 48 (31): B14.

Kaplan, Elaine Bell. 1997. *Not Our Kind of Girl: Unraveling the Myths of Black Teenage Motherhood.* Berkeley: University of California Press.

Keup, Jennifer R., and Ellen Bara Stolzenberg. 2004. *The 2003 Your First College Year Survey: Exploring the Academic and Personal Experiences of First-Year Students.* Monograph no. 40. Columbia: University of South Carolina, National Resource Center for the First-Year Experience and Students in Transition.

Kleiber, Douglas, Reed Larson, and Mihaly Csikszentmihaly. 1986. "The Experience of Leisure in Adolescence." *Journal of Leisure Research* 18 (3): 169–76.

Lareau, Annette. 2003. *Unequal Childhoods: Class, Race, and Family Life.* Berkeley: University of California Press.

Larson, Reed W., Suzanne Wilson, B. Bradford Brown, Frank F. Furstenberg, and Suman Verma. 2002. "Changes in Adolescents' Interpersonal Experiences: Are They Being Prepared for Adult Relationships in the Twenty-First Century?" In *Adolescents' Preparation for the Future: Perils and Promise*, ed. Reed Larson, B. Bradford Brown, and Jeylan Mortimer, 31–68. Malden, MA: Blackwell Publishing.

Laumann, Edward O., John H. Gagnon, Robert T. Michel, and Stuarts Michael. 1994. *The Social Organization of Sexuality: Sexual Practices in the United States.* Chicago: University of Chicago Press.

Levine, Arthur, and Jeanette Cureton. 1998a. "Collegiate Life: An Obituary." *Change* 30 (3): 12ff.

———. 1998b. *When Hope and Fear Collide: A Portrait of Today's College Student.* San Francisco: Jossey-Bass.

Light, Richard. 2001. *Making the Most of College.* Cambridge, MA: Harvard University Press.

Lipset, Seymour Martin. 1972. *Rebellion in the University.* Boston: Little, Brown.

Lipset, Seymour Martin, and Philip Altbach. 1967. "Student Politics and Higher Education in the United States." In *Student Politics*, ed. Seymour Martin Lipset, 199–252. New York: Basic Books.

Lynd, Robert S., and Helen Merrell Lynd. 1929. *Middletown: A Study in Modern American Culture.* New York: Harcourt, Brace, & World.

Lytch, Carol E. 2004. *Choosing Church: What Makes a Difference for Teens.* Louisville, KY: Westminster/John Knox.

Malesic, Jonathan. 2005. "The Smell of Indoctrination in the Morning." *Chronicle of Higher Education* 52 (9): C3.

Marchese, Ted. 1998a. "Disengaged Students." *Change* 30 (2): 4.

———. 1998b. "Disengaged Students II." *Change* 30 (3): 4.

McAdam, Doug. 1988. *Freedom Summer.* New York: Oxford University Press.

McCabe, Donald L. 1993. "Academic Integrity: What the Latest Research Shows." *Synthesis: Law and Policy in Higher Education* 5:340–43.

Miller, Vincent J. 2003. *Consuming Religion: Christian Faith and Practice in a Consumer Culture.* New York: Continuum.

Milner, Murray, Jr. 2004. *Freaks, Geeks, and Cool Kids: American Teenagers, Schools, and the Culture of Consumption.* New York: Routledge.

Mishel, Lawrence, Jared Bernstein, and Sylvia Allegretto. 2005. *The State of Working America 2004/2005.* Ithaca, NY: Cornell University Press.

Moffat, Michael. 1989. *Coming of Age in New Jersey.* New Brunswick, NJ: Rutgers University Press.

Mortimer, Jeylan. 2003. *Working and Growing Up in America*. Cambridge, MA: Harvard University Press.

Nathan, Rebekah. 2005. *My Freshman Year: What a Professor Learned by Becoming a Student*. Ithaca, NY: Cornell University Press.

National Governors Association. 2005. "Rate Your Future Survey." Results released July 16, 2005, at www.nga.org (summary results at http://www.nga.org/Files/ppt /rateyourfuturesurvey.ppt). (Survey results were described in many major media publications, including Michael Janofsky, "Students Say High Schools Let Them Down," *New York Times*, July 16, 2005.)

Newman, Katherine. 1988. *Falling from Grace: The Experience of Downward Mobility in the American Middle Class*. New York: Free Press.

Newman, Katherine, Cybelle Fox, David Harding, Jal Mehta, and Wendy Roth. 2004. *Rampage: The Social Roots of School Shootings*. New York: Basic Books.

Oesterle, Sabrina, Monica Kirkpatrick Johnson, and Jeylan T. Mortimer. 2004. "Volunteerism during the Transition to Adulthood: A Life Course Perspective." *Social Forces* 82 (3): 1123–49.

Pascarella, Ernest T., and Patrick T. Terenzini. 1991. *How College Affects Students: Findings and Insights from Twenty Years of Research*. San Francisco: Jossey-Bass.

———. 2005. *How College Affects Students: A Third Decade of Research*. San Francisco: Jossey-Bass.

Paul, Elizabeth L., Brian McManus, and Allison Hayes. 2000. "'Hookups': Characteristics and Correlates of College Students' Spontaneous and Anonymous Sexual Experiences." *Journal of Sex Research* 37 (1): 76–88.

Paul, Elizabeth L., and Kristen A. Hayes. 2002. "The Casualties of 'Casual' Sex: A Qualitative Exploration of the Phenomenology of College Student Hookups." *Journal of Social and Personal Relationships* 19 (5): 639–61.

Penning, James, and Corwin Smidt. 2002. *Evangelicalism: The Next Generation*. Grand Rapids, MI: Baker Academic.

Peterson, Richard. 1966. *The Scope of Organized Student Protest in 1964–1965*. Princeton, NJ: Educational Testing Service.

Pope, Denise Clark. 2001. *Doing School: How We Are Creating a Generation of Stressed-Out, Materialistic, and Miseducated Students*. New Haven, CT: Yale University Press.

Pope, Loren. 1996. *Colleges That Change Lives*. New York: Penguin.

Potvin, Raymond H., Dean R. Hoge, and Hart M. Nelson. 1976. *Religion and American Youth: With Emphasis on Catholic Adolescents and Young Adults*. Washington, DC: U.S. Catholic Conference.

Putnam, Robert D. 2000. *Bowling Alone: The Collapse and Revival of American Community*. New York: Simon & Schuster.

Raymore, Leslie A., Bonnie L. Barber, and Jacqueline S. Eccles. 2001. "Leaving Home, Attending College, Partnership, and Parenthood: The Role of Life Transition Events in Leisure Pattern Stability from Adolescence to Young Adulthood." *Journal of Youth and Adolescence* 30 (2): 197–223.

Raymore, Leslie A., Bonnie L. Barber, Jacqueline S. Eccles, and Geoffrey C. Godbey. 1999. "Leisure Behavior Pattern Stability during the Transition from Adolescence to Young Adulthood." *Journal of Youth and Adolescence* 28 (1): 79–103.

Regnerus, Mark D. 2003. "Religion and Positive Adolescent Outcomes: A Review of Research and Theory." *Review of Religious Research* 44 (4): 394–413.

Regnerus, Mark D., and Jeremy E. Uecker. 2006. "Finding Faith, Losing Faith: The Prevalence and Context of Religious Transformations during Adolescence." *Review of Religious Research* 47 (3): 217–37.

Rhoads, Robert A. 1998. *Freedom's Web: Student Activism in an Age of Cultural Diversity.* Baltimore: Johns Hopkins University Press.

Riesman, David, with Nathan Glazer and Reuel Denney. 1950. *The Lonely Crowd.* New Haven, CT: Yale University Press.

Riley, Naomi Schaefer. 2005. *God on the Quad: How Religious Colleges and the Missionary Generation Are Changing America.* New York: St. Martin's.

Rojstaczer, Stuart. 2001. "When Intellectual Life Is Optional for Students." *Chronicle of Higher Education* 47 (32): B5.

Roof, Wade Clark. 1993. *A Generation of Seekers.* New York: HarperCollins.

Rosovsky, Henry, and Matthew Hartley. 2002. "Evaluation and the Academy: Are We Doing the Right Thing? Grade Inflation and Letters of Recommendation." Occasional Paper. Cambridge, MA: American Academy of Arts and Sciences.

Schneider, Barbara, and David Stevenson. *The Ambitious Generation: America's Teenagers—Motivated but Directionless.* New Haven, CT: Yale University Press, 1999.

Scholly, Kristen, Alan R. Katz, Jan Gascoigne, and Peter S. Holck. 2005. "Using Social Norms Theory to Explain Perceptions and Sexual Health Behaviors of Undergraduate College Students: An Exploratory Study." *Journal of American College Health* 53 (4): 159–66.

Schor, Juliet. 2004. *Born to Buy: The Commercialized Child and the New Consumer Culture.* New York: Scribner.

———. 1998. *The Overspent American.* New York: Basic Books.

Settersten, Richard A., Frank F. Furstenberg, Jr., and Ruben G. Rumbaut, eds. 2005. *On the Frontier of Adulthood: Theory, Research, and Public Policy.* Chicago: University of Chicago Press.

Shanahan, Michael J. 2000. "Pathways to Adulthood in Changing Societies: Variability and Mechanisms in Life Course Perspective." *Annual Review of Sociology* 26:667–92.

Sherkat, Darren E., and T. Jean Blocker. 1994. "The Political Development of Sixties' Activists: Identifying the Influence of Class, Gender, and Socialization on Protest Participation." *Social Forces* 72 (3): 821–42.

Sherrod, Lonnie R., Robert J. Haggerty, and David L. Featherman. 1993. "Introduction: Late Adolescence and the Transition to Adulthood." *Journal of Research on Adolescence* 3 (3): 217–26.

Smith, Christian. 1998. *American Evangelicalism: Embattled and Thriving.* Chicago: University of Chicago Press.

Smith, Christian, and Robert Faris. 2002. "Religion and American Adolescent Delinquency, Risk Behaviors, and Constructive Social Activities." Chapel Hill: University of North Carolina, National Study of Youth and Religion. www.youthandreligion.org/publications/docs/RiskReport1.pdf.

Smith, Christian, Robert Faris, and Mark Regnerus. 2002. "Mapping American Adolescent Religious Participation." *Journal for the Scientific Study of Religion* 41 (4): 597–612.

Smith, Christian, with Melinda Lundquist Denton. 2005. *Soul Searching: The Religious and Spiritual Lives of American Teenagers.* New York: Oxford University Press.

Sommers, Christina Hoff. 2000. *The War against Boys: How Misguided Feminism Is Harming Our Young Men*. New York: Simon & Schuster.

Stolzenberg, Ross M., Mary Blair-Loy, and Linda J. Waite. 1995. "Religious Participation in Early Adulthood: Age and Family Life Cycle Effects on Church Membership." *American Sociological Review* 60 (1): 84–103.

Swidler, Anne. 2001. *Talk of Love: How Culture Matters*. Chicago: University of Chicago Press.

Thompson, Sharon. 1996. *Going All the Way: Teenage Girls' Tales of Sex, Romance, and Pregnancy*. New York: Hill & Wang.

U.S. Department of Education. 2003. *2003 National Assessment of Adult Literacy Report*. http://nces.ed.gov/naal/. (Results described in Sam Dillon, "Literacy Falls for Graduates from College, Testing Finds," *New York Times*, December 16, 2005.)

Wadsworth, M. E. J., and S. R. Freeman. 1983. "Generation Differences in Beliefs: A Cohort Study of Stability and Change in Religious Beliefs." *British Journal of Sociology* 34 (3): 416–37.

Whyte, William Foote. 1943. *Street Corner Society: The Social Structure of an Italian Slum*. Chicago: University of Chicago Press.

Wuthnow, Robert. 1994. *God and Mammon in America*. New York: Free Press.

———. 1998. *After Heaven: Spirituality in America since the 1950s*. Berkeley: University of California Press.

———. 1999. *Growing Up Religious: Christians and Jews and Their Journeys of Faith*. Boston: Beacon.

Zelizer, Viviana. 1994. *Pricing the Priceless Child: The Changing Social Value of Children*. Princeton, NJ: Princeton University Press.

———. 1997. *The Social Meaning of Money: Pin Money, Paychecks, Poor Relief, and Other Currencies*. Princeton, NJ: Princeton University Press.

Index